access to history

The Later Stuart
the Glorious Revolution

1660–1702

OLIVER BULLOCK

HODDER
EDUCATION
AN HACHETTE UK COMPANY

For Ivy, and a lifetime of learning.

The Publishers would like to thank the following for permission to reproduce copyright material.

Photo credits: p9 Wellcome Collection/Creative Commons Attribution (CC BY 4.0); **p11** Granger Historical Picture Archive/Alamy Stock Photo; **p32** DEA Picture Library/Getty Images; **p52** The Trustees of the British Museum; **p74** Lebrecht Music & Arts/Alamy Stock Photo; **p75** Rijksmuseum/Creative Commons CC0 1.0; **p101** Bridgeman Images/Private collection; **pp122, 173** Granger Historical Picture Archive/Alamy Stock Photo; **p185** Lebrecht Music & Arts/Alamy Stock Photo.

Acknowledgements: Bloomsbury, *The T&T Clark Companion to Nonconformity* edited by Robert Pope, 2013. *British History Online* (www.britishhistory.ac.uk/petitions/cheshire/1678) edited by Sharon Howard. Cambridge University Press, *Popery and Politics in England: 1660–1688* by John Miller, 1973. Clarendon Press, *The Later Stuarts, 1660–1714* by G.N. Clark, 1963. *Eugenics Review*, Gregory King and the population of England and Wales at the end of the seventeenth century, pp. 170–83 by D.V. Glass, 1946. Eyre & Spottiswoode, *English Historical Documents, 1660–1714* edited by Andrew Browning, 1953. Hambledon Continuum, *The Stuarts* by John Miller, 2006. Hodder & Stoughton, *Charles II and James II* by Nicholas Fellows, 1995. Longman & Co., *A Complete Collection of State Trials and Proceedings for High Treason and Other Crimes and Misdemeanors* by Thomas Howell, 1815. Longman's & Green, *The History of England from the Accession of James II* by Thomas Macaulay, 1848. Macmillan, *Britain after the Glorious Revolution, 1689–1714* edited by G. Holmes, 1969. Oxford University Press, *Deliver Us from Evil: The Radical Underground in Britain, 1660–1663* by Richard L. Greaves, 2001; *The First Whigs: The Politics of the Exclusion Crisis, 1678–1683* by J.R. Jones, 1961. Penguin, *Restoration: Charles II and his Kingdoms* by Tim Harris, 2005. Routledge, *The Stuart Age* by Barry Coward and Peter Gaunt, 2017; *The Century of Revolution 1603–1714* by Christopher Hill, 1969. University of Liverpool Press, *The Declaration of Indulgence 1672: A Study in the Rise of Organised Dissent* by Frank Bate, 1908.

Although every effort has been made to ensure that website addresses are correct at time of going to press, Hodder Education cannot be held responsible for the content of any website mentioned in this book. It is sometimes possible to find a relocated web page by typing in the address of the home page for a website in the URL window of your browser.

Hachette UK's policy is to use papers that are natural, renewable and recyclable products and made from wood grown in well-managed forests and other controlled sources. The logging and manufacturing processes are expected to conform to the environmental regulations of the country of origin.

Orders: please contact Bookpoint Ltd, 130 Park Drive, Milton Park, Abingdon, Oxon OX14 4SE. Telephone: +44 (0)1235 827827. Fax: +44 (0)1235 400401. Email education@bookpoint.co.uk Lines are open from 9 a.m. to 5 p.m., Monday to Saturday, with a 24-hour message answering service. You can also order through our website: www.hoddereducation.co.uk

ISBN: 978 1 5104 5912 0

© Oliver Bullock 2020

First published in 2020 by
Hodder Education,
An Hachette UK Company
Carmelite House
50 Victoria Embankment
London EC4Y 0DZ

www.hoddereducation.co.uk

Impression number   10   9   8   7   6   5   4   3   2   1
Year   2024   2023   2022   2021   2020

Cover photo © Niday Picture Library/Alamy Stock Photo
Typeset by Gray Publishing
Printed in the UK by CPI Group Ltd

A catalogue record for this title is available from the British Library.

Contents

Dedication

Keith Randell (1943–2002)

The *Access to History* series was conceived and developed by Keith, who created a series to 'cater for students as they are, not as we might wish them to be'. He leaves a living legacy of a series that for over 20 years has provided a trusted, stimulating and well-loved accompaniment to post-16 study. Our aim with these new editions is to continue to offer students the best possible support for their studies.

Introduction: about this book

This book has been written primarily to support the study of the following courses:

- AQA: Part 2 of Paper 1D: Stuart Britain and the Crisis of Monarchy, 1603–1702 (the years 1660–1702).
- Pearson Edexcel: Paper 1 Option 1C: Britain, 1625–1701: conflict, revolution and settlement (Themes 1–4 from 1660–88 and the Historical Interpretation on the impact of the Glorious Revolution in the years 1688–1701).

The specification grid on pages ix–x will help you understand how this book's content relates to the course that you are studying.

The writer hopes that student readers will regard the book not simply as an aid to better exam results, but as a study which is enjoyable in itself as an analysis of a very important theme in history.

The following explains the different features of this book and how they will help your study of the course.

Beginning of the book

Context

Starting a new course can be daunting if you are not familiar with the period or topic. This section will give you an overview of the history and will set up some of the key themes. Reading this section will help you get up to speed on the content of the course.

Throughout the book

Key terms

You need to know these to gain an understanding of the period. The appropriate use of specific historical language in your essays will also help you improve the quality of your writing. Key terms are in boldface type the first time they appear in the book. They are defined in the margin and appear in the glossary.

Profiles

Some chapters contain profiles of important individuals. These include a brief biography and information about the importance and impact of the individual. This information can be very useful in understanding certain events and providing supporting evidence to your arguments.

Sources

Historical sources are important in understanding why specific decisions were taken or on what contemporary writers and politicians based their actions. The questions accompanying each source will help you to understand and analyse the source.

Interpretations

These extracts from historians will help bring awareness of the debates and issues that surround this fascinating history topic.

Chapter summaries

These written summaries are intended to help you revise and consolidate your knowledge and understanding of the content.

Summary diagrams

These visual summaries at the end of each section are useful for revision.

Refresher questions

The refresher questions are quick knowledge checks to make sure you have understood and remembered the material that is covered in the chapter.

Question practice

There are opportunities at the end of each chapter to practise exam-style questions arranged by exam board. The exam hint below each question will help you if you get stuck.

End of the book

Timeline

Understanding chronology (the order in which events took place) is an essential part of history. Knowing the order of events is one thing, but it is also important to know how events relate to each other. This timeline will help you put events into context and will be helpful for quick reference or as a revision tool.

Exam focus

This section gives advice on how to answer questions in your exam, focusing on the different requirements of your exam paper. The guidance in this book has been based on detailed examiner reports since 2017. It models best practice in terms of answering exam questions and shows the most common pitfalls to help ensure you get the best grade possible.

Glossary

All key terms in the book are defined in the glossary.

Further reading

To achieve top marks in history, you will need to read beyond this textbook. This section contains a list of books and articles for you to explore. The list may also be helpful for an extended essay or piece of coursework.

Online extras

This new edition is accompanied by online material to support you in your study. Throughout the book you will find the online extras icon to prompt you to make use of the relevant online resources for your course. By going to www. hodderhistory.co.uk/accesstohistory/extras you will find the following:

Activity worksheets

These activities will help you develop the skills you need for the exam. The thinking that you do to complete the activities, and the notes you make from answering the questions, will prove valuable in your learning journey and helping you get the best grade possible. Your teacher may decide to print the entire series of worksheets to create an activity booklet to accompany the course. Alternatively they may be used as standalone activities for class work or homework. However, don't hesitate to go online and print off a worksheet yourself to get the most from this book.

Who's who

A level history covers a lot of key figures so it's perfectly understandable if you find yourself confused by all the different names. This document organises the individuals mentioned throughout the book by categories so you know your Thomas Osborne from your Thomas Venner!

Further research

While further reading of books and articles is helpful to achieve your best, there's a wealth of material online, including useful websites, digital archives and documentaries on YouTube. This page lists resources that may help further your understanding of the topic. It may also prove a valuable reference for research if you decide to choose this period for the coursework element of your course.

Specification grid

Chapter	AQA	Pearson Edexcel
Chapter 1 Context		
Chapter 2 The Restoration Settlement, 1660–5	✓	✓
1 Background to the Restoration Settlement	✓	✓
2 The political settlement	✓	✓
3 The financial settlement	✓	✓
4 The religious settlement	✓	✓
Chapter 3 Ministers and parliament, 1660–78	✓	✓
1 Clarendon's ministry	✓	✓
2 The rise of the Cabal	✓	✓
3 The rise of Danby	✓	✓
4 The fall of Danby	✓	✓
Chapter 4 Religious divisions, 1660–78	✓	✓
1 Charles's quest for religious toleration, 1660–70	✓	✓
2 The Catholic threat	✓	✓
3 The experience of Protestant Dissenters	✓	✓
4 The second Declaration of Indulgence and the Test Acts	✓	✓
5 Key debate: Why did religious dissent survive the Restoration?	✓	✓
Chapter 5 The Catholic threat and Exclusion, 1678–81	✓	✓
1 The Popish Plot	✓	✓
2 Government action against Catholics	✓	✓
3 The Exclusion Crisis	✓	✓
4 The end of the crisis	✓	✓
5 Key debate: Why did Exclusion fail?	✓	✓
Chapter 6 Charles II to James II, 1681–7	✓	✓
1 The Tory reaction, 1681–5	✓	✓
2 James II: political settlement	✓	✓
3 James II and Catholicism	✓	✓
Chapter 7 How revolutionary was the Glorious Revolution, 1688–1701?	✓	✓
1 Causes of the Glorious Revolution	✓	✓
2 The Bill of Rights and political settlement	✓	✓
3 The Revolution in Ireland and Scotland	✓	✓
4 Monarchy and parliament	✓	✓
5 Key debate: How revolutionary was the Glorious Revolution?	✓	✓

CHAPTER 1

Context

In the seventeenth century, the monarch was the most important individual in the political system. The organisation of elections and parliaments bore little resemblance to the democracy we know today, although many of the institutions appear to be the same. The **prerogative powers** possessed by monarchs enabled them to control the following areas of government:

- they could declare war
- they could sign treaties with foreign powers
- they had the power to call parliament when they wished (and dissolve it)
- they could appoint a **Privy Council** of their own choosing, for the day-to-day running of government
- they controlled some sources of income such as money received from **feudal dues** and customs duties.

> **KEY TERMS**
>
> **Prerogative powers** Powers that are unique to the monarch.
>
> **Privy Council** A body of advisers appointed by the monarch.
>
> **Feudal dues** Taxes traditionally paid by a lower class to a higher class under the feudal system.

Parliament

Despite the vast powers that could be wielded by the monarchs, they faced restrictions:

- In order to pass legislation, a parliament had to be called. This meant that members of parliament (MPs) could scrutinise and debate proposed laws. This often led to conflict and division. In the early Stuart era, parliament had grown more assertive and these conflicts became increasingly regular.
- When a new parliament was called, a general election would take place. Like today, the country was divided up into a number of geographical constituencies with members elected at county and borough level. In the early Stuart period, it was rare for these constituencies to be contested by more than one person as the local gentry tended to agree who would stand for election among themselves. Later in the period, however, election contests became more common.
- Normal Crown revenue was often not enough for a monarch, especially in times of war. This meant that parliament was relied on to approve new taxes and make grants of money. If parliament did not agree to funding, a political stalemate could occur.

Society

The population of England had roughly doubled between 1500 and 1660, from around 2.5 million to more than 5 million. The population was scattered unevenly, with around three-quarters of people living in the southeast. Large swathes of the north were effectively uninhabited, and in all areas, large towns

Table 1.1 Society in 1660

Group	Description	Involvement in political life
Nobility	The elite class with titles (earls, dukes and so on) and extensive lands. Made up a tiny fraction of society	Many of the nobility had close associations with royalty and they could sit in the House of Lords in parliament
Gentry	Large landowners who dominated county government. Numbers had risen from 5000 to 15,000 in the century before the Civil Wars	Many greater gentry sat in the House of Commons in parliament. Many lesser gentry became office holders in local government
Yeomen	Normally landholders and farmers, and from the late sixteenth century expected to hold land worth over £6 (over £2500 in today's money)	They could sit on juries and wealthier yeomen could take part in elections for MPs
Merchants and professionals	Increased international trade resulted in the growth of a merchant class, many of whom were based in London. The growth of this class, and that of the gentry, created a need for the services of professionals such as doctors, architects and lawyers	Never commanded the same amount of respect and prestige as the landed elites. Entered public office as aldermen on town councils and could become mayors
Husbandmen	Farmers who worked their own land and produced enough to sell some of their surplus at market	Very little involvement in political affairs outside their immediate parish
Labourers	Worked for others for a wage. Made up the majority of the population	Most were illiterate and could not become involved in political life

KEY TERM

Stratified Arranged into groups or classes.

were still a rarity. London bucked this trend as it continued to dominate in terms of population, making it the largest city in western Europe.

Rural society was still strictly **stratified** as it had been for centuries. In the towns, a growing merchant and professional class was beginning to challenge the authority of the traditional gentry elites and with the increase in population growth came an increase in inflation and poverty.

The rule of James I

James came to the throne in England in 1603 after becoming James VI of Scotland in 1566. His mother, Mary, Queen of Scots, was a cousin of the childless Elizabeth I, making James the closest living heir. Elizabeth had faced financial difficulties before her death and this meant that James struggled to raise adequate revenue. James also held a strong belief in the **divine right of kings** and held the authority of the Church in high regard.

He was a fiercely loyal **Protestant**, and although he had misgivings about the more extreme **Presbyterian** Reformation that had taken place in Scotland, he was suspicious of **Catholicism**.

Key milestones in the reign of James I

The Hampton Court Conference, 1604

- In 1603, a group of **Puritans** produced the Millenary Petition, containing the signatures of 1000 ministers.
- They argued that the Church of England was too similar to the Catholic Church.
- James called the conference in order to find a compromise between both sides, and it ended with James refusing to reform the Church along Presbyterian lines. He did, however, accept the suggestion that a new translation of the Bible should be made and the new, King James Bible, was completed in 1611.

The Gunpowder Plot, 1605

- A group of Catholics conspired to blow up parliament and remove James.
- The conspirators were caught and punished – eleven were executed.

The Great Contract, 1610

- James agreed to abandon his right to claim a number of feudal taxes in return for an annual grant from parliament.
- Both James and parliament ultimately rejected the terms.

The Cockayne Project, 1614

- Cloth exports decreased drastically in 1614 and the Dutch had been carrying out the final dyeing and finishing of English cloth for many years.
- A merchant, William Cockayne, devised a plan to complete all cloth production in England.
- James granted Cockayne a **monopoly** over cloth exports, but when the Dutch refused to purchase English cloth, sales slumped and failed to recover.

The Statute of Monopolies, 1624

- Greatly reduced the Crown's ability to sell monopolies and patents and caused tension between king and parliament.

KEY TERMS

Divine right of kings The belief that the power of kings is ordained by God.

Protestants Followers of the Christian Churches that had separated from the Catholic Church. They focused on the belief that faith alone was required to enter heaven.

Presbyterian A Church governed by a council of elders rather than a hierarchy of bishops.

Catholicism The dominant form of Christianity under papal (the pope's) authority in Europe before the Protestant Reformation. The Catholic Church was founded on the belief that bishops were the successors of Christ's apostles and that the pope was the successor to Saint Peter.

Puritans Protestants who believed that the Reformation of the Church under Elizabeth I had not gone far enough, and sought to simplify worship and 'purify' it.

Monopoly The exclusive control of trade in a commodity.

The reign of Charles I

Charles inherited the throne from James in 1625 and shared his father's firm belief in divine right. He aimed to restore a sense of order and decorum to the Royal Court, maintain order in the Church and establish a sound financial base in response to debts created during his father's rule. Charles called a number of parliaments in the years 1625–9 and these were defined by conflict over Charles's **Arminian** religion, his right to collect taxes and the funding of foreign wars.

Charles dissolved parliament in 1629 and it did not meet again until 1640. During these eleven years of 'personal rule', Charles allowed the Arminian Archbishop of Canterbury, William Laud, a high degree of personal control over Church affairs, much to the irritation of the Puritans. Without a parliament to provide him with funds, Charles also had to embark on new methods of raising money. He set about reviving long-forgotten taxes. The most notable of these was ship money, a tax originally designed to be levied on coastal counties in times of war. Charles instead imposed it on the entire country at a time when England was at peace.

Build-up to war, 1637–42

Charles's taxes were generally paid as expected, across the counties between 1634 and 1639. There were a small number of complaints, however, with the most high-profile challenge made by the Buckinghamshire gentleman and Puritan, John Hampden, against ship money. Despite losing the case, contemporaries recorded that the reaction of the gentry to the result of the case was generally hostile.

In the same year as Hampden's trial, Charles attempted to impose the **Anglican Book of Common Prayer** on the Presbyterian Scots. When the book was first read in churches, riots erupted, which spread across the lowlands. The Scots formed a national covenant to defend their religious rights and the so-called First Bishops' War broke out in 1639.

Parliament was recalled in 1640 and its leaders, headed by John Pym, secured a number of concessions from Charles, including restrictions to the Arminians and the prohibition of some taxes. When the Catholic Irish launched a rebellion in 1641 against Protestant English rule, the question of who should control the army came to the fore and this led to further suspicion of the Royal Court and attacks on Charles in parliament. When Charles tried and failed to arrest five of the rebellious MPs, including Pym, in January 1642, he was left with no choice but to leave London, fearing for the safety of himself and his family as the London mob grew increasingly enraged. In the following months, both Charles and parliament began to raise armies and Charles formally declared war on parliament in August 1642.

KEY TERMS

Arminian A follower of the Dutch theologian Jacobus Arminius. Arminians were associated with 'high-church' practices (similar to those of the Catholic Church), such as the use of organs, hymns and bowing to the cross.

Anglican The Church of England.

Book of Common Prayer The English prayer book, first introduced in 1549.

Parliamentary victory, 1642–6

Parliament secured victory in the First Civil War in 1646. This success can be attributed to the following:

- *Royalist weaknesses:* Charles struggled to resolve differences between his senior commanders, and the money raised for his cause through traditional levies soon ran out.
- *Parliamentarian strengths:* parliament controlled London, the navy, many of the ports and some of the wealthiest areas of the south and east of England.
- *The formation of the New Model Army:* in February 1645, an ordinance was passed establishing a new parliamentarian army. It was a single, national force of 21,000 men, whose members were well-paid, godly, uniformed and disciplined.

The road to regicide, 1646–9

Charles gave himself up to the Scots – who had made an alliance with parliament – in May 1646. Parliament offered Charles a settlement proposal called the Newcastle Propositions, which outlined a future government where the militia, the Church and many royalists were to be punished for their role in the war. Charles delayed his answer for a year, and after he finally rejected it, the New Model Army revolted and kidnapped the King. A debate began within the army about what a future political settlement should look like, with radical **Levellers** demanding a **republic** and **universal male suffrage**, and senior military commanders, such as Oliver Cromwell, calling for moderation.

Charles escaped from house arrest at Hampton Court and signed the Engagement, a deal whereby the Scots would assist him in starting a Second Civil War. It was during this conflict, in 1648, that the senior commanders of the army, including Cromwell, began to move towards the idea of placing the King on trial. Parliament was purged of members who were hostile to the idea of **regicide** in an episode known as Pride's Purge, leaving what became known as the 'Rump' Parliament. The trial took place in January 1649; Charles was found guilty and beheaded.

The Rump Parliament

The Rump Parliament governed the country for the next four years. Its initial radicalism was soon diluted by the conservative nature of many of its members, who were overwhelmingly from the ranks of the lesser gentry. As the rate of reform slowed, it seemed increasingly clear that the Rump's members were concerned only with self-preservation. Cromwell – now commander of the army – dissolved the Rump by force in April 1653.

KEY TERMS

Levellers A radical movement that was particularly popular in the New Model Army.

Republic A state in which power is vested in elected representatives rather than a monarch.

Universal male suffrage The vote for all men aged over eighteen.

Regicide The action of killing a king.

The Protectorate

After a brief attempt at creating a more godly 'Parliament of Saints', a body that suffered a similar fate to the Rump in December 1653, a new constitution was produced by Major General John Lambert. It was called the Instrument of Government and created a new system called the Protectorate. **Executive** authority was vested in Cromwell as Lord Protector, with a **Council of State** of 21 members.

CHAPTER SUMMARY

In the years before the Restoration, England had seen profound political, social and religious change. Population growth during the previous century led to an increase in poverty and a steady upsurge in public disorder. Against the backdrop of this change, the early Stuart kings faced opposition to their wishes and policies that eventually led to civil war and regicide. The Stuart dynasty had been overthrown (at least for the time being) and replaced with a republic. The new republican system was far from ideal, however, and after eleven years a Stuart king would sit on the throne once more.

CHAPTER 2

The Restoration Settlement, 1660–5

The execution of Charles I in 1649 resulted in an abrupt pause to the Stuart dynasty. Oliver Cromwell rose to become Lord Protector in 1653. After he died in 1658, his son, Richard, struggled to maintain political balance and in less than two years the monarchy was restored once more. This chapter looks at the Restoration and the political settlement that followed it by focusing on the following events:

◆ Background to the Restoration Settlement

◆ The political settlement

◆ The financial settlement

◆ The religious settlement

KEY DATES

1660	Restoration of the monarchy; election of the Convention Parliament	**1663**	Gilbert Sheldon nominated Archbishop of Canterbury
1661	Election of the Cavalier Parliament; Corporation Act	**1664**	Conventicle Act; Triennial Act
1662	Act of Uniformity	**1665**	Five Mile Act

---

1 Background to the Restoration Settlement

■ *Why was the monarchy restored in 1660?*

Following the execution of Charles I in 1649, England was declared a 'commonwealth and free state' under a republican system. The monarchy and House of Lords were abolished and from 1653, executive power was placed in the hands of Cromwell and the Council of State selected by members of parliament (MPs). On Cromwell's death, it was decided that a new Protector would be elected by the Council of State. However, when Cromwell had been offered the Crown under the terms of the *Humble Petition and Advice* (1657), he had rejected it. Consequently, provision had been made for a hereditary succession. Before his death in 1658, Cromwell declared that his inexperienced son, Richard, should become Lord Protector, bypassing his more experienced (although younger) son, Henry. Before this, he may have intended to nominate another major general, Charles Fleetwood, who was married to Cromwell's daughter, Bridget.

Political vacuum after the death of Cromwell

On succeeding his father, Richard Cromwell summoned the brief Third Protectorate Parliament to meet in January 1659. Richard was a civilian and, unlike his father, he had no experience of warfare or politics. He was unacceptable to the **Council of Officers**, who forced him to resign later in 1659 and then recalled the Rump. The newly restored Rump appeared to have learned nothing from its earlier failures and its leading members began to lose enthusiasm. In October, the army closed it down by force.

General Monck and negotiations for the return of the monarchy

George Monck was the leader of the army in Scotland. He was a former royalist, but had worked closely with Cromwell. Fearful that the country was sliding towards military rule, he assembled an army to bring the Rump to power once again. Monck's motives for this remain unclear. He had been loyal to the Republic in 1659 when Sir George Booth mounted a royalist rising in Cheshire, although he was clearly concerned by an upsurge in radicalism in London and the continued intervention of the army in politics.

The return of the Long Parliament

The army sent a force north under Major General Lambert to counter the threat of Monck. Meanwhile, other members of the army in London, fearful of Lambert's potential slide towards military rule, reinstated the Rump once again. Lambert lost support and was imprisoned to the Tower of London, and Monck entered England on 1 January 1660. He arrived in London in February and was met with **petitions** in favour of both a new parliament and a return of the Long Parliament that had existed before its members were purged to clear the way for the trial of Charles I in 1648. Against the wishes of most MPs, Monck moved to reverse Pride's Purge and restored the Long Parliament. The nature of its membership meant that this parliament was always likely to favour a return to monarchy. In March, the restored Long Parliament voted to dissolve itself, leading to elections for the Convention Parliament.

The Convention Parliament

A large number of known royalists were elected to the **Convention Parliament**, and around 100 of the 145 peers who took their seats in the House of Lords were fiercely loyal to the monarchy. This was countered by a number of former republicans who intended to place political and religious conditions on Charles if he was to return to re-establish the monarchy. However, any enthusiasm to place serious conditions on the Crown dissipated quickly, as MPs began to realise the strength of royalism in their **constituencies**.

Edward Hyde, Earl of Clarendon

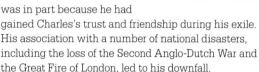

1609	Born to a gentry family in Wiltshire
1626	Graduated from Oxford University and pursued a career in law
1640	Elected as MP for Wootton Bassett in the Short Parliament and Saltash in the Long Parliament
1643	Knighted by Charles I
1660	After a period in exile, returned to England with Charles II at the Restoration
1667	Removed as chief minister and was exiled to France
1671	Began work on his *History of the Rebellion and Civil Wars in England*
1674	Died in Rouen, France

Background

Born into the gentry, Hyde studied law and became adept at establishing influential connections at both parliament and the Royal Court. He took the side of the royalists in the Civil War and joined Charles II in exile. He returned to England with the King and his daughter, Anne, who soon married the future James II.

Career

Until 1667, Clarendon effectively acted as chief minister to Charles. This was in part because he had gained Charles's trust and friendship during his exile. His association with a number of national disasters, including the loss of the Second Anglo-Dutch War and the Great Fire of London, led to his downfall.

Later years

His later years were spent in exile in France. Although keen to maintain good relations with Charles, Louis XIV attempted to have him banished on several occasions. Clarendon began completing and editing his history of the Civil Wars, *The History of the Rebellion and Civil Wars in England*, which he had begun in the 1640s. This was not published until after his death in 1674.

Declaration of Breda

Charles's court was still in exile in the Netherlands, and on 4 April he sent the Declaration of Breda to parliament, along with a series of letters to Monck, the Speakers of each House and the City of London authorities. The Declaration was conveniently timed to coincide with the elections to the Convention, serving to strengthen the position of royalist candidates. The Declaration offered the following:

- An amnesty for those who had taken up arms against Charles I.
- Religious toleration and 'liberty to tender consciences', the details of which were to be settled by parliament.
- Payment of arrears to the army.
- A settlement of land disputes.

The document was deliberately vague, designed to appeal to as many people as possible. Those who had been wavering in their commitment to a restored monarchy out of fear of reprisals were to be reassured by the promise of a general amnesty, and the brief mention of religious toleration was designed to appeal to dissenting Puritans. The ambiguous nature of the proposed settlement was highlighted in parliament, with one MP commenting that, 'as for liberty to tender consciences, no man knew what it was'.

The tone of the Declaration made it seem as though Charles's return was an inevitability. Charles's close adviser, and the man responsible for much of the wording of the document, Edward Hyde (see page 10), deliberately intended to leave many of the matters of detail to a future parliament.

SOURCE QUESTION

How are Charles's skills as a politician illustrated in Source A?

SOURCE A

The Declaration of Breda, 1660

Charles, by the Grace of God, King of England, Scotland, France and Ireland, Defender of the Faith, to all our loving subjects. If the general distraction and confusion which is spread over the whole kingdom does not awaken all men to a desire and longing that those wounds which have so many years together been kept bleeding, may be bound up, all we can say will be to no purpose; however, after this long silence, we have thought it our duty to declare how much we desire to contribute thereunto. And to the end that the fear of punishment may not engage any, we do grant a free and general pardon, excepting only such persons as shall hereafter be excepted by Parliament … All notes of discord, separation and difference of parties be utterly abolished among all our subjects, whom we invite and conjure to a perfect union among themselves, under our protection, for the resettlement of our just rights and theirs in a free parliament.

KEY TERMS

Political nation People able to take part in politics and vote in elections.

Quakers Members of the Religious Society of Friends, a movement founded by George Fox in the early 1650s. Central to their beliefs is the doctrine of the 'Inner Light' of the Holy Spirit that can be accessed by anyone. As a result, their meetings did not follow the same pattern as church services and their organisation did not have a hierarchical leadership structure.

Monarchy restored

The Declaration was formally read to the Convention Parliament, which proceeded to announce Charles as king. Charles landed at Dover in May and was received with a mood of celebration and enthusiasm. However, despite the clear fervour for the Restoration displayed by much of the population, there were still many issues to be resolved, including the funding of the Crown, religious toleration and the future balance of power between Charles and parliament.

Why was Charles restored?

Historians have put forward various arguments to explain why the monarchy was restored in 1660:

- It has been argued that a rejection of the republican governments of the 1650s was inevitable after the return to one-man rule under Cromwell.
- There was fear of another civil war in the context of the political uncertainty of 1659.
- The number of radical religious groups alarmed the **political nation** in the late 1650s. In 1659, there were as many as 60,000 **Quakers**.
- As the Republic had collapsed so quickly, it was essential to men of property that a stable government be restored.
- Charles's Declaration of Breda made him appear as an attractive option, as he offered religious toleration and payment of arrears to the army.

SOURCE B

SOURCE QUESTION

Study Source B. What is the significance of the reference to Charles beginning his reign in 1648?

A contemporary engraving commemorating the Restoration of 1660. The text around the edge includes the words 'honour the King' and 'fear God', as well as references to the regicides who executed Charles's father.

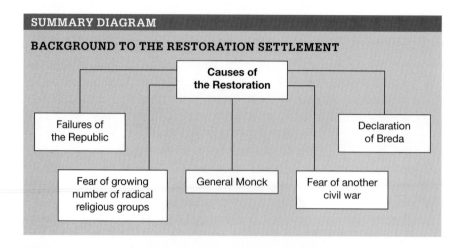

SUMMARY DIAGRAM

BACKGROUND TO THE RESTORATION SETTLEMENT

2 The political settlement

■ *To what extent were the powers of the monarchy fully restored?*

The primary task of the Convention Parliament was to ensure that there was a peaceful and ordered transition to monarchical government. Not all MPs, however, agreed on how this was to be achieved.

The Convention, April to December 1660

The Convention had two important issues to resolve:

■ First, it needed to produce a raft of legislation aimed at providing a settlement that would be acceptable to the majority of the nation, including the settling of land disputes and religious toleration.

■ Second, the issue of the status of the army and its future needed to be determined.

MPs in the Convention can be split into two groups, each of which had different objectives:

■ The Presbyterians were associated with the republican system and did not favour a return to an Anglican national Church.

■ The royalists were Anglicans who were firm supporters of Charles II.

The Act of Indemnity

In the Declaration of Breda, Charles had promised to pardon those who had participated in any rebellious actions against his father. An 'Act of Pardon, Indemnity and Oblivion' was passed in August 1660. This included the following details:

■ All crimes committed during the Civil Wars were pardoned, with the exception of serious offences, such as murder.

- The Act was generally lenient, providing immunity for soldiers who had fought for parliament and the republic, many of whom were still serving in the army.
- The regicides (those who had been involved in the trial and execution of Charles I) and 29 others were exempted from the Act and were liable to punishment.

The Act attempted to solve some of the land issues that had emerged during the Republic. It was routine for the estates of suspected royalists to be confiscated, and lands belonging to the Crown had been sold on the abolition of the monarchy in 1649. In addition, much of the land belonging to the Church of England had been sold off when the national Church became Presbyterian in 1645. In total, £5 million worth of land had been sold. Now that the monarchy was restored, a number of questions needed to be answered:

- What would the new government do to reinstate lands to loyal royalist supporters?
- What would happen to the rights of those who had purchased these lands during the Republic in good faith?

The Convention Parliament attempted to address these questions by adding clauses to the Act of Indemnity that deprived owners of former Church and Crown land of their legal title. Generous compensation was given to those forced to give back land, which resulted in very little opposition.

Land lost by former royalists

The reinstatement of Crown and Church land resolved the issue for some, but much land had been confiscated from private individuals accused of being royalist, and this was not addressed by the Act. In addition, land that was sold to pay for the fines imposed on former royalists was difficult to claim back through the courts because the sales were voluntary. Despite the lack of legal assistance, over 70 per cent of land lost by royalists was reinstated in 1660, normally through a process of negotiation and compromise to produce out-of-court settlements.

Disbanding the New Model Army

The soldiers of the 40,000-strong army were still owed arrears of pay, and there was a consensus at both Court and in parliament that the army should be disbanded in order to facilitate a peaceful political settlement.

In May 1660, there were 57 regiments in the army, together with a number of garrisons in towns across the country. The Indemnity had already guaranteed soldiers immunity from prosecution and Monck was tasked with arranging their demobilisation, with just two regiments surviving to be incorporated into Charles's forces. He arranged for their arrears to be paid, costing £835,000 in total, to be funded from an increase in taxes. As part of the marriage contract that secured Charles's marriage to Catherine of Braganza in 1662, 4500 English troops were required to be sent to Portugal to support the fight for independence from Spain. This came at a convenient time for Monck, who had been struggling to provide enough funds to disband the entire army.

Demobilisation was not wholly successful. An increase in rioting and a spate of robberies in the southeast of England were publicised in the royalist press, with contemporaries blaming ex-soldiers for the increase in crime. In September 1660, Clarendon informed parliament of several seditious plots organised by disbanded veterans. A volunteer militia of 90,000 loyal royalists was raised to undertake many of the policing duties once carried out by Cromwell's troops, which helped to dissipate much of the discontent.

The Cavalier Parliament, February 1661

The Convention Parliament was dissolved in December 1660 and new elections were held in early 1661. In January, the **Fifth Monarchist Thomas Venner** attempted an uprising in London with around 50 supporters. They attempted to seize St Paul's Cathedral and soldiers were given orders to use as much force as necessary to quell the disturbance. Over 40 people were killed in street fighting that lasted several days. With an election only days away, Venner's Rising reminded the political nation that the threat of radical religious groups was still very much alive.

In the same month, there was nearly a Presbyterian coup in the London Corporation elections. When the general election came, these fears of religious radicalism helped to produce a 'Cavalier Parliament', so-called because it contained a royalist and Anglican majority suspicious of both **Protestant Dissenters** and Catholics. At least 73 per cent of the MPs elected in 1661 can be classified as loyal to the Royal Court. There were exceptions, for example, in London where all four seats were won by Presbyterians opposed to the Anglican Church. Away from London, the government intervened to block Presbyterian candidates. It was rare for constituencies to be contested by more than one candidate, but in the elections for the Cavalier Parliament, eleven counties and 32 boroughs saw opponents stand in defiance of the expected MPs.

Prerogative powers

The Cavalier Parliament continued with the task of restoring the monarchy and its associated institutions, although the prerogative courts that had helped to maintain Charles I in power were not revived. The monarch was, however, given the power to appoint his own ministers and state officials, and the Sedition Act (1661) made it a treasonous offence to levy war against the King or encourage a foreign power to mount a war against the monarchy. The Privy Council remained the most important organ of government and Charles doubled its size to 120 in order to accommodate an increasing number of different factions. This made it difficult to manage, so Charles relied on a small inner circle, headed by Clarendon.

KEY TERMS

Fifth Monarchist
A radical Puritan sect whose members believed that Christ's return to Earth was imminent. They had supported the Republic at first, but turned against one-man rule under Cromwell. They wanted a new parliament to be elected based on godly principles.

Protestant Dissenters Members of Nonconformist churches who did not follow the Church of England.

KEY FIGURE

Thomas Venner (c.1609–61)
Venner worked as a cooper (barrel maker) in London before spending time at a number of Puritan colonies in New England. Venner returned to London in 1651, and became the leader of a militant Fifth Monarchist congregation located in Swan Alley. He was involved in several plots against Cromwell and the Protectorate government. After his uprising, Venner unsuccessfully defended himself in court by claiming that Jesus was the true leader of his congregation.

Restrictions on the press

A Licensing Act – fully titled *An Act for Preventing the frequent Abuses in Printing Seditious, Treasonable and Unlicensed Books and Pamphlets* – was introduced in 1662. Restrictions on the press were nothing new, and the Act mirrored similar moves taken by the government of Charles I. All intended publications had to be accepted by the government-approved Stationers' Company, and the number of London printing presses was limited to twenty. Houses and shops could be searched to confiscate unlawful material and imported books were the target of particular suspicion. To remove the threat of the kind of large-scale petitioning seen during the Civil Wars, an Act against Tumultuous Petitioning was passed in 1661.

Restrictions on printed material were only partially successful. Despite attempts to limit the number of printing presses to twenty, there is evidence that many more were in operation in the years immediately following the Restoration and countless critical pamphlets were produced that were read and discussed far from London.

The Militia Act

The status of the army had been partially resolved by the Convention, although the King's role in commanding the militia was a major issue that remained unresolved. In July 1661, parliament agreed that the King had the sole authority to control the militia. This put to rest an issue that had been integral in causing the breakdown in relations between king and parliament in the early 1640s. The organisation of the militia under this Act essentially mirrored arrangements put forward by the Rump in an ordinance of 1659:

- Each county was required to levy a tax to pay for soldiers, horses and arms.
- All men of military age (normally those aged between sixteen and 60) were required to attend an annual **muster**.
- In times of emergency, the King could levy a tax of £70,000 to prepare the militia for war.

The reformed militia was far from an instant success. The Act reduced the total strength of the militia and there were delays in its implementation. Continued rumour of plots and rebellions led to Charles establishing five new regular regiments in late 1662. This was criticised by some MPs as the beginnings of a return to the professional and powerful army of the Republic.

> **KEY TERM**
>
> **Muster** A formal gathering of troops.

The Triennial Act, 1664

Historians who have sought to emphasise the growing power of the monarchy, as opposed to parliament, after the Restoration, have pointed to the 1664 Triennial Act as a key piece of evidence. During the prelude to Civil War in 1641, a Triennial Act had been passed, ensuring that parliament was compelled

> **ONLINE EXTRAS**
> **AQA** **WWW**
>
> Test your knowledge of the political settlement by completing Worksheet 2 at **www.hoddereducation. co.uk/accesstohistory/extras**

ONLINE EXTRAS
Pearson Edexcel **WWW**

Ensure you have grasped the key features of the political settlement by completing Worksheet 2 at **www. hoddereducation.co.uk/ accesstohistory/extras**

to assemble at least once every three years. This major constitutional shift had been carried out in order to avoid any future return to personal rule. In 1664, the Act was renewed and although it stated that 'there should be a frequent calling, assembling and holding of parliament once in three years at the least', Charles II modified the terms, ensuring that there were no legal mechanisms to enforce the Act. Both he and James II would later act in contravention of the Triennial Act.

SUMMARY DIAGRAM

THE POLITICAL SETTLEMENT

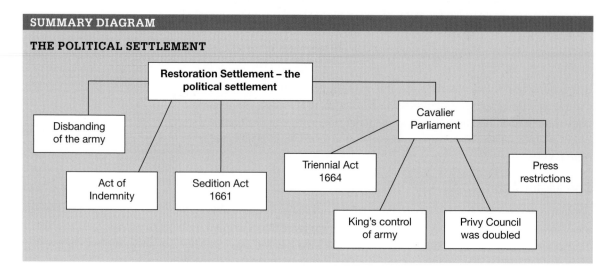

3 The financial settlement

■ *Was Charles II provided with adequate funding?*

If parliament was content to restore Charles to the throne with political powers close to those possessed by his father in 1642, its members were more divided over the issue of government finances. The Convention was more agreeable than the Cavalier Parliament, and its generosity is reflected in the £800,000 raised through extraordinary taxes in the immediate aftermath of the Restoration. This was used to pay for the disbanding of the army. The Convention then approved a permanent Crown revenue of £1.2 million.

Government income

It soon became clear that the Convention had significantly overvalued the proceeds Charles would receive from the various strands of revenue that had been projected. In reality, the average revenue received in the 1660s was around £700,000 (see Table 2.1, page 17). Even in years when England did not have to pay for wars, Charles would need at least £1 million to cover government expenditure. This shortfall was the result of a number of factors:

- War with Spain in the 1650s had disrupted trade and affected the many industries that relied on Spanish raw materials.
- The political upheavals of 1658–60 had a depressing impact on trade, leading to a reduction in customs revenues.
- The high taxes levied under the Republic had led to an economic slump that had continued.
- Poor harvests between 1658 and 1662 led to an increase in food prices.
- Apart from economic factors, there was a genuine desire from many MPs to deliberately restrict the King's revenue so he would have no choice but to work closely with them.

Table 2.1 Projected sources of Crown revenue in 1660.

Sources of revenue	Revenue raised
Customs duties	£400,000
Compensation for the removal of some feudal revenues	£100,000
Rents on Crown land	£263,598
Income from the Office of Postage	£21,500
Wine licences	£22,300
Tax on exported coal	£8,000
Proceeds from the Dean Forest	£4,000
Income from the Queen Mother's estate	£87,929
Liquor excise	£300,000
Total	**£1,207,327**

Mercantile legislation

With the general consensus that the majority of the King's revenue should now come from sources approved by parliament, Charles hoped to gain from a renewed parliamentarian focus on **mercantilism**, which might bolster the inadequate revenue he had been given. Mercantilism was popular with many of the European powers and had been prioritised by Cromwell in the 1650s. A Navigation Act had been passed in 1651, which stated that goods being transported to English colonies could be carried only on English ships. This was designed to break a developing Dutch monopoly on transatlantic trade. In the years immediately following the Restoration, further legislation was passed:

- Another Navigation Act in 1660 was designed to strengthen the original legislation. It stated that a number of goods produced in the colonies (see Chapter 10), including sugar and tobacco, could be supplied only to England. It also required English vessels to be manned by crews of at least three-quarters English by nationality.
- The Statute of Frauds (1662) introduced tight controls on ships carrying goods that became subject to customs duties on arrival in England. Government agents were given permission to board ships suspected of withholding goods liable to taxation.

KEY TERM

Mercantilism
A economic policy that attempts to achieve self-sufficiency and surplus wealth for a state by regulating trade and acquiring overseas possessions and colonies.

- A further Navigation Act, also known as the Staple Act, was passed in 1663. It stated that all foreign goods being shipped to England's American colonies had to first be routed through English ports. This ensured that the appropriate customs duties could be collected.

The increased revenue raised from this legislation resulted in an improved financial position for Charles, although the enhanced customs duties did not make much difference until the 1670s.

Court and government expenditure

As Table 2.2 shows, Charles's personal expenditure was high. His reputation as the 'Merry Monarch' is reflected in the £58,000 spent on his wardrobe in 1664. This amount is significantly higher than the £30,000 spent by his father in the 1630s. On top of this, the arrival of his new queen in 1662 and her associated household expenses added further to Charles's financial burden. The Royal Court was inefficient and Charles provided salaries and pensions to courtiers based on their friendship rather than their ability to dispense valuable advice.

Table 2.2 Expenditure on the Royal Court in 1664

Item	Cost
Households	£117,000
Wardrobe	£58,000
Stables	£2,700
Art	£12,000
Private expenses	£21,000
Other departments	£12,700
Meetings and associated expenditure	£32,000
Pensions to courtiers	£83,000
Total	**£338,400**

Charles would have to wait for an improvement in trade in the mid-1660s to see his income come close to matching expenditure. Any optimism about the government's long-term financial position was soon dampened when Charles committed England to war with the Dutch in 1665.

Sale of Dunkirk, 1662

Charles could still raise money independently of parliament, but this came with the disadvantage of eating into his capital. The sale of most of the remaining Crown lands in the 1670s raised £800,000, leaving Charles with only the estates used by the royal family. The inadequate nature of the financial settlement is reflected in his decision to sell Dunkirk in 1662. Dunkirk, in northern France, had been captured from Spain in 1658 and maintained a garrison of former Republican soldiers. Charles agreed to sell the town to Louis XIV of France for £320,000.

The Hearth Tax

Another blow to Charles's hopes of accessing more funding was the initial failure of the Hearth Tax. The tax was based on the number of hearths (fireplaces) in a house, with each hearth being liable to one shilling (5p), collected twice a year. Parliament approved this in November 1661 and the tax was first levied in 1662, with contemporaries often calling it the 'chimney tax'.

Constables acted as local tax collectors and faced significant opposition, as well as pressure to overlook hearths. Only one-third of the expected revenue of £250,000 was collected in the first year. In 1664, the local officials were replaced with independently appointed subcontractors, but they found it even more difficult to obtain local cooperation. It took several more years for the tax to become lucrative enough to make up the shortfall for which it had been originally intended.

ONLINE EXTRAS WWW
AQA

Learn how to write effective introductions by completing Worksheet 3 at **www. hoddereducation.co.uk/ accesstohistory/extras**

ONLINE EXTRAS WWW
Pearson Edexcel

Learn how to structure essays that address the concept of significance by completing Worksheet 3 at **www. hoddereducation.co.uk/ accesstohistory/extras**

SUMMARY DIAGRAM

THE FINANCIAL SETTLEMENT

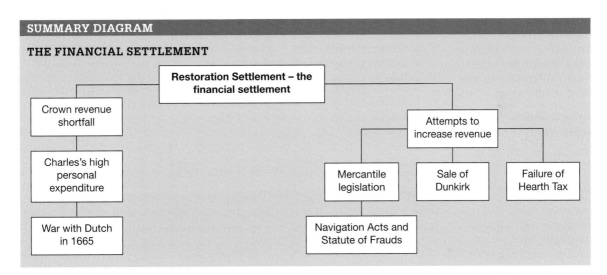

4 The religious settlement

■ *How was Anglicanism restored to a position of pre-eminence?*

Because of Charles's reliance on parliament's support to raise revenue and the shortfall in the financial settlement, parliament was able to exert influence on Charles over the future of the Church. As the Cavalier Parliament was overwhelmingly Anglican, it was inevitable that its members would insist on the full restoration of the Church of England to a form similar to that inherited by Charles I in 1625. It did seem, however, that a compromise might be found when the Convention arranged the Worcester House Conference in October 1660.

Worcester House Conference, 1660

The meeting included Presbyterian and Anglican clergy and resulted in the Worcester House Declaration. This proposed that the bishops be reinstated in an Anglican hierarchy, but with a Presbyterian to be appointed as royal chaplain and several concessions made to the Presbyterians. Clarendon suggested a clause that would allow 'others' to meet so long as they did not disturb the peace, but the Presbyterians' leader, **Richard Baxter**, opposed it as allowing liberty to Catholics. Less than six weeks after the publication of the Declaration, a motion transferring it into law lost in parliament by 183 votes to 157. Ultimately, the recommendations in the Declaration were not implemented for the following reasons:

- Charles supported the Worcester House Declaration because he had hoped to appeal to as many people as possible until he was secured on the throne. As his position became safer, he was able to distance himself from the negotiations.

- Charles was aware of the large number of Presbyterians in Monck's army and in the Convention Parliament, so had no choice but to support a more enhanced role for them in late 1660.

- Many of Charles's advisers, including Lord Chancellor Hyde, believed that the monarchy would survive only if the Anglican Church was restored on a broad, rather than a narrow basis.

Savoy Palace Conference, 1661

Charles issued a warrant for a conference at the Savoy Palace – the residence of **Gilbert Sheldon**, Bishop of London – in March 1661 to revise the *Book of Common Prayer* (see below) and discuss details of the long-term religious settlement. Baxter was once again the most vocal of the Presbyterians, and although he was asked to prepare a new form of worship for consideration, his suggestions were rejected outright.

No concessions were offered by the Anglicans and no compromises were made. Any hope for an inclusive Church of England was now lost and it was only a matter of time before Puritan clergy like Baxter would be ejected from the Church. Although both the high-church and low-church factions had been represented at the Conference, the impact of Venner's Rising and the election of the Cavalier Parliament meant that High Anglicanism would now dominate. The four Acts of the Clarendon Code (discussed on page 21) reflected the nature of this settlement.

(discussed on page 21)

KEY FIGURES

Richard Baxter (1615–91)

Baxter worked as a chaplain in the parliamentarian army and became a high-profile Presbyterian writer and preacher during the Republic. After the Restoration, he called for a national Church that could encompass both Presbyterian and Anglican views, but was cast aside when the Anglicans became the dominant religious force.

Gilbert Sheldon (1598–1677)

Sheldon was ordained as a priest in the 1620s and became a royal chaplain to Charles I. He was nominated Bishop of London in 1660 and joined the Privy Council. He became a key figure in the High Anglican movement and was a strong supporter of the Act of Uniformity. He became Archbishop of Canterbury in 1663 and held the post until his death.

Restoration of the *Book of Common Prayer*, 1662

The *Book of Common Prayer* of 1549 (see page 4) had been the target of Puritan scorn in the 1630s, and when a variant of it was imposed on the Scots in 1637, it caused widespread rebellion that ultimately led to two wars between Charles and the Scottish Presbyterians. It was agreed at the Savoy Palace Conference that the book should be used by the clergy once again. The only Presbyterian suggestion that made it into the book was the recommendation that the King James version of the Bible should be used in sermons, although this was already widely accepted. The book did remove some ceremonies from church services for their associations with Catholicism, but most – including baptism, Holy Communion and making the sign of the cross in Church – were kept.

The Clarendon Code

Charles demonstrated in the Declaration of Breda that his aim was to allow a measure of religious toleration. This initially relieved the fears of radical Protestants and was a view shared with Clarendon, who was primarily concerned with achieving unity in Church and State. The Worcester House Conference had promised a degree of cooperation and Charles even listened to the sermons of Richard Baxter.

As the Cavalier Parliament was overwhelmingly Anglican, its members moved to restore the Church of England to its former status and Charles and Clarendon's quest for toleration began to unravel. The result, as put forward at the Savoy Conference, was a Church with a narrow, exclusively Anglican view. Between 1661 and 1665, four Acts were passed that became known as the Clarendon Code:

- *The Corporation Act of 1661* restricted non-Anglicans from sitting on borough corporations. This gave Anglicans political domination in local government.
- *The Act of Uniformity of 1662* stated that parish priests should once again accept the *Book of Common Prayer.* The 1800 ministers, including Baxter, who were unable to conform were expelled and deprived of their livings in a process known as 'the Great Ejection'.
- *The Conventicle Act of 1664* restricted Dissenters from meeting in groups outside the Church of England. The most severe penalty for contravening this Act was transportation to the American colonies. An earlier Conventicle Act from 1593 was still in place, but it was rarely enforced.
- *The Five Mile Act of 1665* forbade ministers expelled under the Act of Uniformity from going within five miles of their former parishes.

Although this collection of Acts takes its name from Edward Hyde, Earl of Clarendon, he was less concerned about Nonconformity than most MPs were. He had promised senior offices in the Church to Nonconformists in order to smooth the way for the Restoration and was pragmatic when it came to both political and religious matters.

The Quaker Act, 1662

Further evidence of the Cavalier Parliament's reluctance to allow toleration can be found in the passing of the Quaker Act in 1662. Its full title was *An Act for preventing mischiefs and dangers that may arise by certain persons called Quakers and others refusing to take lawful oaths.* The Act banned Quaker meetings and made it illegal for people to refuse to take the oath of allegiance to the Church of England, something that was contrary to fundamental Quaker beliefs.

Extracts from the Clarendon Code

? SOURCE QUESTION

Read Sources C–E. How do you think the Puritans would react to the Acts of the Clarendon Code? Which sections would particularly irritate them?

SOURCE C

Extract from the Corporation Act, 1661.

No person or persons shall for ever hereafter be placed, elected or chosen in or to any offices that shall not have within one year next before such an election or choice taken the Sacrament of the Lord's Supper according to the rites of the Church of England. And in default hereof every such placing, election and choice is hereby enacted and declared to be void.

SOURCE D

Extract from the Act of Uniformity, 1662.

All ministers in any cathedral, collegiate or parish church or chapel shall be bound to say and use the Morning Prayer, Evening Prayer, celebration and administration of both the Sacraments. And to the end that uniformity in the public worship of God may be speedily effected, be it further enacted that every parson, vicar or other minister before the Feast of St Bartholomew [24 August], 1662, openly and publicly declare his unfeigned assent and consent to the use of all things in the said Prayer Book. And that all and every such person who shall neglect or refuse to do the same shall be deprived of all his spiritual promotions.

ONLINE EXTRAS **WWW**
AQA

Test your understanding of the religious settlement by completing Worksheet 4 at **www.hoddereducation. co.uk/accesstohistory/extras**

ONLINE EXTRAS **WWW**
Pearson Edexcel

Test your understanding of the Restoration Settlement by completing Worksheet 4 at **www.hoddereducation. co.uk/accesstohistory/extras**

SOURCE E

Extract from the Conventicle Act, 1664.

Be it enacted that if any person of the age of sixteen years or upwards, being a subject of this realm, shall be present at any assembly, conventicle or meeting under colour or pretence of any exercise of religion in other manner than according to the liturgy and practice of the Church of England, at which conventicle, there shall be five persons or more assembled, the justice shall impose on every such offender so convicted a fine of five shillings for such first offence.

SUMMARY DIAGRAM

THE RELIGIOUS SETTLEMENT

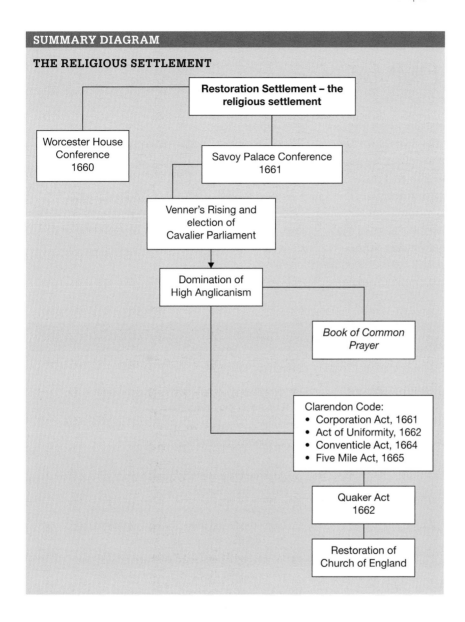

CHAPTER SUMMARY

Politically, the Restoration Settlement was able to provide a degree of harmony to the political nation after almost two decades of conflict and strife. The monarchy was restored with many of its former prerogative powers intact. The religious and financial issues, however, were far from resolved, and the inadequate nature of the financial settlement meant that Charles would spend much of his reign seeking new sources of funding. In the end, this would bring him into an ever-closer alliance with his cousin, Louis XIV of France. Religious matters were equally pressing and the Anglican-dominated Cavalier Parliament failed to comply with Charles's desire for religious toleration by passing the Acts of the Clarendon Code. This would also store up problems for later, as many of the conflicts between king and parliament in the years 1665–85 were founded on religious divisions.

Refresher questions

Use these questions to remind yourself of the key material covered in this chapter.

1 What was General Monck's role in restoring the monarchy?

2 Why was the Declaration of Breda appealing to the majority of English people?

3 In what ways did Venner's Rising affect political opinion?

4 How did the Act of Indemnity attempt to solve the problem of land ownership?

5 What are the main features of the Cavalier Parliament's membership?

6 How was the press restricted after the Restoration?

7 Why was the political settlement inadequate?

8 How was the Triennial Act of 1664 different from its predecessor?

9 Why was government income insufficient in the years after the Restoration?

10 What is mercantile legislation and how did it help to improve government income?

11 How did Charles II contribute towards increased government expenditure in the years immediately following the Restoration?

12 What were the outcomes of the Worcester House Conference and Savoy Palace Conference and how did they shape religious policy?

13 Which groups would have disagreed with the restoration of the Book of Common Prayer?

14 Who were the Acts of the Clarendon Code aimed at restricting?

15 What was the aim of the Quaker Act?

CHAPTER 3

Ministers and parliament, 1660–78

The Restoration Settlement failed to solve the problems that had led to war and revolution. Given the lack of clarity over the relative balance of power between monarch and parliament, it is not surprising that conflict re-emerged. What made matters worse was the growing suspicion that Charles was pursuing a pro-Catholic and absolutist agenda. This chapter focuses on the changing fortunes of Charles, his advisers and parliament before the Popish Plot of 1678, under the following headings:

◆ Clarendon's ministry

◆ The rise of the Cabal

◆ The rise of Danby

◆ The fall of Danby

KEY DATES

1660	Declaration of Breda	**1669**	James, Duke of York, converted to Catholicism
1662	Charles attempted to suspend the Act of Uniformity	**1670**	Treaty of Dover
1665	Second Anglo-Dutch War broke out	**1673**	Rise of Danby
1667	Fall of Clarendon	**1677**	Marriage of William of Orange and Mary Stuart
	End of Anglo-Dutch War		

1 Clarendon's ministry

■ *Why was Clarendon replaced as chief minister in 1667?*

Edward Hyde came from a gentry family and had trained as a lawyer before being elected to the Long Parliament in 1640. Although he was originally associated with the anti-court party, he felt that the increasing attacks on Charles I in the Long Parliament were a step too far. He became one of the **Constitutional Royalists** and fought for the King in the Civil War. He joined Charles II in exile in France in the 1650s and became his closest adviser.

Clarendon as chief minister, 1660–7

Hyde ensured that he was well placed to become chief minister on the Restoration of the monarchy in 1660:

■ Charles had already appointed him Lord Chancellor while still in exile.

■ He was a key author of the Declaration of Breda (see page 9).

KEY TERM

Constitutional Royalists A group which believed that the concessions won by parliament in the years 1640–2 were adequate and that the King's powers should not be limited any further. Many had fought for Charles I in the Civil War.

- His daughter, Anne Hyde, married Charles's brother James, Duke of York, in 1660. Their two daughters became the future monarchs Mary II and Queen Anne.

- He was created Earl of Clarendon at Charles's coronation in 1661.

SOURCE QUESTION

According to Source A, what negative qualities did Clarendon possess?

SOURCE A

From Gilbert Burnet's (1643–1715) reflections on Clarendon's qualities in *History of My Own Time*, published in 1724. Burnet was a clergyman and royal courtier and was closely associated with the Whig Party.

Charles did so entirely trust the Earl of Clarendon, that he left all to his care, and submitted to his advices as to so many oracles. The Earl of Clarendon distinguished himself so in the House of Commons, that he became considerable, and was much trusted all the while the King was at Oxford. He stayed beyond the sea following the King's fortune till the Restoration; and was now an absolute favourite, and the chief or the only Minister, but with too magisterial a way. He was always pressing the King to mind his affairs, but in vain. He was a good Chancellor, only a little too rough, but very impartial in the administration of justice. He never seemed to understand foreign affairs well: And yet he meddled too much in them. He had too much levity in his wit, and did not always observe the decorum of his post. He was high, and was apt to reject those who addressed themselves to him with too much contempt. He had such a regard to the King, that when places were disposed of, even otherwise than as he advised, yet he would justify what the King did, and disparage the pretensions of others, not without much scorn; which created him many enemies. He was indefatigable in business, tho' the gout did often disable him from waiting on the King: Yet, during his credit, the King came constantly to him when he was laid up by it.

Implementing the Declaration of Breda, 1660

As one of the architects of the Declaration of Breda, Clarendon worked tirelessly to ensure that its promises were carried out. At the behest of Charles, he spoke out in the Lords to minimise the number of former parliamentarians to be executed under the terms of the Act of Indemnity. Working closely with Charles to fulfil the king's wishes, Burnet (see Source A) claimed that the Declaration could not have been carried out without him, and 'the work from beginning to end was entirely Clarendon's'.

Clarendon disagreed with Charles on the implementation of the religious settlement. Charles preferred full toleration for all religious groups, whereas Clarendon favoured one national Church that could incorporate both Anglicans and Presbyterians.

Catherine of Braganza

Clarendon wished the King to marry, but was keen for his new wife to be a Protestant. This meant that when a Catholic match was first suggested, he was reluctant. The marriage between Charles and **Catherine of Braganza** was first proposed by the Portuguese ambassador in June 1660. Despite Clarendon's

KEY FIGURE

Catherine of Braganza (1638–1705)

Catherine was the daughter of the Portuguese king, John IV. She suffered three miscarriages and failed to produce a legitimate heir for Charles. Although their relationship was cold at first (he had twelve illegitimate children with a number of mistresses), Charles defended her vigorously when she was accused as part of the fictitious Popish Plot in 1678 (see page 72).

KEY TERM

Great Tew Circle
A group that assembled at the house of Lucius Cary, Viscount Falkland, in the 1630s. Many of its members had unorthodox and tolerant religious beliefs, although they tended to support a strong monarchy.

reluctance, when the Privy Council unanimously approved of the marriage he had no choice but to provide open backing.

In part to maintain his position as chief minister, Clarendon took a leading role in the arrangements and formally announced the King's marriage to parliament in May 1661. Catherine proved to be infertile, which meant that Charles's brother, James, was next in line to the throne. This was damaging to Clarendon because of his own grandchildren's position in the line of succession, as they were the daughters of James. He was later accused of deliberately arranging for Charles to marry an infertile bride in order to advance himself and his family members.

Clarendon Code

Despite its name, Clarendon was not particularly involved in the drafting of the Clarendon Code (see page 21). The zealously Anglican Cavalier Parliament enforced the Code, and although Clarendon accepted the necessity of establishing a level of conformity in the Church, he worked tirelessly in an attempt to pass an Act that would see Presbyterian ministers continue in their livings. He had been deeply involved in theological debate from an early age as a member of the **Great Tew Circle** of religious moderates and felt that a broad-based Church, rather than one that was strictly Anglican, would result in the most positive outcome for the nation. In addition, he joined the majority of the Lords in proposing a bill intended to provide financial protection for those ministers removed under the terms of the Act of Uniformity.

Tensions with other ministers

While Clarendon was essentially a religious moderate, he was torn between a firmly Anglican parliament that insisted on uniformity, and a King intent on providing religious toleration for Catholics. **Henry Bennet**, who became the first Earl of Arlington in 1665, spearheaded a move among the pro-Catholic party to suspend the laws enforcing Anglicanism, which Clarendon firmly opposed. This opposition was founded primarily on grounds of personal hostility rather than any strong disapproval of the religious content. **George Digby**, Earl of Bristol, had long hoped to bring a prosecution of treason against Clarendon, and although discouraged by Charles, he made a formal accusation on 10 July 1663. Clarendon completely denied the charges and the judges stated that even if the accusations were true, they did not amount to high treason. Charles further defended his chief minister, telling the Lords that many of the alleged facts of the case – including an accusation that he profited from Irish land sales – were fictitious.

The diarist **Samuel Pepys**, who took a close interest in Court affairs, wrote that 'Bennet and Bristol and their friends have cast my Lord Chancellor [Clarendon] on his back, past ever getting up again'. Despite these attacks, Clarendon was still of the firm belief that Nonconformists were a danger to the peace of the state, writing, 'their faction is their religion, which makes them cling inseparably together'.

KEY FIGURES
Henry Bennet (1618–85)
Arlington supported the royalist cause in the Civil War and joined Charles and James in exile in the 1650s. He became especially close to Charles and firmly established himself as a royal favourite, with responsibility for procuring Charles's many mistresses. He was made Secretary of State in 1662 and his influence grew further, before establishing himself as a member of the Cabal ministry (page 31) from 1667.

George Digby (1612–77)
Digby was loyal to Charles I in the Civil War and joined Charles II during his exile, converting to Catholicism in 1657. His religion excluded him from senior government posts in the early years of the Restoration and he became extremely active in the House of Lords in an attempt to undermine Clarendon. After his attempted impeachment of Clarendon, Digby removed himself from public life, but was welcomed back to the Royal Court on the fall of Clarendon in 1667.

Samuel Pepys (1633–1703)
Pepys worked as a government and then naval administrator from the late 1650s and began making a diary in 1660. He recorded both his personal life and the major national events that he experienced first hand, including the Great Fire of London, the Great Plague and the coronation of Charles II.

The failure of the Second Anglo–Dutch War, 1665–7

Anglo-Dutch commercial rivalries were long-standing by the time of the Restoration, in part because both countries had economic interests in the American colonies. This rivalry came to a head in 1663, when England seized the Dutch fort on Cape Verde. This was followed by the capture of New Amsterdam (renamed New York) in 1664. Parliament voted funding for a conflict in February 1665 and war was promptly declared. The Battle of Lowestoft (June 1665) was a rare English victory in a war dominated by the Dutch, and when, in early 1666, the French and the Danes joined the Dutch, English fortunes spiralled into decline. During the raid on the Medway in June 1667, the Thames was blockaded, resulting in the price of coal briefly increasing by 900 per cent. Sailors were left unpaid, and the government had to purchase supplies at prices that had increased by as much as 40 per cent in two years.

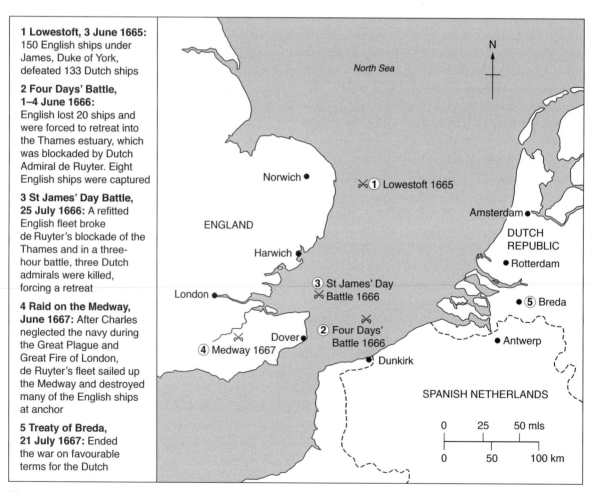

1 Lowestoft, 3 June 1665: 150 English ships under James, Duke of York, defeated 133 Dutch ships

2 Four Days' Battle, 1–4 June 1666: English lost 20 ships and were forced to retreat into the Thames estuary, which was blockaded by Dutch Admiral de Ruyter. Eight English ships were captured

3 St James' Day Battle, 25 July 1666: A refitted English fleet broke de Ruyter's blockade of the Thames and in a three-hour battle, three Dutch admirals were killed, forcing a retreat

4 Raid on the Medway, June 1667: After Charles neglected the navy during the Great Plague and Great Fire of London, de Ruyter's fleet sailed up the Medway and destroyed many of the English ships at anchor

5 Treaty of Breda, 21 July 1667: Ended the war on favourable terms for the Dutch

Figure 3.1 The major battles of the Second Anglo-Dutch War.

The terms of the resulting Treaty of Breda were humiliating for Charles. The Navigation Acts were modified to allow the Dutch access to English ports and most colonies taken during the war were returned. Clarendon became a scapegoat for the defeat, and although he was not directly involved in operational decisions, government incompetence had certainly contributed to the outcome. He wrote that he was unable to travel freely in London and the trees outside his home were pulled up by the mob.

The Great Plague

English performance in the war was hampered by the Great Plague (1665–6) and the Great Fire of London (September 1666). Plagues were relatively common in the seventeenth century; however, a combination of insanitary conditions and hot summers in 1665 and 1666 caused a serious outbreak. This **bubonic plague** was most likely spread by fleas and brought to England in merchant ships. It reached its height in September 1666, when 30,000 deaths were recorded nationally in one month.

> **KEY TERM**
>
> **Bubonic plague**
> The most common form of plague, typified by fever and swollen lymph nodes (called buboes). The disease killed around half of those who contracted it in the seventeenth century.

The Great Fire of London

Early in the morning of 2 September 1666, a fire started on Pudding Lane, London. Within a few hours the fire was a mile long, and in very dry conditions, with wells almost out of water, the fire continued for several days. There was little loss of life, but the material damage was enormous. Eighty-nine churches were destroyed, including St Paul's Cathedral. Other public buildings, such as the Guildhall and Royal Exchange, were also lost, as well as 3200 houses. The reconstruction came at great expense, with the Navigation Act relaxed in order to import large amounts of timber. The fire was another major economic setback that put further pressure on Charles to find new solutions to his financial problems and again, as chief minister, Clarendon was associated with this period of misfortune.

Clarendon's fall

One of Clarendon's fundamental flaws as chief minister was his lack of commitment to the role. He did not believe in the concept of a chief minister and failed to grasp some of the more subtle aspects of the role that could have led to his cultivating a wider following. For example, he neglected to understand the importance of attending banquets and royal entertainments in order to establish informal contacts with the newer members of the Royal Court, whom he always viewed with suspicion.

This lack of personal support was magnified in the wake of the Anglo-Dutch War and the Great Fire. The accusations against him in parliament, which would later be presented in impeachment proceedings, mounted:

- He had suggested in 1666 that parliament be dissolved in order for it to be replaced with a more obedient assembly.

- He was accused of saying that the House of Commons was useful only for raising money and that it should not interfere with the affairs of state.
- His suggestion during the raid on the Medway that additional taxes should be levied on coastal counties to pay for defence was interpreted as his ambition to control an army.
- It was even rumoured that he had called the King a papist (Catholic).
- He had corruptly sold offices in government.

Although nearly all the accusations were baseless, Clarendon was removed as Chancellor in October 1667, and Charles assured parliament that he would never be employed again in public office.

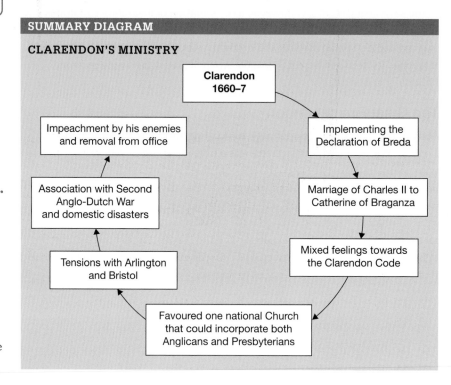

SUMMARY DIAGRAM

CLARENDON'S MINISTRY

Clarendon
1660–7

Implementing the
Declaration of Breda

Marriage of Charles II to
Catherine of Braganza

Mixed feelings towards
the Clarendon Code

Favoured one national Church
that could incorporate both
Anglicans and Presbyterians

Tensions with Arlington
and Bristol

Association with Second
Anglo-Dutch War
and domestic disasters

Impeachment by his enemies
and removal from office

KEY FIGURE

**Louis XIV of France
(1638–1715)**

Louis reigned for over 72 years, from 1643 until his death in 1715. He and Charles II were cousins, as Louis' aunt was Henrietta Maria, Charles's mother. Like the Stuart monarchs, he believed firmly in the divine right of kings, but unlike the Stuarts he was not expected to consult a parliament. He became a champion of absolutist rule and centralised all the power of the state in himself and a small group of advisers. He spent much of his reign at war, and through massive investment in the army and navy, France became the leading military power in Europe.

2 The rise of the Cabal

■ *Were the members of the Cabal united in their objectives?*

Even before the Treaty of Breda had been signed, it was clear that Charles favoured a pro-French foreign policy. He had written to his cousin, **Louis XIV**, towards the end of the war, promising to support him in any way he could. His choice of advisers began to reflect this preference, and in the months preceding the fall of his chief minister, an informal network had developed around Charles that had one thing in common: a shared loathing of Clarendon. This 'Cabal' took its name from the initials of its members' names. However, recent research has suggested that the group, rather than providing decisive and united leadership, was disjointed and possessed little cohesion.

Members of the Cabal ministry

- *Thomas Clifford*. A committed Catholic, Clifford joined the Privy Council in 1666 and was a chief promoter of French interests in the Cabal. He signed the secret part of the Treaty of Dover and his support for royal despotism and Catholicism is summed up in his advice to Charles: 'rather to be in slavery to one man [Louis] than to five hundred [parliament]'.
- *Henry Bennet, Earl of Arlington*. Although not a Catholic, Arlington's religious preferences were for the High Church tradition. He did much to promote Clifford and the two became close allies. Together with Buckingham, he was perhaps the most powerful member of the Cabal.
- *George Villiers, Duke of Buckingham*. Buckingham had close links with Nonconformists and had long been a prominent opponent of Clarendon. Jealousy and rivalry with Arlington prevented the two men from cooperating, despite the fact that many of their foreign policy objectives were the same.
- *Anthony Ashley Cooper*. A supporter of Protestant Nonconformity, Ashley was Chancellor of the Exchequer from 1661 to 1672 and had opposed the imposition of the Clarendon Code, instead preferring the religious toleration offered by Charles's Declaration of Indulgence.
- *John Maitland, Duke of Lauderdale*. Served as Secretary of State in Scotland from 1661 to 1680. He was from a Scottish noble family and was a committed Presbyterian in his younger years, switching allegiance to Charles during his exile. He spent most of his time in Scotland and engaged little in English affairs.

Foreign policy under the Cabal

The chief architect of English foreign policy in these years was Arlington. Always keen to please Charles, he was credited with urging England's entry into the Second Anglo-Dutch War. Under the Republic, he had acted as Charles's agent in Madrid, but in the years after the Restoration he failed to achieve his aim of forging an alliance with Spain.

Charles and Buckingham ensured that when the French ambassador Henri de Ruvigny visited England in August 1667, no secret was made of the fact that their preference was for a much closer Anglo-French alliance. Meanwhile, a clear rift in the foreign policy objectives of the Cabal began to emerge when Arlington entered into negotiations with the Dutch in order to form an alliance against France in a move that would satisfy Spain. As a consequence, the Triple Alliance between England, the Dutch Republic and another Protestant power, Sweden, was created in early 1668. This was aimed at restricting French territorial claims after Louis had attacked the Spanish Netherlands. The alliance was popular in England, and despite offering it his support in public, Charles continued to assure Louis that it made no difference to their relations.

SOURCE QUESTION

Study Source B. De Medina's painting was produced after 1688. Why do you think there was such an interest in the Cabal so many years after its demise?

SOURCE B

The Crimson Bedchamber by John Baptist de Medina (1659–1710), traditionally said to depict the members of the Cabal ministry. De Medina spent most of his career in Scotland producing portraits of Whig politicians and this work was probably painted after the Glorious Revolution of 1688. Left to right: Thomas Clifford, Henry Bennet, George Villiers, Anthony Ashley Cooper and John Maitland.

In the late 1660s, then, popular sentiment had become increasingly pro-Dutch and anti-French. This was reflected in parliament:

- Parliament agreed to supply Charles with ships to bolster his fleet in early 1688.
- A sum of £310,000 was voted to support Charles in the alliance. The tax to pay for this was intended to come primarily from French imports.
- Existing suspicions of the French and Catholics were heightened in parliament. In 1668, the Anglican majority petitioned Charles to issue a proclamation against religious meetings outside the Church of England, aimed specifically at Catholics.

Continued dependence on parliamentary finance

In early 1669, Charles ordered a review of his financial situation so he could determine whether he might be able to free himself of parliamentary support.

It was found that his debts were too high and his income too low from hereditary sources. If his personal and Court expenditure was reduced he would still need at least £1 million per year. When parliament assembled in October 1669, Charles told them that the £310,000 they had granted for the Triple Alliance had been spent, and he urged them to consider offering more money to help him pay off his debts. Instead of offering supply, members of parliament (MPs) insisted that the financial affairs of Charles's associates should be scrutinised more closely. Parliament was promptly prorogued by Charles for several months.

Key parliamentary procedures and terminology

- *Supply.* The granting of government income from parliament, normally through the raising of new taxes.
- *Prorogation.* When a session of parliament is discontinued without being formally dissolved.
- *Dissolution.* The official term for the formal end to a parliament. When parliament is dissolved, every seat in the House of Commons becomes vacant until a general election is held.
- *Adjournment.* The end of a meeting of parliament with the intention of resuming it at a later date.
- *Session.* The period for which parliament convenes in order to discuss legislation. There may be a number of sessions between elections and they are of no fixed length.
- *Bill.* A proposed law, before it has received the royal assent to become an Act of Parliament.

The Treaty of Dover, 1670

The increasingly pro-French foreign policy of Charles and the Cabal climaxed in the signing of the Treaty of Dover with Louis in 1670. This established a formal military alliance between the two countries against the Dutch.

French motives

As well as border disputes, economic rivalry had developed between France and the Dutch Republic that would result in Louis seeking support from Charles. France had important overseas possessions, but the Dutch had started to develop a monopoly over international trade. Furs from Canada, sugar from French colonies in the Caribbean and slaves from Africa were all traded in Dutch ships. To compete with the English Navigation Acts, the French imposed high tariffs on Dutch imports. In addition, Louis, who tended to leave economic policy to his advisers, but viewed himself as a defender of the Catholic faith, supported the establishment of Catholicism in England and felt that Charles would be open to the idea. Negotiations in London soon began over the terms of a formal treaty.

English motives

The French ambassador, Charles Colbert de Croissy, arrived in England in August 1668 with instructions to negotiate an alliance. He found Buckingham to be greatly supportive of the idea, but Arlington – who was both pro-Spanish and pro-Dutch – strove to block it. Early in 1669, Charles's brother James, Duke of York, publicly announced his conversion to Catholicism, having taken advice on the matter from both Clifford and Arlington. This was followed by a meeting between Charles and the three men, whereby Charles expressed his regret at not being in a position to personally convert, and asked for their views on the best means of promoting Catholicism in England.

The secret treaty

There were two versions of the resulting Treaty of Dover, signed by both parties in 1670, with only one version containing the 'secret' clauses. Only a small inner circle around Charles and Louis had knowledge of the secret Treaty. It included three main objectives:

- France would assist Charles in restoring Catholicism in England.

- The two countries would renew hostilities against the Dutch and a French subsidy of £800,000 would be paid for English participation (in the final draft this was reduced to £300,000).

- Charles would announce his own conversion to Catholicism at an appropriate time, in exchange for French subsidies that would free Charles from dependence on parliaments, beginning with a gift of £200,000. A second pact with Louis, in 1675, committed more money to Charles, with the first payment of £100,000 being made in 1681, enabling Charles to embark on personal rule for the last four years of his reign.

The public treaty

It had been found impossible to show the secret version of the treaty to the Protestant members of the Cabal (it had been signed only by Clifford and Arlington), as they would never agree to the clause stating that Charles would declare himself a Catholic. A second treaty was therefore prepared in which funding and a commercial alliance were still promised by the French, but nothing was said of the Catholic conversion or the promise to bring French troops to England to help Charles.

Why did Charles believe the treaty would succeed?

It seems strange that the sovereign of a Protestant country would consider converting the nation back to Catholicism against the wishes of the majority. Charles may appear to be blinkered and out of touch, but in fact there was some logic behind his decision to move forward with the alliance:

- He was assured of the devotion of his troops, and as a result of the Militia Act (see page 15) he had sole control of the army.

- A number of senior officers were Catholic, including governors of several military garrisons.
- He believed that as Protestant Nonconformists hated the Anglicans more than the Catholics, they would support him, as they would have a greater chance of achieving religious toleration.

The aftermath of the treaty

Although parliament had no knowledge of the secret treaty, when it met again MPs seemed aware that the situation was beginning to favour an increase in monarchical power. They voted an additional tax on wine and vinegar, estimated to provide about £400,000 a year to Charles, and dropped the financial investigations into Charles's advisers.

Preparations for another Dutch war

The Cavalier Parliament met for its ninth session in October 1670. Charles told parliament that £800,000 would be required to equip an adequate fleet. The Commons was agreeable and provided this sum through new taxes on beer and property transactions. Six months later, however, this harmony between parliament and Charles was interrupted when MPs presented the King with a petition against the growth of Catholicism, particularly in relation to the large numbers of Catholics found in London. Charles was able to satisfy parliament by issuing a proclamation requiring all Catholic priests to leave England within two months.

Preparations without parliament

In April 1671, Charles prorogued parliament once again until February 1673. During this interval of nearly two years, Charles faced the prospect of fighting a war he was financially underprepared for. The most pressing problem was his debts, which now amounted to £2 million. Knowing that he would be unable convert the country to Catholicism, but still intent on Catholic toleration, he passed a Declaration of Indulgence in March 1672, which suspended penal laws against Nonconformists and Catholics (see page 63).

The Stop of the Exchequer

As a result of the major debts faced by Charles and the need to find savings to fight the war, it was decided that all payments to his creditors would be suspended in what became known as the **Stop of the Exchequer** (20 January). This move was initially suggested by Clifford and in the proclamation made by Charles to his creditors he stated that for a period of one year he would continue to pay interest on his loans, but would not pay any of the capital. This ensured that enough funding remained in place to continue the war for the time being, but any goodwill between Charles and his financiers – particularly the **goldsmith bankers** – was lost.

KEY TERMS

Stop of the Exchequer
The suspension of loan repayments to creditors. Charles used a loophole in the law to declare his debts illegal and void because they were charged at a rate of more than six per cent.

Goldsmith bankers
The London goldsmiths were able to provide safe storage for valuable items and in the early seventeenth century began to accept deposits and made loans with the funds they kept. After the Stop of the Exchequer a number of goldsmith bankers went out of business completely.

The Third Anglo-Dutch War

At the outbreak of war, the French and English had the superior forces. The Dutch did not initially view this as a problem because they were convinced that their two opponents would not be able to work efficiently together. James, Duke of York, took a leading role as commander of the fleet once again. The Battle of Solebay (7 June 1672) was claimed as a victory on both sides and was the first of a number of failed attempts by the English to make a landing on the Dutch coast. By the time the autumn 1672 session of parliament had arrived, the war was becoming increasingly unpopular.

Table 3.1 Comparison of forces in the Third Anglo-Dutch War

Item	French and English	Dutch
Warships	98	75
Cannons	6,000	4,500
Troops	34,000	20,000
Casualities	2,500	2,600

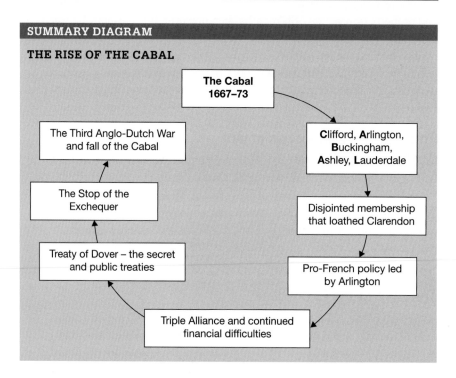

SUMMARY DIAGRAM

THE RISE OF THE CABAL

3 The rise of Danby

■ *How successful was Danby at managing king and parliament?*

The members of the Cabal were never united and generally pursued their own individual political interests. From 1672, their factional rivalries and failures became increasingly exposed and their influence waned.

The fall of the Cabal

With a shifting political climate, the members soon lost their official appointments or, at the very least, the substantial patronage of the King that they once enjoyed.

Clifford

Only Clifford and Arlington were privy to the secret Treaty of Dover, and as a Catholic, Clifford was closely involved in Charles's various negotiations with the French. He was made Baron Clifford of Chudleigh in April 1672, in part because of his role in arranging the Stop of the Exchequer. Promoted to Lord Treasurer in November, Arlington began to conspire against Clifford in fear that he was being promoted too far. Before Arlington was able to push for his removal, the Test Act was passed, requiring Catholic office holders to take Anglican Communion. This signalled Clifford's downfall and he was forced to resign from the Privy Council. He died a few months later, possibly by his own hand.

Arlington

Clifford's promotions came while Arlington was busy attempting to negotiate peace terms with the Dutch, which ultimately ended in failure. Arlington's jealously became too much, and he began to associate himself with the opposition. He supported the Test Act, in part because he knew this would result in Clifford's resignation. In order to ingratiate himself with his new allies, he revealed his knowledge of the secret Treaty of Dover to Ashley. This was too late for him to build up a new support base and he was impeached by the Commons for leading the pro-French policy and promoting Catholicism.

Buckingham

Buckingham travelled with Arlington to take part in peace negotiations with the Dutch, which failed. He was made aware of the secret Treaty of Dover and this led to increased resentment and suspicion of Arlington. Before he could build support to discredit Arlington further, Buckingham was, like his new opponent, impeached in the Commons on charges of promoting the pro-French alliance and arbitrary government. Charles was now keen for an opportunity to remove Buckingham, partly because of his policy failures and partly because of a high-profile affair Buckingham had been conducting with the Countess of Shrewsbury, which had been embarrassing for the Court. He was removed from the Privy Council.

Ashley

In February 1673, Ashley, now made Earl of Shaftesbury, delivered a speech declaring the Dutch 'England's eternal enemy' and showing support for the Declaration of Indulgence. His support for Nonconformists was not well received by the Commons, and when Ashley organised elections to fill the 36 seats that had become vacant since 1661, he was attacked for offering these to his supporters. He conformed to the Test Act later in 1673, but it was now clear that the Cabal was falling apart and he began to align himself with the pro-Dutch Country opposition (see below). When the Duke of York married the Catholic Mary of Modena, Ashley moved to condemn the marriage in parliament. This led to strong criticisms from James, and Charles removed Ashley from the post of Lord Chancellor in November 1673.

Lauderdale

While in Scotland, Lauderdale passed a number of measures to strengthen the Crown's position, including the raising of troops and a measure of toleration for ministers who submitted to the authority of the King. Because of his absence from London, he was never truly a member of the Cabal in the same way the 'English ministers' were. He was included because of his closeness to Charles, and this perhaps explains why his career continued while the other members' declined. On James's resignation as Lord Admiral following the passing of the Test Act in 1673, Lauderdale was promoted at the Admiralty; and his political opponents in Scotland – led by the Duke of Hamilton – attempted to remove him from office. On 13 January 1674, he was attacked in the Commons, primarily because he had declared that 'the king's edicts are equal with the law'. Before Lauderdale could be impeached, Charles prorogued parliament, saving his political career.

The emergence of parties

Since the beginning of Charles I's reign, a division had begun to emerge between 'Court' and 'Country' interests. Members of the political nation – particularly in parliament – who were suspicious of Charles's links to Catholic powers and the Arminians, formed the Country faction against Court interests. These divisions had acted as one of the grounds for side-taking in the Civil Wars, where many of the opposition joined the parliamentarian side and Court loyalists formed the core of the royalist army.

The two factions became more defined from the early 1670s. The Country faction believed that Charles II's pro-French policies were damaging to the nation, and his attempts to provide toleration to both Catholics and Dissenters were dangerous. The Court faction were on the whole fiercely loyal to Charles and supported the pro-French policy of creeping absolutism. In the autumn 1673 session of parliament, a determined opposition began to take shape, led by Lord Cavendish, William Russell, the Earl of Shaftesbury (Ashley), Sir William Coventry and the Earl of Halifax.

Table 3.2 The development of factions in parliament

Tension	When?	Reason
'Court' vs 'Country'	Early seventeenth century	• Suspicion of Arminianism and Catholic influence at Court • Arbitrary government of Charles I
Royalists vs parliamentarians	The Civil Wars (1642–51)	• Side-taking in the Civil Wars was determined by a number of factors, including loyalty, religious allegiance or economic motives
Tories vs Whigs	After the Popish Plot and Exclusion Crisis (1678–81)	• The Tories were loyal to the Royal Court and favoured a strengthened monarchy • The Whigs favoured excluding James from the line of succession and were associated with Nonconformist Protestants and a limited monarchy

The Duke of York demoted

At this point, Charles's brother James, Duke of York, might appear to have been in the most trusted position to assist Charles in fulfilling his policy objectives. However, he possessed neither political wisdom nor knowledge of the country he would one day rule. As a Catholic, he would always have a prospective following among Nonconformist Dissenters prepared to welcome his resistance to Anglicanism, and, although one of his great strengths was his focus and seriousness, at this stage in his political life he lacked the ambition to become closely involved in government strategy.

Danby as chief minister

At this juncture, Charles told friends that he was fortunate to be able to advance a minister who, he felt, possessed many of the qualities of Clarendon. What made Sir Thomas Osborne (as he was known before being made Earl of Danby) different from Clarendon was his firm commitment to Anglicanism and a genuine desire to reduce religious dissent. He replaced Clifford as Lord High Treasurer in June 1673, and took to the task of placing Charles's government on a more sound financial footing:

- He was able to negotiate with Charles's creditors to reduce the rate of interest on government loans by promising a payment of £77,000 per annum to cover losses incurred after the Stop of the Exchequer.
- By securing efficiencies in the collection of excise taxes he was able to increase income from this source by £20,000 per annum.
- He improved yields from the Hearth Tax, which helped to pay off old debts and increased revenue by a further £100,000.
- He was able to secure a total revenue of £1.4 million in 1674–5. For the first time, Charles was not in debt and a future without the need for parliaments was a possibility.

Thomas Osborne, Earl of Danby

1632	Born to Sir Edward and Anne Osborne at Kiveton, Yorkshire
1661	Elected High Sheriff of Yorkshire
1668	Appointed Treasurer of the Navy
1673–9	Lord High Treasurer
1679–84	Imprisoned in the Tower of London after impeachment
1688	Acted as one of the seven politicians who invited William of Orange to invade in the Glorious Revolution
1694	Created Duke of Leeds
1712	After remaining as an active member of the House of Lords for many years, died at the age of 80

Background

Danby was born in Yorkshire and his estates neighboured those of the Duke of Buckingham. His father had been a staunch royalist in the Civil War and Danby enjoyed the patronage of Buckingham during his early political career, followed by a series of promotions orchestrated by him. He was even referred to by Pepys in 1668 as 'the creature of Buckingham'.

Career

Before rising to become chief minister he served as Treasurer of the Navy in 1668, and Commissioner for the State Treasury in 1669. As chief minister he was able to dictate much government policy, and despite his successes (including arranging the marriage of William and Mary and putting the government on a sound financial footing), his determination to increase royal authority made him many enemies, eventually leading to his impeachment.

Later years

After spending nearly five years in the Tower of London, Danby was released shortly before the death of Charles II. He became a moderate Tory, and after becoming disillusioned with the rule of James II, was one of the seven signatories of the letter inviting William of Orange to invade in 1688.

KEY FIGURE

William of Orange (1650–1702)

William was the son of William II, Prince of Orange, and Mary, the eldest daughter of Charles I. Although his father died shortly before his birth, political conditions in the Netherlands prevented William becoming *Stadtholder* (head of state) until 1672. Marriage to his first cousin, Mary, in 1677 brought him closer still to the Stuarts and this helped to pave the way for him succeeding to the English throne in the Glorious Revolution.

Pro-Dutch policy

Danby had a gift for both accountancy and affability and by March 1675 was firmly established as chief minister. Despite his dedication to Anglicanism he was supported by both the Duke of York and Buckingham and was given relative freedom to change the direction of government policy. Most notably, he favoured an alliance with **William of Orange**, rather than Louis XIV. This stemmed from a commitment to a religious alliance; Danby was a realist, and as the Dutch economic model (based on state support for increased international trade) appeared to be reaping great rewards, he felt England should follow suit.

Religious differences with Charles

Danby hoped to establish royal independence from parliament, but unlike Charles, he felt that French assistance was not the way to achieve financial security. In Danby's view, another drawback of the French alliance was the likely outcome of increased religious toleration. Like the majority of members of the Cavalier Parliament, Danby was uncompromisingly Anglican and in private he strongly disapproved of the Declaration of Indulgence.

Continued French negotiations, 1674–5

Charles felt regret that he had been obliged to abandon the French alliance, and, in order to buy time while he decided on his next move, he prorogued parliament from July 1674 to April 1675. Despite the officially pro-Dutch policy,

Charles continued his secret negotiations with French ambassador Ruvigny. The French pushed for a complete dissolution of parliament, which Danby strongly opposed, and he was instrumental in ensuring that a French offer of £100,000 to prorogue parliament for longer was rejected.

By the time parliament met again, Danby had issued a number of edicts against Catholics and Nonconformists in the hope that MPs would receive him favourably. One of the edicts introduced financial rewards for those who reported the locations where mass was being said. In return, Charles asked, in his first speech to the reassembled parliament, for sufficient finance to strengthen the fleet. Parliament's response was not what Charles expected. They called for the impeachment of Danby, and accused him of amassing far more personal power than was appropriate. The charges were ultimately dropped, in part because Danby had bribed many of the members to support his cause.

ONLINE EXTRAS **WWW**
AQA

Test your knowledge of the differences between Clarendon and Danby by completing Worksheet 7 at **www.hoddereducation. co.uk/accesstohistory/extras**

ONLINE EXTRAS **WWW**
Pearson Edexcel

Test your knowledge of Danby's ministry by completing Worksheet 7 at **www.hoddereducation. co.uk/accesstohistory/extras**

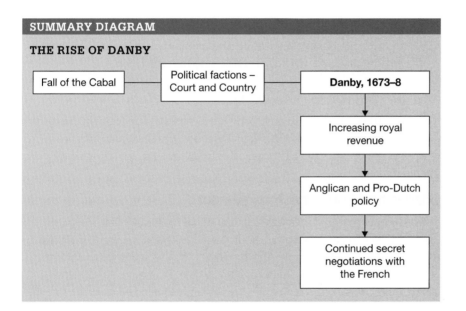

SUMMARY DIAGRAM

THE RISE OF DANBY

Fall of the Cabal — Political factions – Court and Country — **Danby, 1673–8**

↓

Increasing royal revenue

↓

Anglican and Pro-Dutch policy

↓

Continued secret negotiations with the French

4 The fall of Danby

◼ *Why did Danby fall out of favour?*

In 1675, Charles was still maintaining a number of English soldiers in France who were fighting for Louis. This created further animosity from sections of parliament, and how evenly parties were divided was demonstrated when the question of whether to recall these soldiers was put to the House, with 135 votes counted on each side. The soldiers remained in France for the time being.

The consolidation of parties in parliament

Danby has been accused of being inadvertently responsible for solidifying the two parties in parliament that would become Whig and Tory. He attempted to pass a bill imposing a new oath on all office holders, including MPs, stating their loyalty to the government and the Church of England. With this bill, Danby intended to confine membership of high office to Anglicans, with one anonymous letter to parliament stating that 'they [the Anglicans] wish to fight the old quarrel over again now that they have the arms and forts of the nation'. This move was short-sighted and led to a number of problems:

- By attempting to pass the bill, Danby was opening up old wounds and effectively making political criticism and opposition illegal.
- Shaftesbury, now a key leader of the opposition, pushed for parliament to be prorogued in order to block the bill becoming law. On 9 June, he was successful and parliament was closed for several months.
- Danby's true ambition of increasing royal authority had been made public by the bill and this gave more determination to the opposition.

Danby survives, 1675–6

It could be argued that Danby was fortunate to survive impeachment; however, despite the growth of opposition, Charles was always reluctant to sacrifice him. After all, Danby had been responsible for increasing royal revenue to unprecedented levels.

Charles and Louis reach agreement

In the summer of 1675, Louis was still fighting an increasingly bloody war with the Dutch. If parliament was recalled again at this stage, there was a real possibility that bribery from the Dutch – via Danby – would result in a majority of MPs voting to support hostilities against France. To remove this possibility, Charles and Louis agreed in August that parliament would be recalled, with the instruction that its members vote money to Charles without conditions. In the event, parliament failed to do this; therefore, it was agreed that the French would provide an annual subsidy to Charles of £100,000.

Danby's influence attacked in parliament

The Commons voted 172 to 165 to refuse a large grant of money to Charles, again demonstrating how evenly divided the Court and Country parties were. A second bill to provide £400,000 to bolster the navy was narrowly passed. Danby's overbearing influence was still the overriding concern for MPs, and a group consisting of both Catholics and Nonconformists (including the Duke of York, Buckingham and Shaftesbury) tabled a motion asking for Charles to dissolve parliament entirely and hold new elections. Rather than dissolve parliament, in November 1675 it was prorogued for fifteen months. Although the conditions attached to the payment of French subsidies had not been fulfilled, Louis grudgingly agreed to pay his first instalment to Charles in March 1676.

Danby's downfall, 1677–8

Despite Danby securing much additional income for Charles from 1673–5, by 1677 Charles faced an all too familiar situation:

- In November 1676, he attempted to obtain a loan from the City of London merchants. As Charles had broken his contracts with them in the 1672 Stop of the Exchequer, they were reluctant and duly failed to provide him with funds.

- In Virginia in July 1676, a rebellion against the colonial governor began, led by Nathaniel Bacon. 'Bacon's Rebellion' took several months to suppress, and while military costs reached £200,000, the impact on transatlantic trade resulted in vastly reduced customs revenues.

- Charles's debts now totalled around £1 million, rising to £2.2 million in 1678.

Louis promised Charles an additional £100,000 for 1677, with the promise of more money if he prorogued parliament until 1678.

1677 session of parliament

When parliament eventually met again in February 1677, Buckingham and Shaftesbury, along with Lords Salisbury and Wharton, repeated the demand for a complete dissolution with the justification that in the sixteen years since a general election was last held, the political sympathies of the nation had changed significantly. They were sent to the Tower of London for 'contempt of the House'.

MPs did show goodwill to Charles with a vote of £600,000 for the building of ships, but the distraction of the Franco-Dutch war was soon at the top of the agenda once more. In May, the Commons issued an address refusing to grant further supply until the King issued a statement outlining which alliances he was still party to and urging a military union with Holland. Charles's reply was a direct refusal, and he reminded the House that the ability to make peace and war was part of the royal prerogative and he was under no obligation to consult parliament on the matter.

A series of adjournments meant that parliament could not resume proceedings until January 1678. In the intervening months, Danby attempted to distance Charles from the French alliance for a final time when he began making arrangements for the marriage of William of Orange and **Mary Stuart**.

The marriage of William and Mary

The marriage had been on the political agenda for a number of years when William – in need of support following a number of disastrous defeats by the French – decided this would be an appropriate time to finalise the arrangements. England was the only country that could help William to end the European deadlock, and as Danby strongly favoured the marriage in order to restore Protestant confidence in the Stuarts, arrangements were made quickly. The final decision lay with Charles, and he approved the marriage because he believed

KEY FIGURE

Mary Stuart (1662–94)

Mary was the eldest daughter of James, Duke of York, and his first wife, Anne Hyde, and was therefore niece to Charles II. She was raised a Protestant and, because Charles II had no legitimate children, she spent much of her life as second in line to the throne. After her father converted to Catholicism, Charles restricted contact between her and James.

that it would remove suspicions that he was intent on converting England to Catholicism.

The betrothal was announced on 22 October 1677 and the wedding took place two months later. Thus, Charles had made a swift turnaround in policy, and the king who had signed the Treaty of Dover committing himself and his country to the Catholic faith had, nevertheless, brought his government into an alliance with the leader of European Protestantism.

Formal alliance with Holland and Danby's fall from grace

Danby's confidence was buoyed by the marriage, and he petitioned Charles to enter into a more formal treaty arrangement with the Dutch. On 31 December 1677, Charles agreed in principle to a treaty ending the Franco-Dutch War that would pave the way for an offensive alliance with William in the future. In reality, Charles had no desire for an alliance with the Dutch and played for time, never ratifying the final arrangements of the treaty. He continued his talks with the French, and proposed to stay out of the conflict on the side of the Dutch in return for continued subsidies from Louis.

A complicated arrangement now ensued. Louis gave the French ambassador large amounts of cash with which to bribe MPs to resist a war against France, and high-profile members of the Country opposition, such as Buckingham and Shaftesbury, gave their support to this cause, despite the fact they had previously supported a Dutch alliance. Meanwhile, Danby borrowed £60,000 from the City of London merchants for a campaign of counter-bribery.

Louis signed a peace treaty with the Dutch in July 1678 and, when he discovered that Danby had attempted to block his alliance with Charles for several years, took the opportunity to leak details of Danby's role in secretly securing French subsidies. In addition, two issues contributed to Danby's final fall:

- His character. Although he had a sound financial mind, he never commanded the respect of the political nation and had few political friends. He often moved to exclude talented men from office as a result of his jealousies.
- The excessive profits he appeared to be making from his office. These amounted to around £20,000 a year.

Impeachment

One of the men Danby attempted to exclude from high office was Ralph Montagu, who had been serving as ambassador to France. Danby overlooked him for the position of Secretary of State, instead preferring William Temple, who had assisted Danby in arranging the marriage of William and Mary.

While in Paris, Montagu received a number of letters from Danby containing instructions on how to proceed in the secret negotiations with Louis. All the letters contained a postscript in Charles's handwriting: 'I approve of this letter, C.R.' Montagu was elected to parliament in 1678 with the intention of bringing about Danby's fall, and gave two of the letters to the Speaker to read to the House of Commons. The Speaker made no reference to the King's consent to the letters being sent, and their contents were enough to incriminate Danby.

> ### SOURCE C
>
> The Articles of Impeachment for High Treason against the Earl of Danby, drawn up by a committee of MPs and Lords, 21 December 1678; 179 members proceeded to vote in favour of the impeachment and 116 against.
>
> I. He has traitorously encroached to himself regal power, by treating in matters of peace and war with foreign princes and ambassadors, and giving Instructions to his Majesty's ambassadors abroad, without communicating the same to the Secretaries of State, and the rest of his Majesty's Council.
>
> II. That he has traitorously endeavoured to subvert the ancient and well-established form of government in this Kingdom; and instead thereof to introduce an arbitrary and tyrannical way of government. And the better to effect this purpose, he did design the raising of an army, upon pretence of a war against the French King; and then to continue the same as a standing army within this kingdom.
>
> III. That he did propose and negotiate a peace for the French King, upon terms disadvantageous to the interest of his Majesty and his kingdoms, for the doing whereof he did endeavour to procure a great sum of money from the French King, for enabling of him to carry on and maintain his said traitorous Designs and Purposes.
>
> IV. That he has wasted the king's treasury, by issuing unnecessary pensions and secret services to the value of £231,000 in two years.

SOURCE QUESTION

According to Source C, why did parliament want to impeach Danby?

Danby was impeached for negotiating matters of war and peace without the knowledge of the Privy Council, as well as corruption and embezzlement. Although Charles soon dissolved parliament, halting the impeachment proceedings, Danby was forced to resign as Lord Treasurer and spent several years in the Tower of London. Danby's downfall was welcomed by most of his former parliamentary colleagues, with one MP writing that 'never was a man less pitied in his fall than he'.

ONLINE EXTRAS WWW
AQA

Test your knowledge of the fall of Danby by completing Worksheet 8 at **www.hoddereducation.co.uk/accesstohistory/extras**

ONLINE EXTRAS WWW
Pearson Edexcel

Test your knowledge of the last years of Danby's ministry by completing Worksheet 8 at **www.hoddereducation.co.uk/accesstohistory/extras**

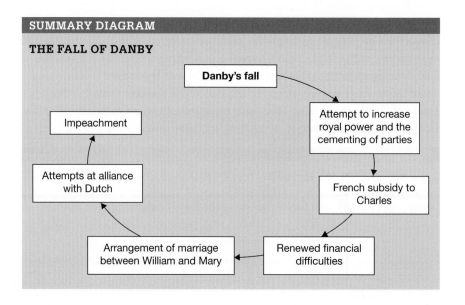

SUMMARY DIAGRAM

THE FALL OF DANBY

CHAPTER SUMMARY

With Clarendon as chief minister in the years 1660–7, Charles was able to implement many of the promises made in the Declaration of Breda. Clarendon's fall owed more to circumstance than personal failure, as his years in office coincided with the disasters of the Second Anglo-Dutch War, the Great Plague and the Great Fire of London. Charles was encouraged in his subsequent pro-French policy by members of the Cabal ministry, although the growing gulf between Court and parliament became increasingly evident in the years 1667–73. Charles's desire to free himself of the need to call parliaments became his overriding objective in the 1670s, and he was fortunate to find a minister in Danby who could help him settle his finances. The price Charles had to pay for this improved financial situation was the pro-Dutch policy favoured by Danby, but even this did not prevent the King from continuing his secret negotiations with Louis XIV.

Refresher questions

Use these questions to remind yourself of the key material covered in this chapter.

1 What were the achievements of Clarendon as chief minister?

2 How did the Second Anglo-Dutch War affect Clarendon's position?

3 Why was Clarendon impeached?

4 Why was the Cabal ministry disjointed?

5 How would you describe the foreign policy of the Cabal?

6 Why was the Treaty of Dover controversial?

7 What was the Stop of the Exchequer?

8 Why did the Cabal decline in significance and power?

9 What were the achievements of Danby?

10 Why did Danby favour a pro-Dutch policy?

11 How did Danby inadvertently strengthen loyalty to the two parties in parliament?

12 How did Charles demonstrate his continuing loyalty to Louis in the mid-1670s?

13 Why was Danby impeached?

Question practice: Pearson Edexcel

Essay questions

1 To what extent was there conflict between Charles II and parliament in the years 1660–78? [AS level]

EXAM HINT Examine the ways in which the Restoration Settlement failed to clarify the powers of both king and parliament, and the extent to which it caused problems during Charles's reign, especially on religious toleration and financial matters.

2 'Financial issues in Charles II's government were at the heart of the political instability that existed in the years 1660–78.' How far do you agree with this statement? [A level]

EXAM HINT Explain how the Restoration Settlement left Charles short of funds, forcing him to negotiate parliamentary subsidies. Other factors causing instability might include religious toleration and foreign policy.

3 'The continued dominance of Anglicanism meant that political stability would never be possible in the years 1660–78.' How far do you agree with this statement? [A level]

EXAM HINT Compare Charles's hopes for religious toleration with the narrow Anglicanism of the Cavalier Parliament. Explain how this led to political instability, especially in the 1670s.

CHAPTER 4

Religious divisions, 1660–78

Religious belief was at the heart of life for people of all classes in the seventeenth century. By the time Charles II came to the throne it had been nearly 130 years since Henry VIII had broken from Rome to establish the Church of England. Religious issues contributed to both political and social instability in these years, and government policy had a direct impact on freedom of worship for dissenting groups. The interplay between Anglicans, Nonconformists and the Catholic-leaning royal family is examined under the following sections:

◆ Charles's quest for religious toleration, 1660–70

◆ The Catholic threat

◆ The experience of Protestant Dissenters

◆ The second Declaration of Indulgence and the Test Acts

The key debate on page 67 of this chapter asks the question: Why did religious dissent survive the Restoration?

KEY DATES

1661–5	The Acts of the Clarendon Code passed	**1672**	Declaration of Indulgence
1662	Charles attempted to suspend the Act of Uniformity	**1673**	The Test Act
			James's marriage to Mary of Modena
1667	The First Conventicle Act expired	**1676**	The Compton Census of Dissenters
1670	Second Conventicle Act	**1678**	Second Test Act

1 Charles's quest for religious toleration, 1660–70

■ *How successful was Charles in establishing religious toleration in the early years of his reign?*

Table 4.1 (see page 49) shows the percentage of the population who followed Anglicanism, Puritanism (Nonconformist Dissenters) and Catholicism. Jewish people were generally excluded from religious toleration and made up a very small fraction of the population both in the 1670s and at the end of the period. Although non-Anglicans made up only a small proportion of Christians when Charles II came to power, he put much effort into his attempts to ensure that they were given religious toleration. Why was Charles so enthusiastic about toleration?

- Charles has been accused of putting pleasure before business, particularly in the early years of his reign. His social circle included individuals who took a variety of religious and moral viewpoints and this instilled in him an open-mindedness not often seen in monarchs of the period.

- Charles was a Catholic sympathiser. He was grateful for Catholic loyalty and assistance during the Civil Wars and during his time in exile. Furthermore, his mother, Henrietta Maria, was a Catholic. His dealings with the French suggest that he was interested in converting, and he probably did so on his deathbed.

Table 4.1 Religious affiliation in the late seventeenth and early eighteenth centuries

Faith	1670s	1720
Anglican	94.4%	92.0%
Nonconformist Dissenter	4.4%	6.6%
Catholic	1.1%	1.3%
Jewish	<0.1%	0.1%

The Act of Uniformity

Within eight months of Charles's return, **episcopacy** had been effectively restored and Anglicanism was dominant once again. Charles reluctantly gave his assent to the Act of Uniformity in the spring of 1662 in exchange for supply. This gave virtually no concessions to the Dissenters, essentially providing them with the option of conforming or leaving the Church.

Before the passing of the Act of Uniformity, Charles had shown his natural leniency by ordering many Quakers and other imprisoned Dissenters to be released, to mark the arrival in England of his new wife. After the passing of the Act, Clarendon and Charles attempted to dilute its impact. Clarendon reminded parliament that it was up to the King to execute the laws, and he urged Charles to use his **dispensing power** to stop the law being enforced against moderate Dissenters.

The Act came into operation on 24 August 1662. This day was chosen specifically to deprive outgoing ministers of the **tithes** which they would have been entitled to collect had they been able to remain in post for longer. A week before the deadline, many Presbyterian ministers resigned from their congregations, some without even reading the new prayer book to which they were expected to conform. Although 25 per cent of ministers resigned within a year, disturbances among the **laity** were few and far between. Samuel Pepys recorded a case where a group of young people at a church in London shouted 'Porridge!' instead of listening silently to the new prayer book, and one newspaper stated that 'a few fanatics laboured to disturb the ministers in one or two churches'.

KEY TERMS

Episcopacy Government of a Church by bishops.

Dispensing power A long-standing prerogative power allowing monarchs to discard laws in certain cases. It was exercised widely in the medieval and Tudor periods, but came under attack during the reigns of James I and Charles I.

Tithe A tax paid to support the Church and the clergy.

Laity People who belong to a religion, but are not members of the clergy.

Charles finds support for toleration

The Catholic Earl of Bristol, as well as Charles's mother, Henrietta Maria, pressed for a full and permanent suspension of the Act. When Arlington became Secretary of State, he provided additional support for the policy of toleration. There were also a number of **Independents** at Court who favoured the policy and further bolstered Charles.

On 26 December 1662, Charles issued a Declaration of Indulgence in favour of toleration, which suspended the Act of Uniformity. This came too late for the Puritan ministers already ejected for failing to conform.

The Declaration failed for a number of reasons:

- As dispensing power was part of the royal prerogative and had been a subject of controversy for many years, it attracted legal challenges.
- Both Anglicans and Presbyterians resented its grateful references to Catholic loyalty.
- Clarendon, as chief adviser, had considerable reservations about the wording of the Declaration.
- The new Archbishop of Canterbury, Gilbert Sheldon, strongly opposed the Declaration.

KEY TERM

Independents People who believed in the local control of churches without a national hierarchy.

? SOURCE QUESTION

According to Source A, why was Sheldon so critical of the Declaration?

SOURCE A

A letter from Gilbert Sheldon to Charles II, January 1663.

Your Majesty has propounded a toleration of religion. I beseech you sir, take into consideration what the act is, and next what the consequences may be. By your act you labour to set up that most damnable and heretical doctrine of the Church of Rome. If you fail in your design your kingdom will suffer God's heavy wrath and indignation.

Exceptions to the Act of Uniformity

Despite the failure of Charles's Declaration, some dissenting ministers were able to maintain their posts. John Angier continued to preach at Denton Chapel, Lancashire, because he was greatly respected by his parishioners, with one contemporary writing, 'the worst of men had no heart to meddle with him, and the justices held him in great respect'. Because the two principal families in the neighbourhood were Puritans, Angier was never reported to the authorities.

A number of dissenting ministers preached at Anglican churches and chapels, including Thomas Gregg of St Helens. Once again, popularity among their congregations seems to be the overriding factor in their survival.

Across the country, judges refused to convict lawbreakers, in part to gain favour with the King. At Hereford, for example, only 150 were presented to court for breaking the Conventicle Act, just twenty of whom were Puritans. This was despite the fact that there were over 1000 recorded Dissenters attending meetings in the county. Sir Thomas Bridges, a local official from Bristol, was summoned before the Privy Council and told that his rigorous proceedings against Dissenters were not agreeable to the King. Edmund Calamy, who was imprisoned in January 1663 for preaching without a licence, was released after a week by order of Charles, on the grounds that his offence had been committed with the approval of several members of the Privy Council.

Suspicion and persecution of Dissenters, 1664

The year 1664 saw a number of plots and rumoured plots. It was reported that in Lancashire and Cheshire alone, 5000 Nonconformists were ready to rise against the government. The Farnley Wood Plot resulted in the execution of twenty suspects in January 1664. The aim of the plotters was to force the King to grant religious liberty to all but Catholics, and to remove most taxes. This led to a renewed backlash against Dissenters from the Cavalier Parliament.

The Five Mile Act, 1665

In October 1665, in the midst of the Second Anglo-Dutch War, parliament assembled and Clarendon urged members to increase the persecution of Nonconformists. He told them that this was necessary because of recent plots and that 'if you suppress your enemies at home, you will find your enemies abroad more inclined to peace'. The Five Mile Act (see page 21) was soon passed, arguably the cruellest of the persecuting Acts of the Clarendon Code. A significant feature of the Act was the clause stating that those who acted as informers against former ministers were to be granted one-third of any fines imposed.

The years 1665–6 saw the coming of the Anglo-Dutch War, the Great Plague and the Great Fire of London. The cause of toleration hit a new low as Puritans and Catholics were blamed for the disasters. Since the majority of the churches in London had perished in the fire, many of the meeting houses of Nonconformists were seized by the Church of England to be used for worship.

Toleration under the Cabal, 1667–70

The members of the Cabal ministry (see page 30) took a markedly different approach from Clarendon. Clifford and Arlington leaned towards Catholicism, Ashley was firmly on the side of the Nonconformists and Buckingham had been accused of having no religion at all. These appointments were, in part, made as a political move by Charles to obtain toleration. Charles was assisted especially by Buckingham in this task:

- He secured the release of many Republicans and some former officers from Cromwell's army.
- **Conventicles** were allowed and large numbers flocked to these meetings quite openly.

However, despite the allowances made for Dissenters, Sheldon was still Archbishop of Canterbury and would grant no such allowances. He sent letters to his bishops and clergy, instructing them to continue their persecutions.

> **KEY TERM**
>
> **Conventicles** Religious meetings outside the Church of England.

SOURCE B

SOURCE QUESTION
What statement do you think the artist of Source B is making about the religious issues that existed in 1673?

THE PRESENT STATE OF ENGLAND

Frontispiece to Edward Chamberlayne's *Angliae Notitia*; or 'the Present State of England' (1673). Charles is enthroned, holding an orb and sceptre. Standing beside him are Gilbert Sheldon, Archbishop of Canterbury, and a figure who has been identified as either Sir Orlando Bridgeman or Anthony Ashley Cooper, Earl of Shaftesbury.

Bridgeman's bill for toleration

The **Lord Keeper**, **Orlando Bridgeman**, was favourable towards toleration and in January 1668, on behalf of Charles, he consulted leading Presbyterians about their potential role in a future religious settlement. The question of reordination became a stumbling block. As Presbyterians did not believe in a Church hierarchy of bishops, they refused to be **ordained** by one. A draft bill was drawn up merely requiring the laying-on of hands by the bishops rather than full reordination.

A second bill was drafted which would provide **comprehension** for Presbyterians and Charles's opening speech to parliament in 1668 spoke of his desire to create 'a union in the minds of my Protestant subjects'. Suspicion of the intentions of the Cabal helped to unite the Commons against all these schemes for toleration. Ultimately the proposal was voted down by 176 votes to 70.

1668–9

Nonconformists were generally free from persecution as long as parliament was not sitting, so the long adjournments in 1668 and 1669 helped Charles in his objective. In a series of meetings with Nonconformist leaders, Charles shared his view that he was more desirous of toleration than he had ever been, and they should bide their time until a solution was made possible.

The situation in Scotland

In 1669, Charles offered reinstatement to ministers whose previous positions had been vacant for the seven years since the passing of the Act of Uniformity. The only condition was that ministers behave in an 'orderly manner' and attend Church courts when necessary. This was made possible because the nobility in Scotland were more open to toleration than the English parliament, and Charles had expended much effort in forging alliances with high-profile Scottish Presbyterians.

Assessment: how successful was Charles in promoting religious toleration in the early years of his reign?

Despite the Anglicanism of the Cavalier Parliament, Charles was reasonably successful in securing a measure of religious toleration between 1660 and 1670. Even when his attempted Declaration of Indulgence failed in parliament, he maintained the loyalty of many local government officials who refused to convict lawbreakers. However, any formal legal measures to assist the Dissenters in these years failed, and parliament generally united and voted down bills for further toleration.

KEY TERMS

Lord Keeper
A high-ranking Privy Councillor with particular responsibility for the care of the king's great seal, with the authority to affix it to public documents.

Ordain To make someone a priest or minister.

Comprehension
The process of accepting different religious denominations into the national Church.

KEY FIGURE

Orlando Bridgeman (1606–74)
Bridgeman trained in the law and gained a significant reputation as a lawyer during the reign of Charles I. Excluded from working in government under Cromwell, he practised as a property lawyer. He was made Lord Chief Justice of the Common Pleas 1660–7 and became Lord Keeper, and therefore a high-ranking Privy Council member and main mouthpiece of Charles to parliament, after the fall of Clarendon.

ONLINE EXTRAS WWW
AQA
Develop your analysis of the quest for toleration by completing Worksheet 9 at **www.hoddereducation. co.uk/accesstohistory/extras**

ONLINE EXTRAS WWW
Pearson Edexcel
Get to grips with the quest for toleration by completing Worksheet 9 at **www. hoddereducation.co.uk/ accesstohistory/extras**

SUMMARY DIAGRAM

CHARLES'S QUEST FOR RELIGIOUS TOLERATION, 1660–70

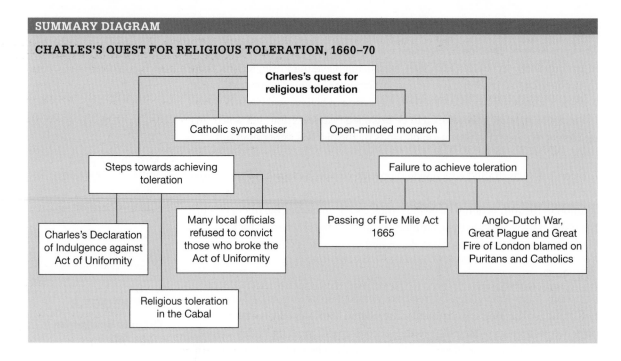

2 The Catholic threat

■ *How serious was the threat of Catholicism in the early years of Charles's reign?*

Since the Protestant Reformation there had developed a deep-rooted suspicion of Catholics in English society. They remained a small minority in the later Stuart era, but in both parliament and wider society they were deeply mistrusted.

Anti-Catholicism in English society

Anti-Catholicism is a persistent theme in the history of the early Stuarts and the Civil War years. At all levels of society, Catholicism was unpopular. Why was this the case?

■ Since the Protestant Reformation, the Catholic Church had been viewed with increasing suspicion. New Catholic religious orders, ceremonies and Church taxes had been imposed across Catholic Europe and the dangerous ambition of popes and priests was seen as to blame.

■ To Protestants, an individual relationship with God was central to their religious beliefs. They believed that the spiritual essence of Christianity was lost in the Catholic Church due to an increased bureaucracy and what they saw as the continuation of vain and irrelevant ceremonies.

- The Gunpowder Plot of 1605 had reinforced the negative perception of Catholics. Stories of Protestant settlers in Ireland being massacred in 1641 added to the horrific accounts already circulating of Catholic brutality in Europe.

- A Counter-Reformation had taken place in Europe, centred in the German territories of the Holy Roman Empire. In 1618, the Thirty Years' War broke out between Protestant and Catholic forces and Protestantism appeared to be in retreat. Both James I and Charles I sent troops to fight for the Protestant cause.

- After the Protestant Reformation, much land belonging to the Catholic Church was sold off. The buyers had a vested interest in maintaining Protestantism and rejected Catholicism because a return to the old faith would have made the land forfeit. Religious belief came second to economic considerations.

SOURCE C

John Flavel, *Tidings from Rome, or, England's Alarm*, published in 1667. A Puritan clergyman who preached in Devon, Flavel intended to prepare the Protestants of England for the possibility of a Catholic succession.

Your fears cannot help but increase, when you consider the preparation and progress these Catholic enemies have already made. Have they been sleeping all this while? No; they have digged as deep as hell in their counsels, their numbers among us are already formidable, their confidences high, and their foreign assistants ready.

Two considerable advantages they have already obtained. First, the removal of so many able and godly ministers out of the way. Second, the destruction of our famous city, the strength and glory of the nation, which they have laid to dust. A design, no doubt, contrived in the popish conclave. My heart bleeds for London.

It was Queen Elizabeth's motto, no peace with Spain; and it should be ours, no peace with Rome. And what cause have you to abhor popery? It is a false, bloody, blasphemous, uncomfortable and damnable religion. Prepare yourselves for the worst, that if times should alter, yet your hearts may not be turned back.

SOURCE QUESTION

Study Source C. Why were Catholics a threat to England, according to Flavel?

The Catholic population

Any estimate of the number of Catholics in England under Charles II must at best be an educated guess. One survey carried out on behalf of the Church of England in 1660 gave a figure of 100,000 (two per cent), and another in 1664 reported that there were 200,000 (four per cent of the population). An estimate from the Earl of Castlemaine in 1679 puts the figure at 50,000 (one per cent). Modern estimates put the number at approximately 60,000, which is around 1.1 per cent of the population.

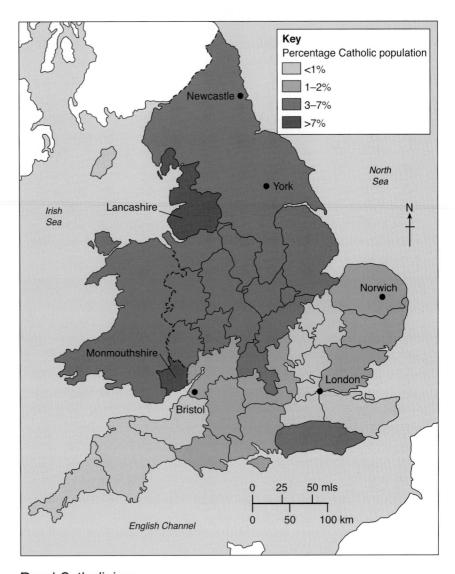

Figure 4.1 Distribution of Catholics in England and Wales, 1660–88, based on Church census data.

Rural Catholicism

Catholicism tended to be strongest in the more rural areas of the country where traditional landlord–tenant relationships had survived the longest. In some counties in the north of England, nearly ten per cent of people were Catholic. Even in rural areas, the reasons for this continued survival varied greatly:

- In Monmouthshire, local politics and society were dominated by the Catholic Somerset family, who included the Earls of Worcester. There were several complaints to parliament about the continuing protection of Catholics by the family.

- In Lancashire, there was no single dominant family. The survival of Catholicism was helped by the geographical isolation of some of the most strongly Catholic areas. These areas were often large and sparsely populated, and it was therefore difficult for the clergy to maintain control.

Urban Catholicism

Catholicism was weaker in towns. In more densely populated towns, it was difficult for Catholics to thrive as they did in the relative isolation of the Lancashire countryside. Many town authorities actively supported Puritanism by appointing Puritan ministers to town churches. The main strength of urban Catholicism in the larger towns came from the servants and business associates of the Catholic gentry who lived in towns for part of the year. There were also some professionals – particularly doctors – who had trained abroad and had either converted or become more steadfast in their Catholicism as a result.

Catholics in London had the benefit of being able to access a number of royal chapels and foreign embassies, where they could attend mass more openly. Two royal chapels opened by Catherine of Braganza were active from 1662 and chapels in the French, Spanish, Venetian and Portuguese embassies operated with little interference. In 1671, the Venetian ambassador reported that the four embassy chapels could not hold all those wishing to use them. The social status of these individuals varied, although most of those convicted of **recusancy** were members of the gentry.

Reasons for continued belief

Despite the recusancy laws and continued exclusion from public office, Catholic numbers were static. Most Catholic landed families remained steadfast in their faith. Many Protestants claimed that Catholics clung to their faith because of blinkered conservatism and the fact that it was the religion their ancestors had followed. There is some truth in this, but Catholics also thought carefully about their decision to maintain loyalty to the old religion. Part of their belief was that the Catholic Church was the sole legitimate source of spiritual authority and they should have absolute unquestioning faith. Catholics put principle before convenience and by doing so ensured the survival of their religion in England.

Clarendon's attitude to Catholics

While Clarendon's views on Dissenters were relatively tolerant, his attitude to the Catholics was more complicated. In 1660, he twice expressed approval of the idea that Catholics should have a bishop in England; however, he was later accused of opposing the King's attempted Declaration of Indulgence in 1662. This was because his primary aim was to achieve a religious settlement acceptable to the Presbyterians, as this would help to avoid serious unrest. He was prepared to consider some relief for Catholics, but not at the expense of his main objective.

Extent of persecution in the 1660s

In towns, municipal authorities tried hard to suppress Catholicism. In York, for instance, the council on its own initiative doubled the one shilling a week fine for absence from church. Some county sheriffs demanded the maximum fine of £20 per month from recusants, in addition to confiscating two-thirds of

> **KEY TERM**
>
> **Recusant** A person who refused to attend Anglican Church services.

Table 4.2 Types of London residents convicted of recusancy under Charles II

Description	Number
Women	411
Gentry	192
Textile workers	94
Medicine	30
Labourers	33
Jewellers	21
Architects and builders	18
Domestic servants	13
Merchants	9

their property. However, the 1641 abolition of the **Court of High Commission** and the **Council of the North** was not reversed at the Restoration, removing the two main agencies for the persecution of Catholics. Many Protestants had an ambivalent attitude towards the Catholics who lived near them and were able to distinguish between what they viewed as the malign political force of Catholicism at Court and ordinary Catholic neighbours with whom they had much in common.

Even the Anglican clergy were often indifferent towards Catholics in the early part of Charles's reign. In 1665, the Bishop of Chester wrote of Catholics, 'it is a great scandal and offence to let them alone, though I wish the **sectaries** were but as quiet and as inoffensive as the Catholics are'. At parish level, the churchwardens who were supposed to report the names of recusants were often reluctant to do so. In Wiltshire, for example, churchwardens routinely presented recusants for a fine of one shilling per week, rather than the £20 a month they were required to impose. Even this smaller fine was not usually collected. In areas dominated by Catholic gentry it was easier to avoid prosecution. In Monmouthshire, 40 Catholics brought before a judge for recusancy simply walked out of court when they were asked why judgment should not be passed on them. The sheriff in charge of their detention refused to fetch them back.

The impact of the Great Fire of London

The Privy Council was sure that the Great Fire of 1666 was an accident, but this did not prevent rumours spreading that pointed the blame at the French and Catholics. Stories of thousands of Catholics in arms spread around London, and foreigners – especially Frenchmen – were attacked in the streets. At the request of parliament but, as usual, against his own conscience, Charles ordered that all Catholic priests should be banished and all soldiers who refused to take Anglican Communion be dismissed. This response soon softened, and in April 1667 the Privy Council ordered that new recruits to the army were to take Anglican Communion within a year, rather than immediately.

James's conversion, 1669

It is not certain exactly when James's conversion to Catholicism took place, but it was probably in late 1668 or early 1669. His first wife, Anne Hyde, had almost certainly converted before he did, and she made the single biggest impact on his thinking about the issue. His conversion was not made public immediately, and he continued to attend Anglican services until 1676.

Assessment: how successful was government action against Catholics?

Despite their small numbers, the perceived threat from Catholics was long-standing and Catholic gentry had a disproportionate amount of influence in some counties. Charles's preference for toleration was backed up by the apathy of many local officials and their failure to persecute Catholics as they were instructed. Despite the sympathetic attitude of those in government, popular sentiment against Catholics was still strong and as the Duke of York became increasingly influential in the 1670s, the question of his potential future succession to the throne became the main political issue.

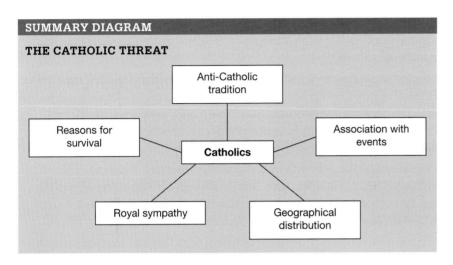

SUMMARY DIAGRAM

THE CATHOLIC THREAT

Anti-Catholic tradition

Reasons for survival

Catholics

Association with events

Royal sympathy

Geographical distribution

3 The experience of Protestant Dissenters

■ *How successful were Dissenters in the years following the Restoration?*

Under the Republic, the national Church had been based on a Presbyterian structure; however, after the demise of Cromwell and the return of the monarchy, all Puritans, including the Presbyterians, were classified as Dissenters as they were not able to adhere to all aspects of the Anglican national Church. Several Presbyterians were offered bishoprics and the Worcester House Declaration (see page 20) had suggested that there would be generous terms offered to the Puritans, although the Savoy Conference made it clear that as Archbishop, Gilbert Sheldon was determined to reduce their influence.

The impact of the Clarendon Code

The Act of Uniformity resulted in 25 per cent of clergy being ejected from their parishes. This wholesale purge of Puritan ministers was a dramatic break with the Church's recent past.

A typical example of the experiences of the expelled clergy can be found in the case of Richard Steele, who was a minister in north Wales at the time of the Restoration. In September 1660, he was presented to a judge for refusing to read the *Book of Common Prayer* to his congregation. This prosecution fell through after the King's Worcester House Declaration, which had given a brief promise of respite to Puritan ministers. Steele resigned as a consequence of the Act of Uniformity in 1662, but continued to hold meetings near his home in Wrexham. Like many dissenting ministers, he was harassed by the authorities and was ultimately arrested on suspicion of treason. In early 1665, he was made a 'collector of the royal aid', a local government position that could be taken up only by laymen and was virtually impossible to refuse. This position was conferred on him in an attempt to secure his complete removal from any ministerial activity.

Even ministers close to the King were not spared. Thomas Case had travelled to Holland in 1660 as a representative of a Presbyterian group who were supportive of the Restoration, and he was subsequently made a royal chaplain. He was ejected for Nonconformity in 1662 and did not enter employment in the Church of England again.

Puritan clergy who did conform faced hostility from their former friends. William Gurnall, a minister from Suffolk, did sign the declaration required by the Act of Uniformity and was subject to attacks from other ministers, including a libellous pamphlet called *Covenant-Renouncers Desperate Apostates.*

Some ministers were able to continue their work if they had connections with high-profile individuals. After Nathaniel Vincent was expelled from his parish in Buckinghamshire he became chaplain to Sir Henry Blount and worked in his household. Others became teachers, one of the few professions left open to expelled clergy.

The Conventicle Act, 1664

In 1668, Clarendon remarked that the Conventicle Act would have transformed the religious make-up of England 'if it had been vigorously executed'. He was clearly of the opinion that its primary aim of restricting religious meetings outside the Church of England had not been achieved. In reality, it had mixed success.

Evidence of persecution

- At any time the meeting houses of Dissenters were liable to be forcibly entered and those found inside might incur heavy fines.
- If Dissenters could not afford the fines, household goods, farm equipment or cattle were confiscated and sold far below their actual value. George Pye of Lydiate, Lancashire, faced a demand of £3, but ended up losing six cows worth £20.
- For a third offence, Dissenters could be imprisoned for seven years.
- Informers were rewarded for giving information on meetings, which resulted in the net spreading more widely in some areas.
- Between 1664 and 1665, there were 909 convictions in London alone.
- Some individuals, particularly those with some existing notoriety, were repeatedly targeted. Oliver Heywood, a Nonconformist minister based in the north of England, was arrested four times.

Evidence of success for Dissenters

- There was little popular enthusiasm for the Clarendon Code and the maximum penalty of £5 for the first offence was very rarely imposed, with the usual fines ranging from one shilling to five shillings. As Source D below shows, Dissenters were able to continue their worship in relative freedom.

- The maximum penalty of £10 for a second offence was never imposed.

- Some dissenting ministers benefited from association with wealthy merchants or landowners, and were offered payments for preaching.

- The main beneficiaries of this generosity were the Presbyterians, with a group founded by John Canne receiving £20 a year from Lady Dorothy Norcliffe. The domestic chapel of Sir Edward Rodes employed two Puritan ministers, and in 1669 it was reported that conventicles were being held there on a regular basis. Thomas Trenchard, who died in 1670, left £100 in his will to the Puritan minister Samuel Poole, who had served as his chaplain both before and after 1662.

- In London, there were numerous examples of conventicles continuing, often led by ministers who had been expelled in 1662. After Ralph Venning's ejection he led an independent congregation for a further twelve years with very little disturbance from the authorities.

SOURCE QUESTION

Study Source D. Why do you think the Bishop of Chester produced this report?

SOURCE D

An account of the conventicles held in Lancashire, drawn up by the Bishop of Chester for Archbishop Sheldon, 1669.

Blackburn Deanery:
Blackburn. Several conventicles of nonconformists usually to the number of 100. There have also been conventicles at Darwen chapel.
Churchkirke. A meeting of Independents to the number of about 30.
Haslingden. Quakers to the number of about 20.
Whalley. Several conventicles, some very numerous. Their last meeting consisting of 200 persons or above.
Clitheroe. No conventicles.
Newchurch in Pendle. No conventicles.
Colne. No conventicles.

Leyland Deanery:
Brindle. Weekly meetings of Papists.
Standish. Monthly meetings of Quakers, their numbers about 40 or 50 and several other conventicles.

Manchester Deanery:
Manchester. Frequent conventicles of nonconformists (which are the most numerous). Others of Anabaptists and Quakers. The persons are tradesmen and mostly women.
Gorton. Frequent and numerous conventicles consisting chiefly of Presbyterians.

The Quaker Act

Passed in 1662, the Quaker Act subjected Quakers to severe penalties if they refused to take the oath of allegiance, which the authorities knew their beliefs would not allow them to do. They were particularly vulnerable because they met in silence and this aroused suspicions that they met for other, secret purposes. The founder of the Quaker movement, George Fox, was arrested in 1664.

The expiration of the Conventicle Act, 1667

In 1667, the first Conventicle Act expired, resulting in a flurry of activity for Dissenters:

- Meeting houses could be built again. At Canterbury, there were two groups that each contained more than 600 members. At Dover, there was a group of more than 500.

- At Kendal, it was reported that Dissenters had so much freedom that 'a man might hear 6 or 7 sermons every Sunday, and make nothing of it'.

- **Dissenting academies** could be founded. One opened in London in 1667, which was attended by the novelist Daniel Defoe. In 1669, a Presbyterian academy was founded to formally train Puritan ministers.

- Further training academies were later built, and ministers' associations were formed in the early 1670s.

Although the Act had expired, persecution was not stopped entirely. Sheldon was still archbishop, and his office poured out letters urging the bishops and clergy not to give Dissenters any respite. As most bishops followed the lead of Sheldon, it is not surprising that arrests continued. Between 1667 and 1668, 1400 cases of Nonconformity were heard in Lincolnshire alone. When parliament met in 1668, members of parliament (MPs) compelled Charles to issue a proclamation ordering the strict enforcement of the laws against Catholics and Protestant Dissenters.

The second Conventicle Act, 1670

In February 1670, the Commons met in a rage. It had been reported that dangerous meetings were now being held near Westminster. A second Conventicle Act was passed in 1670. It was even stricter than the first:

- Each person caught attending a conventicle was fined five shillings.

- Any minister found leading meetings could be fined £20.

- If a magistrates were aware of a conventicle but did not prosecute they were liable for a £100 fine.

While parliament sat between May 1670 and April 1671, Dissenters suffered as they had never done before. The army was called to break up meetings and, in London at least, deaths resulted. Convictions were often rushed through and a contemporary reported that 'men might be convicted and fined without having any notice or knowledge of it till the officers came and took away their goods'.

KEY TERM

Dissenting academies
Educational institutions established to teach Dissenters. As Oxford and Cambridge barred Dissenters from taking degrees, the academies were the only places where they could receive a formal education.

There were also reports that some juries were forbidden to return verdicts in favour of the accused. It was possible to appeal, although offenders who failed in this were subjected to having their fines trebled.

Assessment: how successful were Dissenters?

It is true that many ministers and ordinary people were harassed and persecuted for religious dissent in the 1660s and 1670s. Both Conventicle Acts included harsh punishments and there were many convictions in these years, with notorious Dissenters being rarely left alone for long. However, religious dissent survived and the laws were not always carried out with enthusiasm.

ONLINE EXTRAS WWW
AQA

Test your essay technique by completing Worksheet 11 at **www.hoddereducation. co.uk/accesstohistory/extras**

ONLINE EXTRAS WWW
Pearson Edexcel

Ensure you have understood the strengths and weaknesses of Dissenters by completing Worksheet 11 at **www.hoddereducation. co.uk/accesstohistory/extras**

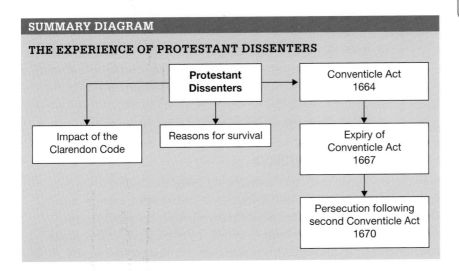

SUMMARY DIAGRAM

THE EXPERIENCE OF PROTESTANT DISSENTERS

4 The second Declaration of Indulgence and the Test Acts

■ *To what extent was Charles able to achieve religious toleration in the 1670s?*

Despite Charles's struggles to achieve toleration in the 1660s, his resolve did not diminish in the early 1670s and he issued a Declaration of Indulgence in 1672.

Second Declaration of Indulgence, 1672

In the wake of the second Conventicle Act, many members of Charles's Court urged the King to take matters into his own hands and grant toleration for both Catholics and Protestant Nonconformists by the exercise of his prerogative powers. The only reason Charles had consented to any of the persecuting Acts was because he needed supply from parliament. By December 1671, it was taken for granted by those close to the King that a Declaration was only a matter of time, and it was formally presented on 15 March 1672.

 SOURCE QUESTION

Study Source E. Does the Declaration appear to be more tolerant towards Catholics or Protestants?

> **SOURCE E**
>
> **An extract from Charles's second Declaration of Indulgence, March 1672.**
>
> *We do declare our will and pleasure to be, that the execution of all penal laws in matters ecclesiastical against whatsoever sort of nonconformists or recusants, be immediately suspended. And all judges, sheriffs, justices of the peace, mayors, bailiffs and other officers are to take notice of it and pay due obedience to it.*
>
> *And there may be no reason for any of our subjects to continue their illegal meetings and conventicles. We shall from time to time allow a sufficient number of places, as they shall be desired, in all parts of the country, for the use of such as do not conform to the Church of England, to meet and assemble. These places shall be free and open to all persons.*
>
> *This shall extend to all sorts of nonconformists, except the recusants of the Roman Catholic religion, to whom we shall in no way allow public places of worship, but only indulge them their share in the common exemption from the penal laws, and the exercise of their worship in their private houses only.*

Reaction to the Declaration

Both Catholics and Protestant Dissenters welcomed the Declaration in large numbers. Having survived the first feelings of intense relief, however, some Dissenters began to experience doubts about whether they should accept the same toleration that was being extended to Catholics, whom they hated and feared in equal measure. Others wrestled with their conscience and welcomed the Declaration as the fulfilment of biblical prophecy. Thomas Jolly, a Nonconformist from Lancashire, saw 'a great hand of God in it for special good'.

The Independents, in particular, received the Declaration with great excitement. What set them apart from the Presbyterians was their lack of support for the notion of a national Church, and the Declaration promised freedom for each individual congregation. The offer of preaching licences in the Declaration made little difference to the Quakers. Despite the heavy persecution they had endured, they had never ceased to preach and write boldly and with little attempt to hide their activities. Over 500 Quakers were also released from prison in the wake of the Declaration.

The granting of licences

Addresses and petitions for licences poured into the Privy Council from all over the country. A significant number of these came from the clergy who had been expelled in 1662 – many of whom had continued preaching in some capacity – but there were also requests to build meeting houses from cobblers, tinkers, tailors, joiners and tanners. For the most part, private houses were used, but barns, vacant churches and large public halls were also requested in the petitions.

In total, 1508 licences were issued in little under a year, with 848 being granted to Presbyterians, 368 to Independents and 101 to **Baptists**. The southeastern and western corners of England saw the most licences granted and this is no surprise, as these regions were traditionally the greatest strongholds of dissent.

Despite the granting of licences, some judges continued to hear cases against Dissenters and conventicles. One Nonconformist complained that, when he was fined by the courts, he 'pleaded the King's declaration suspending the execution of the penal laws, but they said that old scores must be wiped off'.

The withdrawal of the Declaration

Despite the enthusiasm of Charles's Court and the Dissenters for the Declaration of Indulgence, most MPs were hostile towards it. They expressed their contempt for toleration, and even some dissenting MPs argued that the Declaration should be withdrawn to protect against popery. As Charles was in desperate need of funds for the Third Anglo-Dutch War, he had no choice but to cancel the Declaration on 7 March 1673. However, the licences were not recalled until 1675, which meant that the years 1672–5 were some of the most active and tolerant for Dissenters in the Stuart era.

Test Act, February to March 1673

When parliament met in February 1673, members stressed how dangerous Catholicism was to the state, and how the Declaration had helped it to spread. On 29 March, Charles gave his assent to the Test Act. It stated that all public office holders should publicly swear an oath of allegiance, take Anglican Communion and subscribe to a declaration denying the Catholic doctrine of **transubstantiation**. The most high-profile victim of the Test Act was James, Duke of York, who resigned his position as Lord Admiral, effectively publicising his conversion to Catholicism (although by this time his religious preferences were common knowledge). In addition, Clifford resigned from the Privy Council, bringing to an end his leading role in the Cabal ministry.

James's second marriage, November 1673

Despite Charles's opposition to his brother's conversion to Catholicism and insistence that his daughters be raised as Protestant, James, like Charles, was permitted to marry a Catholic. James married **Mary of Modena** by proxy, in a Catholic service in September 1673, and she arrived in England in November, where an Anglican ceremony was carried out. She was immediately unpopular in England and parliament even threatened to have the marriage annulled.

The Compton Census, 1676

With the demise of the Cabal and Danby's preference for uniformity and Anglicanism, the Dissenters faced the threat of increased persecution once again. In order to convince Charles that he did not need to take further steps to allow toleration, Danby decided to commission a census of Dissenters in order

> **KEY TERMS**
>
> **Baptists** A Protestant sect that practised adult baptism.
>
> **Transubstantiation** The belief that the bread and wine consumed during Holy Communion change their essence to become the body and blood of Christ.

> **KEY FIGURE**
>
> **Mary of Modena (1658–1718)**
>
> The daughter of the Duke of Modena, Mary married James at the age of fifteen. She had a string of children who died in infancy but two survived to adulthood, including James Francis Edward Stuart, the future Jacobite claimant to the English throne.

to prove that their numbers were so small they were not worthy of significant attention. By this time, the Archbishop of Canterbury, Sheldon, was elderly and frail, so the task was taken up by the Bishop of London, Henry Compton. Many of the clergy who were expected to count the numbers of Dissenters clearly misunderstood their instructions, with some failing to count women, some clearly missing out large areas of their parishes, and others counting those under the age of sixteen who were not meant to be included. However, Compton reported that four per cent of the population were Protestant Dissenters and around 0.5 per cent were Catholics in 1676.

The number of Dissenters had been underestimated, which both helped and hindered their cause. Their calls for toleration were usually backed by their own claim that England contained a million Dissenters, a number so large that they should be listened to, but the census put the number at around 108,000. However, as the numbers did appear to be so low, there was no immediate call for further persecution.

Second Test Act, 1678

A second Test Act passed in 1678 stated that members of both the House of Commons and the House of Lords had to take the same tests as the public office holders in the 1673 Act. This effectively excluded Catholics from parliament. The Lords delayed the passing of the Act for several months and inserted an amendment that exempted James from being barred from the House of Lords.

ONLINE EXTRAS WWW
AQA

Test your understanding of the survival of dissent by completing Worksheet 12 at **www.hoddereducation. co.uk/accesstohistory/extras**

ONLINE EXTRAS WWW
Pearson Edexcel

Get to grips with the second Declaration of Indulgence by completing Worksheet 12 at **www.hoddereducation. co.uk/accesstohistory/extras**

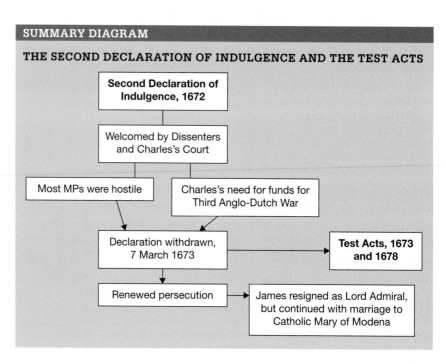

SUMMARY DIAGRAM

THE SECOND DECLARATION OF INDULGENCE AND THE TEST ACTS

Second Declaration of Indulgence, 1672

Welcomed by Dissenters and Charles's Court

Most MPs were hostile

Charles's need for funds for Third Anglo-Dutch War

Declaration withdrawn, 7 March 1673

Test Acts, 1673 and 1678

Renewed persecution

James resigned as Lord Admiral, but continued with marriage to Catholic Mary of Modena

5 Key debate

■ *Why did religious dissent survive the Restoration?*

Despite the exhaustive actions taken by parliament to clamp down on Dissenters, they managed to survive the reign of Charles II and by the early eighteenth century they were flourishing. Historians have put forward a number of arguments to explain this survival. In the late nineteenth and early twentieth centuries, **Whig historians** put forward the view that there was a large body of people willing to assist the Dissenters and this explains their persistence. The Whigs tended to disapprove of Charles's Catholicism and desire for absolutism, but sympathised with the Protestant Nonconformists. As the Whigs believed that the Stuart kings were blocking the inevitable rise of modern democracy and toleration, they also believed that most people in England were sympathetic to both parliamentary reform and religious liberty. In more recent years, some historians have come to the conclusion that the simple commitment of the Dissenters explains their survival. Others point to the failure of the authorities to adequately investigate cases of Nonconformity and a lack of enthusiasm for the Clarendon Code.

Assistance from sympathisers

Even after the particularly harsh second Conventicle Act had been passed, dissenting groups continued to increase in numbers. A report to the Privy Council in 1671 stated that the Lord Mayor of London had 'laid the laws to sleep' and was in fact sympathetic to their cause. Generally speaking, magistrates, knowing that Charles was averse to persecution, were content with enforcing the laws only periodically. In addition, Protestant dissent could not have survived without the patronage and support of powerful landowners and, in the towns, wealthy merchants. Frank Bate focuses on this interpretation, arguing that the generosity of friends and sympathisers maintained dissenting ministers in employment.

> **KEY TERM**
>
> **Whig historians**
> Historians who presented the seventeenth century as the inevitable rise of a constitutional monarchy and increased religious liberty. They believed that the Stuart kings who attempted to block reform were tyrants, and tended to revere institutions such as parliament and the legal system as the key components of a balanced constitution.

> **INTERPRETATION QUESTION**
>
> Read Extracts 1–4. What are the different views put forward to explain why religious dissent survived the Restoration?

> **ONLINE EXTRAS** WWW
> AQA
>
> Get to grips with historical interpretations by completing Worksheet 13 at **www.hoddereducation.co.uk/accesstohistory/extras**

> **ONLINE EXTRAS** WWW
> Pearson Edexcel
>
> Get to grips with historical interpretations by completing Worksheet 13 at **www.hoddereducation.co.uk/accesstohistory/extras**

EXTRACT 1

From Frank Bate, *The Declaration of Indulgence 1672: A Study in the Rise of Organised Dissent*, University of Liverpool Press, 1908, p. 32.

Some ministers taught in schools, some managed to get into families, some cut tobacco and obtained other mean employments. Such of the gentry as adhered to the non-conformist party very liberally supported and relieved distressed ministers. In the diary of John Argor, ejected from Braintree, Essex, are many entries noting the kindness he received from friends. 'Jan. 2, 1663, I received £5 2s. This was when I was laid aside for not conforming. And I received £3 15s. which was gathered for me by my friends.' Indeed, so generously were they treated that some ventured to hint that they lost nothing by their nonconformity, but were fed as well and lived as they had before.

The commitment of Dissenters

Some historians argue that Dissenters survived these years because of a zealous commitment to their cause. Dissident minority groups tend to flourish under conditions of oppression, and many of the leaders who were arrested for Nonconformity, such as George Fox, William Penn and John Bunyan, wrote their most impassioned defences of their beliefs while they were in prison. Whatever the motives behind the attempts to crush Dissenters, they failed. Twenty years of unchecked growth before the Restoration had given the sects strength, organisation and self-confidence, which the state's apparatus of coercion could never completely destroy. Richard L. Greaves concentrates on the reasons why the radical religious underground survived the early years of the Restoration, noting that those who had held radical beliefs during the Republic did not change their ways.

> **EXTRACT 2**
>
> From Richard L. Greaves, *Deliver Us from Evil: The Radical Underground in Britain, 1660–1663*, Oxford University Press, 2001, p. 4.
>
> *No amount of penal legislation could eradicate dissent from the restored church, nor did the return of the Cromwellian officers and men to their traditional occupations quench their thirst for a government more responsive to their needs and aspirations. The more radical among them not only grumbled and schemed, but girded on their swords to fight for the* **Good Old Cause**. *The dissidents kept alive the ideas and traditions of the Interregnum. The Quakers must have numbered at least 35,000, and by early 1661 more than 4,200 were in jail. Repeatedly imprisoned, they refused to be broken by penal legislation.*

KEY TERM

Good Old Cause

A phrase used by former parliamentarians and republicans in reference to the reasons that motivated them to fight during the English Civil Wars.

Attitude of the authorities

As uniformity was defined on a narrow basis in the acts of the Clarendon Code (accepting the *Book of Common Prayer* as the main criteria), the number of people classified as Dissenters was relatively high and they were, therefore, not as isolated as they might be. This made the job of the authorities very difficult, as tracking down all Dissenters and punishing them was an impossible task. The fact that some magistrates followed the lead of the King and were sympathetic to Dissenters – as discussed by John Coffey in Extract 3 – meant that persecution fluctuated. Some magistrates, particularly in towns, were even Dissenters themselves; however, most were Anglican. They were inclined to turn a blind eye to Dissenters because most of the Puritans they knew were respectable citizens, many of whom attended parish churches as well as their own meetings. In the eyes of the magistrates, the Catholics were the real enemy.

The sympathetic magistrates were also able to take advantage of loopholes in the law. The Five Mile Act applied to towns governed by corporations. Some centres of Nonconformity, such as Manchester, were not governed by a corporation and were, therefore, exempt from the provisions of the Act. The actions of the King undoubtedly contributed to more compassionate decisions being made in courts across the country. In addition to his Declaration of Indulgence and repeated public support for toleration, Charles's attitude was shown in the decisions taken by his Privy Council. When the leaders of conventicles appeared before them to answer for their misdeeds, they invariably escaped with nothing worse than a reprimand.

EXTRACT 3

From John Coffey, 'Church and State, 1550–1750: The Emergence of Dissent' in Robert Pope, editor, *The T&T Clark Companion to Nonconformity*, Bloomsbury, 2013, Chapter 4.

Persecution fluctuated according to geography and denomination. In many communities, local magistrates were sympathetic to Dissent, and some bishops favoured a policy of lenience too. Elsewhere, the law was rigorously implemented. As for the denominations, militant Anglicans tended to see all Dissenters as dangerous, but others recognised that there was a broad spectrum extending from moderate Presbyterians to radical Quakers, with Congregationalists [churches that were self-governing] and Baptists somewhere in between. Presbyterians like Baxter acknowledged that Quakers bore the brunt of the repression, though no group was immune.

Structural problems in the Church of England

Barry Coward and Peter Gaunt point to the failure of the Church of England to provide enough resources to deal with Dissenters, especially as so many were defined as such according to the narrow uniformity expected in the Clarendon Code. In some parts of the country, there were simply not enough clergy to oversee the activities of the local population. It is no coincidence that areas like Lancashire, where Dissenters worshipped in relative freedom and their ministers were able to travel easily, contained large parishes with few clergy.

EXTRACT 4

From Barry Coward and Peter Gaunt, *The Stuart Age*, Routledge, 2017, p. 508.

In some areas, dissent flourished primarily because of the failure of the Church of England to provide enough churches and vicars. Mostly these were areas where the Church had always been weakest, in forest, pastoral and fenland areas, for example, where parishes were large and communities scattered, and where there was a long tradition of opposition or apathy to the Church. Although the Church had made some attempts to fill these gaps in large parishes by building 'chapels of ease', these were often poorly endowed and there were not enough of them. In these areas dissent grew by default. The Yorkshire parish of Halifax, for example, covered 124 square miles in which there was only one parish church.

Conclusion: why did dissent survive?

On balance, it is clear that religious dissent survived as a result of a combination of reasons, but it is vital to recognise the recent history of Puritanism in order to fully understand the plight of Dissenters. They had already survived the particularly severe persecutions of Charles I, primarily because of their commitment and the sympathy of local officials. What marked their experience in the 1660s and 1670s as different from the 1630s was the attitude of the King. Charles II was determined to allow as much toleration as possible and this meant that Dissenters were able to cope with the sustained attacks that came from the hostile Cavalier Parliament.

CHAPTER SUMMARY

Charles had made religious toleration one of the cornerstones of the Declaration of Breda and he strove to promote religious freedom for both Protestant Dissenters and Catholics. Despite opposition in parliament to virtually all of his religious policies, both Catholics and Puritans continued to worship. Anti-Catholicism in English society reached a high point in the wake of the Great Fire of London and Charles's continued alliance with Louis XIV; however, the authorities were lax in their application of the recusancy laws. Dissenters were persecuted via the Acts of the Clarendon Code, and the second Conventicle Act of 1670 was even harsher than the first. Through a combination of royal support, assistance from sympathisers and the failures of the authorities, Dissenters survived the early years of Charles's reign, and their threat, as well as the danger of Catholicism, is a theme that would be reignited in the later 1670s and 1680s.

Refresher questions

Use these questions to remind yourself of the key material covered in this chapter.

1 Why did Charles's attempted Declaration of Indulgence fail in 1662?

2 What was the attitude of the Cabal to religious toleration?

3 Why were Catholics disliked in England?

4 Why had Catholicism survived in both towns and the countryside?

5 Why did the Catholic threat appear to be heightened in the early years of Charles's reign?

6 What evidence is there of success for Dissenters?

7 What is the significance of the Conventicle Act's expiring in 1667?

8 Why was the second Conventicle Act harsher than the first?

9 What was the key message of the second Declaration of Indulgence in 1672?

10 Why was the Declaration withdrawn?

11 What is the Test Act?

12 What did the Compton Census demonstrate about religion in England?

Question practice: AQA

Interpretation question

1 Using your understanding of the historical context, assess how convincing the arguments in Extracts 1 (page 67), 2 (page 68) and 3 (page 69) are in relation to the reasons for the survival of religious dissent under Charles II. [A level]

EXAM HINT You need to analyse each extract in turn. Find the main argument (or arguments) and, using your contextual knowledge, assess how convincing each extract is. There should be no development of provenance in answers, and there is no need for an overall judgement.

Question practice: Pearson Edexcel

Essay questions

1 'The Cavalier Parliament was successful in restoring the authority of the Church of England in the years 1660–78.' How far do you agree with this statement? [AS level]

EXAM HINT Examine the measures taken in 1661–5 to establish a narrow form of Anglicanism, and the Church's persecution of dissenters in later years. Evaluate the extent to which the Church's authority had been firmly established.

2 How accurate is it to describe Charles II's government as sympathetic to Dissenters in the years 1660–78? [AS level]

EXAM HINT Examine Charles's aim of furthering toleration for dissenters, and also for Catholics in the 1670s. You might want to compare the government's attitude with the Church's policy of persecuting dissenters, notably the Quakers.

3 How far do you agree that religious dissent survived in the years 1660–78 because of the actions of Charles II? [AS level]

EXAM HINT Evaluate the importance of some MPs who favoured toleration and a broader Church. Note the importance of individuals such as Shaftesbury and Fox.

4 'The fear of Catholicism was central to the discontent faced by the government in the years 1660–78.' Assess the validity of this view. [A level]

EXAM HINT Evaluate the importance of the stated factor along with other reasons for discontent. These might include divisions over foreign policy and financial matters, and fears concerning the drift towards absolutism.

CHAPTER 5

The Catholic threat and Exclusion, 1678–81

Suspicion of the Catholic minority in England reached a new peak in 1678 with the invention of the fictitious Popish Plot by Titus Oates and Israel Tonge. Whether the plot was real or not was of no consequence to many in the political nation, particularly the followers of Shaftesbury who would soon form the Whig faction in parliament. They had been hostile towards James and his Catholic associates for many years and now used the plot as an excuse to mount a campaign to exclude him from the throne. This chapter explains the issues around Catholicism and Exclusion in these years under the following headings:

◆ The Popish Plot

◆ Government action against Catholics

◆ The Exclusion Crisis

◆ The end of the crisis

The key debate on page 87 of this chapter asks the question: Why did Exclusion fail?

KEY DATES

1678	**Aug.**	Charles informed of the suspected Popish Plot
	Sept.	Titus Oates gave evidence before the Privy Council
	Oct.	Murder of Edmund Berry Godfrey
1679	**March**	Charles dissolved the Cavalier Parliament and new elections were held for the First Exclusion Parliament

1679	**May**	First Exclusion bill introduced by Shaftesbury
1680	**Oct.**	James exiled to Scotland
	Nov.	Second Exclusion bill
1681	**March**	Oxford Parliament
	July	Shaftesbury sent to the Tower of London

1 The Popish Plot

■ *How did the Popish Plot begin and develop?*

In August 1678, an Anglican priest named Titus Oates (see page 75), who had been educated at a **Jesuit** school in France, concocted a story of a Catholic plot. The main details of the alleged plot are as follows:

■ Jesuits disguised as Presbyterians were to be sent to stir the Scots to revolt.

■ Jesuit funds and French troops would be sent to Ireland to assist in a Catholic rebellion.

- There was a threat to the King's life, assisted by the French and several named Catholics in England, including **Edward Coleman**, Mary of Modena's secretary.

- James, Duke of York, was to become king under the direction of the Jesuits.

Oates's patron was Israel Tonge, a Protestant fanatic and fervent anti-Catholic. Although he was the first to persuade Oates to betray the Catholics to the government, Tonge does not seem to have been involved in the authorship of the accusations. Tonge eagerly accepted Oates's statements, and their next task was to bring the accusations to the attention of the King. They contacted Christopher Kirkby, a royal courtier and chemist who was prepared to help them. Kirkby was able to secure a short audience with Charles and this was attended by Tonge. Charles was initially dismissive of the accusations, but referred the case to Danby, who was in his final months as Lord Treasurer.

In early September, Oates and Tonge took their accusations to the London magistrate **Edmund Berry Godfrey**. Godfrey was clearly distressed by the accounts he read and on 28 September the government, possibly at the instigation of the Duke of York, decided to investigate the matter.

Involvement of the Privy Council

At a Council meeting presided over by Charles, a bundle of papers received from Tonge was reviewed. Included in it were letters, supposedly written to a Jesuit priest, that were obviously forgeries. Tonge was questioned and claimed that he knew very little, as any information he possessed had been given to him by Oates. He was asked to fetch Oates, who was consequently interrogated.

Oates swore under oath that the contents of the letters were genuine, and he presented himself with such confidence that the arrest was ordered of all the men whom he named. Oates was questioned over the course of two days, and his accusations became increasingly elaborate. He cited a letter from the Jesuit leader, Thomas White, as proof that Sir George Wakeman, doctor to Catherine of Braganza, had agreed to poison the King for £15,000 (£1.7 million in today's money), £5000 of which had already been paid by Coleman. Impressively, he managed to juggle several narratives involving many named individuals:

- 24 English Jesuits
- nineteen foreign Jesuits
- twelve Scottish Jesuits
- 23 monks
- four laymen: Wakeman and Coleman, as well as Oates's doctor, William Fogarty and John Grove, who lived in a house where the plot was supposedly planned.

The historian John Kenyon (1972) has observed that Oates's apparently incredible powers of recall are less impressive when it is realised that he had written the letters himself, something the Council was slow to appreciate.

SOURCE QUESTION

Playing cards featuring images of the plot became very popular. Why do you think this was the case?

Titus Oates tells Charles II of the Popish Plot, from a playing card designed by the English painter and engraver Francis Barlow in 1679.

Titus Oates

1649	Born in Oakham, Rutland, son of a Baptist preacher
1665	Expelled from the Merchant Taylors' School, London
1669	Left Cambridge University without a degree
1670	Ordained as a priest in the Church of England
1675–6	Served in the Royal Navy as a chaplain
1677	Converted to Catholicism
1678	Leading role in Popish Plot allegations
1681	Imprisoned after opinion turned against him
1689	Pardoned by William III
1705	Died in London

Background

Oates was the son of the Baptist preacher Samuel Oates and although he left Cambridge without a degree, he became a priest in the Church of England. In a time when homosexuality was illegal, his sexuality saw him reprimanded for misconduct several times. He also faced charges of perjury (lying under oath) when he attempted to discredit a schoolmaster in order to take his job. His reputation as a fantasist and a liar was well established by the time he was appointed chaplain of the ship *Adventurer* in the Royal Navy in 1675.

Popish Plot

In 1677, Oates became a chaplain to the Protestants in the household of the Catholic Duke of Norfolk. He soon gained the acquaintance of the anti-Jesuit Israel Tonge, who urged him to betray the Catholics to the government, even though Oates had recently converted himself. He spent some time in Jesuit seminaries in Europe before being expelled, and on his return he and Tonge concocted the details of the plot.

Aftermath of the plot

After three years as a leading accuser of Catholics, Oates fell out of favour in 1681 and an increasing number of those tried were found to be innocent. He was imprisoned after denouncing Charles and James and was not released until after the Glorious Revolution in 1689 (see Chapter 7).

Death of Godfrey

Godfrey left his house on the morning of 12 October and did not return. On 17 October, his body was found on Primrose Hill with his own sword in his back. He had been stabbed with the sword after his death, possibly days afterwards. The surgeons who inspected the body and gave evidence at his inquest suggested that Godfrey had been strangled, and there is still no consensus among historians about the exact motive for his death, although it is unlikely that it had anything to do with Oates or the Catholics named in the plot accusations. The significant sum of £500 (£58,000 in today's money) was offered for the discovery of the murderers.

William Bedloe soon came forward to claim the money after travelling from Bristol to London. A committee of the Lords was created to investigate the murder and Bedloe gave evidence before its members. Bedloe claimed that he was supposed to have assisted in the murder and had been taken to see the body, where he saw Samuel Atkins, a clerk to Samuel Pepys, as well as a servant of Lord Belasyse. Another arrest of a Catholic named Miles Prance helped Bedloe to substantiate his story. Prance fell under suspicion for the murder because his lodger claimed that Prance was out of his house on the night of Godfrey's disappearance. After being held in a freezing cell in Newgate prison, Prance confessed to involvement in the murder. It was on his evidence that three other men were hanged in February 1679.

> **KEY FIGURE**
>
> **William Bedloe (1650–80)**
>
> A serial fraudster who was close to a number of Jesuits in London. He was involved with the criminal underworld and through this may have had some legitimate knowledge of Godfrey's murder.

Contemporary reactions to the Popish Plot

SOURCE QUESTION

How can you account for the contrasting reactions to the Popish Plot found in Sources B–E?

SOURCE B

An Anglican loyalist view, from William Lloyd's funeral sermon for Edmund Berry Godfrey, 31 October 1678. Lloyd was chaplain to Mary Stuart.

Such a sort of men there is, even here in England, and we have them among us. They are the Jesuits I speak of. They hold it lawful to kill men that would prejudice them, or their religion. God still deliver us from your bloody hands. God keep England from your bloody religion. He that saved us in eighty eight [invasion of the Spanish Armada], he that saved us from the Gunpowder Plot, he will deliver us from this cursed conspiracy.

SOURCE C

A Catholic view. William Blundell was a Catholic who fought for Charles I in the Civil Wars. Despite his religious preferences, he voiced criticism of France and Spain and was committed to fight against them in the event of war. This letter was written on 4 April 1679 to a close friend.

Since I wrote to you last, I have been inwardly a little afflicted to see and hear these many astonishing accounts which have filled the world with wonder. I was troubled a little some months ago to see my trusty old sword taken from me on the order to disarm papists, which had been my companion when I lost my limbs, my lands and my liberty for acting against the Rebels on the king's behalf [in the Civil War]. I deny in the presence of God that I have ever entertained any design contrary to the duty of a subject against the king. It has always been my professed principle that all Catholic subjects of a lawful Protestant king are obliged faithfully to adhere to that king. I trust you will pity and pardon me if now, when so many are grown stark mad, I am become a little distracted.

SOURCE D

A Nonconformist view, from Edward Calamy, diarist and the son of a Nonconformist minister. Here he recalls the atmosphere in London after Godfrey's death.

The discovery of this plot put the whole kingdom into a new fermentation and filled people universally with unspeakable terror. To see the posts and chains put up in all parts of the city, and a considerable number of the Trained Bands, night after night, well-armed, watching with much care. And to be entertained from day to day with the talk of massacres designed, and a number of bloody assassins ready to serve such purposes was much surprising. The frequent execution of traitors that ensued and the many dismal stories handed about continually, made the hearts, not only of the younger, but the elder persons to quake for fear.

A Whig view. The Earl of Shaftesbury's reply to a letter asking how people could believe in the plot.

It is no matter. The more nonsensical the better; if we cannot bring them to swallow worse nonsense than that, we shall never do any good with them.

Investigations in London

Parliament reassembled on 21 October and quickly began organising a thorough investigation into the plot.

- Committees were established in order to examine witnesses.
- The vaults under parliament were searched for gunpowder, as 5 November was approaching.
- Fireworks on sale at businesses in Westminster were inspected.
- The walls of parliament were inspected for explosives.
- Houses in the vicinity were searched for arms.
- Shaftesbury, who by now was one of the chief promoters of Oates's narrative, recorded statements made by boys aged fifteen and seventeen of what had been said to them by a child of six. These statements were unreliable, but were presented by Shaftesbury as fact.

Coleman's letters

A parliamentary committee was established specifically to examine the letters of Edward Coleman. Beginning in 1674, he had written numerous letters to his contacts abroad about the prospect of restoring Catholicism in England, and the discovery of these gave the plot yet more legitimacy, especially as many were written in code.

His statements about the prospect of converting England were often vague, but were the proof for which parliament had been looking. One of the councillors wrote, 'the general scope of all these letters tends to bring the Roman Catholic religion into England'.

ONLINE EXTRAS WWW
AQA

Test your knowledge of the Popish Plot by completing Worksheet 14 at **www. hoddereducation.co.uk/ accesstohistory/extras**

ONLINE EXTRAS WWW
Pearson Edexcel

Ensure you have grasped the key features of the Popish Plot by completing Worksheet 14 at **www. hoddereducation.co.uk/ accesstohistory/extras**

SUMMARY DIAGRAM

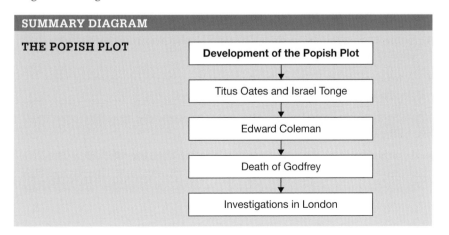

THE POPISH PLOT

Development of the Popish Plot
↓
Titus Oates and Israel Tonge
↓
Edward Coleman
↓
Death of Godfrey
↓
Investigations in London

2 Government action against Catholics

■ *What was the impact of the anti-Catholic hysteria of 1678–9?*

The Lords proceeded with a bill for prohibiting Catholics from sitting in either House. On 20 November, this was modified to exempt the Duke of York, even though some members of parliament (MPs) had spoken in debates of their desire to remove him from government based on the contents of Coleman's letters. Some argued that expelling James would drive him into the hands of the conspirators. In the end, the bill was passed by the fine margin of 158 to 156.

The Five Popish Lords

Five Catholic lords – Arundell, Belasyse, Powis, Petre and Stafford – were sent to the Tower on a fresh accusation from Oates. The Commons resolved 'that there has been and still is a damnable and hellish plot for rooting out and destroying the Protestant religion'. On 28 November, Bedloe was called into parliament and the doors were locked while he gave evidence to the Commons. Having been given a full pardon in advance, he proceeded to relate how a Jesuit meeting had taken place at Somerset House (the occasional residence of Queen Catherine). He claimed that this had been attended by Lord Belasyse, Lord Powis, two French abbots and Coleman. The Queen joined them, as well as a mysterious 'Father Walsh', supposedly an Irish priest, although he was never tracked down. Bedloe continued to claim that it was at this meeting that Catherine consented to the murder of her husband in order to restore the Catholic faith in England. This accusation was subsequently supported by Oates.

The first trials

Many of those mentioned in the testimonies of Oates and Bedloe now began to face legal proceedings.

- Coleman appeared before a court where Oates once again gave evidence against him. He was tried and executed on 3 December.
- Three leading Jesuits, Ireland, Grove and Pickering, were next to be tried and were sentenced to death.
- After a debate on 5 December, parliament resolved to impeach the 'Five Popish Lords' and they were held in the Tower.

Charles refused to listen to suggestions that his own wife be arrested, but the five Catholic lords suffered to varying degrees:

- Lord Stafford was the only one of the accused to be executed. He was tried for treason in the Lords and found guilty by 55 votes to 31. Charles had little sympathy for Stafford and may have initially been convinced by some of the accusations. Even if he did disagree with the execution, the renewed anti-Catholic climate that was in evidence during Stafford's trial in 1680 made it impossible for Charles to question the proceedings.

- Charles burst out laughing when told that Lord Belasyse was a leading conspirator because he was far too infirm to be involved. He was eventually released.
- Lord Petre was held without trial and died in prison in 1684.
- Arundell and Powis were imprisoned in the Tower until their release in 1684.

Explosion of print

When the Licensing Act (see page 15) expired in 1679, there were very few restrictions on print, and material was produced in the form of cheap pamphlets intended for wide public consumption. Recent research has suggested that seventeenth-century audiences were more literate than had once been assumed, and most people would at least know someone who could read. The two previous peaks in printed material were in 1642, when the Civil War broke out, and 1660, when the monarchy was restored. In 1679, more than 2000 printed pamphlets were produced and in 1680 the number increased to nearly 3000. Many of them contained accounts of the trials, as well as satirical ballads and poems critical of Catholics.

Action against Catholics

The King and many of his councillors realised that the evidence from Oates and the other witnesses was inept. However, the plot placed the King and the Court in an unfavourable position because many of the accusations were concerned with the religious and political leanings of the Court. Charles, therefore, had to act vigorously to try to dispel the impression that his Court was implicated in the plot. This way he could safeguard his brother's succession to the throne.

London

Beginning in November 1678, Charles issued several proclamations against Catholics, including one stating that all Catholics should leave London and stay at least ten miles away from the city. In London, the number of convictions for recusancy peaked at 1203 in 1679. Convictions continued into 1680 and 1681, and all but 60 of those convicted came from the City of London, Westminster and the western suburbs. This was the area where most Catholics lived, but was also where there was more sensitivity to the threat, as it was close to parliament and the Court. One of the individuals who appeared before the courts was Joan Page, wife of a butcher called John Page. She was accused of saying she 'hoped to wash her hands in the Protestants' blood, for they are heretics', and was said to have threatened to set fire to her neighbours' houses. She was fined in 1679 and faced similar charges a year later.

Table 5.1 Numbers of Catholics asked to take the oath of allegiance in 1678–80

County	Number of Catholics identified	Number who took the oath of allegiance	Number punished for refusal
Herefordshire	143	38	30
Buckinghamshire	Recorded as 'numerous'	13	1
Lancashire	1406	124	0
Kent	>100	15	0

Outside London

Magistrates in the provinces followed the lead of the Privy Council and in some areas began to enforce the recusancy laws much more vigorously. In Wiltshire, there was a sharp, but short-lived, rise in the number of convictions in 1678–9; however, there were still fewer convictions than in 1673. In Warwickshire, the period 1678–80 saw the only convictions for recusancy in Charles's reign.

The Commons ordered that its members provide lists of all suspected Catholics in their counties. These Catholics were subsequently expected to take the oath of allegiance to the Crown and Church of England. However, the government was often hampered by a lack of cooperation at the local level. Many **justices of the peace** (JPs) felt that the potential penalties involved were too drastic. In Warwickshire, a commission to tender the oath to a number of local Catholics does not seem to have been acted on. In Buckinghamshire, although many people were presented for recusancy, only fourteen suspected Catholics were asked to take the oath. Many Catholics simply failed to turn up to court when summoned and it was rare for action to be taken against them.

KEY TERM

Justices of the peace Magistrates who were responsible for ensuring that law and order was upheld at a local level. They were typically members of the lower gentry.

Action against the clergy

No Catholic priests had been executed between 1660 and 1678 but eighteen, including an Irish archbishop, Oliver Plunkett, were executed between 1678 and 1681. Others died in prison, including another Irish bishop, Peter Talbot. The work of Catholic clergy across the country was disrupted. By 1680, the Catholics of Worcester, who had previously been able to worship in relative peace, had not seen a priest for over a year.

Reduction in hysteria

By Christmas 1678, fear of Catholics had begun to diminish in the provinces because the weeks of rumours appeared not to be amounting to anything. It lasted longer in London, partly because it had the highest concentration of population and partly because it was the centre of the original accusations. In January 1679, many daggers intended for self-defence were sold inscribed with Godfrey's name. When James went out into the streets of the city to organise putting out a large fire, he left for fear of the crowds who called him a 'popish dog'.

After May 1679, the fear in London seems to have diminished. Between March and July the nightly guard was reduced from 2000 to 500. There was to be no recurrence of the panic of late 1678 and early 1679, and tension was only increased again by political events connected with the attempted exclusion of James from the line of succession (see pages 84–7). In total, the Popish Plot had claimed 35 victims, fifteen of whom were hanged at **Tyburn**.

KEY TERM

Tyburn The site of London's gallows, where public hangings took place.

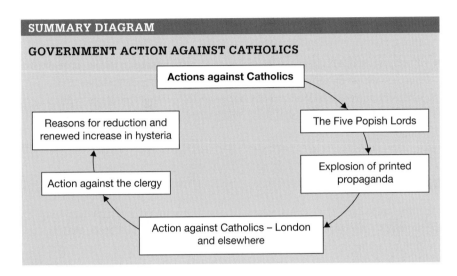

SUMMARY DIAGRAM

GOVERNMENT ACTION AGAINST CATHOLICS

- Actions against Catholics
- Reasons for reduction and renewed increase in hysteria
- The Five Popish Lords
- Action against the clergy
- Explosion of printed propaganda
- Action against Catholics – London and elsewhere

ONLINE EXTRAS
AQA   WWW

Develop your analysis of the actions against Catholics by completing Worksheet 15 at **www.hoddereducation. co.uk/accesstohistory/extras**

ONLINE EXTRAS
Pearson Edexcel   WWW

Test your understanding of the actions against Catholics by completing Worksheet 15 at **www.hoddereducation. co.uk/accesstohistory/extras**

3 The Exclusion Crisis

■ *What action was taken to exclude James from the line of succession?*

During the 1670s, and more particularly after the Popish Plot, anti-Catholic feeling became increasingly focused on the question of the succession to the throne. Charles had several illegitimate but no legitimate children, and according to the ordinary rules of hereditary succession, his brother, James, would be next in line to the throne.

Possible successors

James was now an open Catholic with a Catholic second wife. Although he had two daughters by his first wife who had been brought up Protestant, a son by his second marriage might well be brought up as a Catholic and would have precedence over his daughters. Several solutions to the succession problem were offered by parliament before 1678:

- One plan was for Charles to follow the precedent of Henry VIII. This would involve divorcing and remarrying in order to try to have a male Protestant heir. Charles rejected this idea outright.

- Another was that special legal limitations should be put on a Catholic king, with the understanding that these would only be temporary. Charles said he was prepared to discuss this, but no agreement was reached.

- Some MPs and peers wanted the King's eldest and favourite illegitimate son, **James Scott, Duke of Monmouth**, to be declared the lawful heir. Since the passing of the Test Act in 1673, rumours had been circulating that Charles and Monmouth's mother, Lucy Walter, had legally married, thus making him a legitimate heir. Charles made three formal declarations in 1678 denying that a marriage had taken place.

- The most compelling case was for James to be bypassed in favour of Mary, his own eldest daughter. This became a more serious political question after her marriage to William of Orange in 1677, but at this stage William was unwilling to be a tool of the English opposition and disapproved of the suggestion.

The dissolution of the Cavalier Parliament, March 1679

Over the course of the next two years, Charles summoned and dissolved two parliaments – the third and fourth of his reign – and in each of these, the Commons attempted to pass bills excluding James from the line of succession. At the end of this process, Charles and James were successful in ensuring that the succession remained unchanged. Charles was then able to relieve himself of the need to summon parliaments through a renewal of French subsidies.

The aftermath of dissolution

Charles dissolved parliament on 24 January 1679 amid the debates around Danby's impeachment. It had now been eighteen years since the loyalist enthusiasm of the last election in 1661, and he knew that new elections would not result in such a faithful parliament. In order to pre-empt some of the complaints that would inevitably be made by the opposition in a new parliament, he produced a signed declaration on 3 March to the effect that he had never married anyone except Catherine and therefore Monmouth was illegitimate. Charles remodelled his Privy Council to include loyal courtiers and members of the opposition (including Shaftesbury).

Elections to the First Exclusion Parliament

The election of 1679 was the first to be fought on distinctively party lines. The dividing lines between Whigs (previously known as the Country opposition) and loyal Tories were being cemented, and MPs were generally committed to one of these two sides. The Country opposition issued pamphlets outlining their aims, including one written anonymously called *England's great interest in the choice of this new parliament,* which can be summarised as follows:

- Further action to be taken in response to the Popish Plot.

- Those who have benefited from bribes in parliament to be punished.

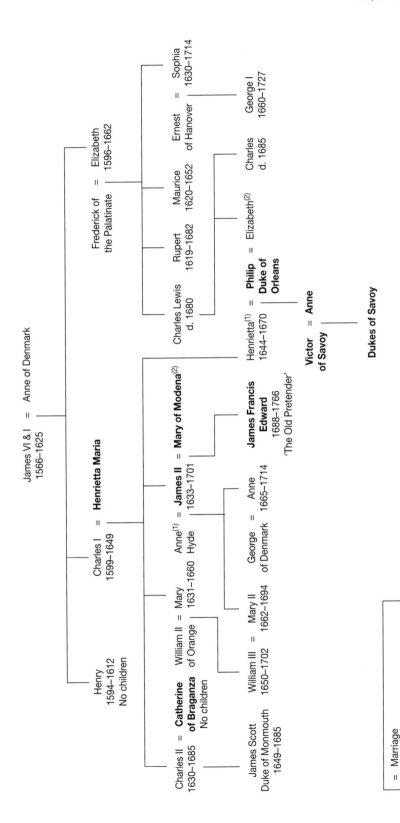

Figure 5.1 The English succession, 1670–89.

- Measures to be adopted for the securing of more frequent parliaments.
- The king's 'evil counsellors', such as Danby, to be brought to justice.

This was one of the first clear statements of party doctrine ever put before the English electorate. The election resulted in no more than 40 MPs on whom the Court could rely, and a large proportion of the opposition members had no parliamentary experience.

First Exclusion bill, May 1679

The new parliament assembled on 6 March, and many of the early exchanges featured debates about the continued influence of Catholicism. On 27 March, the Commons formally resolved that 'the Duke of York being a Papist, and hopes of his coming to the Crown, has given the greatest encouragement to the present conspiracies and designs of the Papists against the King and Protestant religion'.

With each passing week, bitterness towards James from the MPs increased. On 11 May, one of the members for London, Thomas Pilkington, proposed that James should be impeached for high treason. On 15 May, Richard Hampden moved for the introduction of an Exclusion bill to prevent James from becoming king in England, Scotland and Ireland. It was passed in the Commons by 207 votes to 128.

? SOURCE QUESTION

Study Source F. How can the Exclusion bill be linked to the Popish Plot?

SOURCE F

The first Exclusion bill, 1679.

The emissaries, priests and agents for the Pope, have traitorously seduced James Duke of York, presumptive heir to these Crowns, to the Communion of the Church of Rome; and have induced him to enter into several negotiations with the Pope, his Cardinals and Nuncios [diplomats] for promoting the Romish Church and interest; and by his means and procurement, had advanced the power and greatness of the French King, to the manifest hazard of these Kingdoms.

1. James Duke of York, should be incapable of inheriting the Crowns of England, Scotland, and Ireland.
2. In case his Majesty should happen to die, or resign his dominions, they should devolve to the person next in succession, in the same manner as if the Duke was dead.
3. All acts of sovereignty and royalty that the Prince might then happen to perform, are not only declared void, but to be high-treason, and punishable as such.
4. If the Duke himself ever returns into any of these dominions, he should be looked upon as guilty of the same offence; and all persons are authorised and required, to seize upon and imprison him.

Habeas Corpus Act

In order to block the Exclusion bill, Charles appeared personally in parliament on 27 May and spoke to both Houses. As a compromise, he assented to the Habeas Corpus Act, put forward by the opposition to prevent arbitrary imprisonment. The Act was part of Shaftesbury's broader actions against James because he feared that James would rule arbitrarily if he came to the throne. Charles then prorogued parliament and it was later dissolved before its members could meet again.

Dissolution of parliament

At the dissolution, Charles appeared to be in the stronger position. July saw the first sign that the public were beginning to lose faith in the Popish Plot when Sir George Wakeman was found not guilty after the judge, William Scroggs, questioned the evidence of Oates. James now wanted to prove his credentials as king in waiting and favoured using the army to maintain order. Charles knew that this was an extremely dangerous prospect and induced James to depart for Brussels with a promise that his main rival to the throne, Monmouth, would be exiled to Holland.

ONLINE EXTRAS **WWW**
AQA

Get to grips with the Exclusion Crisis by completing Worksheet 16 at **www. hoddereducation.co.uk/ accesstohistory/extras**

ONLINE EXTRAS **WWW**
Pearson Edexcel

Ensure you have grasped the key features of the Exclusion Crisis by completing Worksheet 16 at **www. hoddereducation.co.uk/ accesstohistory/extras**

SUMMARY DIAGRAM

THE EXCLUSION CRISIS

Exclusion and survival

James departed for Belgium and Monmouth was exiled to Holland

The succession problem – rival claims to the throne

First Exclusion bill, 1679, and dissolution

Dissolution of the Cavalier Parliament, 1679

First Exclusion Parliament – first fought on party lines

---

4 The end of the crisis

■ *How did Charles and James survive the Exclusion Crisis?*

The new parliament was summoned for 7 October 1679. However, when it met, it was immediately prorogued by Charles for a year. In the meantime, Charles's immediate objective continued to be the securing of the succession for his brother.

To ensure that his brother could continue in the succession, Charles decided to rule with councillors of his own choosing. Shaftesbury was therefore dismissed from the Privy Council in October 1679. Charles then appointed men who were primarily royalists and opponents of Exclusion, including the Earl of Sunderland, Sidney Godolphin and Lawrence Hyde. This group was the first exclusively Tory cabinet. They were anxious to protect themselves against sudden changes in the political climate and were strong supporters of James.

Increase in anti–Catholic hysteria

The hysteria that had begun to wane in London started to rise once again in the autumn of 1679. On the annual commemoration of Elizabeth's accession to the throne on 17 November, there was a **pope-burning** ceremony reportedly attended by 200,000 people. This was followed by the return of the popular Monmouth on 27 November. The pope-burning had been sponsored by the **Green Ribbon Club** and this enthusiasm spread beyond London to Yorkshire, where another Catholic plot to kill the King was apparently discovered. A network of informers continued to report on apparent conspiracies, including Israel Tonge's son, Simson.

In the months that Charles ruled without parliament, Titus Oates's credibility began to decline as his evidence was more frequently brought into question. In July 1680, his salary was reduced from £12 per week to £2. This was followed by a series of acrimonious disputes with Tonge about the authorship of the original plot accusations.

 SOURCE QUESTION

Study Source G. What does the symbolism of the procession suggest about the reasons for the spread of the Popish Plot?

SOURCE G

A contemporary description of a pope-burning procession, 17 November 1679, from an anonymous pamphlet.

1. *Six whistlers to clear the way.*
2. *A bell-man ringing and shouting, 'Remember Justice Godfrey'.*
3. *A dead body, representing Sir Edmund Berry Godfrey, in the habit he usually wore, the cravat wherewith he was murdered about his neck, with spots of blood on his wrists, shirt and white gloves, riding on a white horse, one of his murderers behind him to keep him from falling, representing the manner he was carried from Somerset House to Primrose Hill.*
4. *A Jesuit giving pardons very freely to those who would murder Protestants.*
5. *Six Jesuits with bloody daggers.*
6. *Four Popish bishops in purple and lawn sleeves.*
7. *Lastly, the Pope, preceded by silk banners with bloody daggers painted on them for murdering heretical kings, and behind him his counsellor the Devil.*

Attempt to pass the second Exclusion bill

Charles had delayed the summoning of parliament in the hope that enthusiasm for Exclusion might have cooled. This was certainly the case among some sections of the public and the Lords, but the Whigs in the Commons were still in a strong position. When parliament finally met in October 1680, another Exclusion bill was presented by the Commons. It passed on 11 November and was sent to the Lords, where Lord Halifax led the opposition to it. He argued that Exclusion would inevitably lead to another civil war and instead backed Charles's offer to limit James's power. As had been the case in the First Exclusion Parliament, Charles attended the debate in person and spoke to Lords individually in an effort to secure their support. The bill was defeated by 63 votes to 30.

The Oxford Parliament, 1681

Charles dissolved parliament in January 1681 and summoned another to meet at the royalist stronghold of Oxford in March. This was an astute political move as it deprived Shaftesbury and the Whigs of the support of the City of London, which was generally more fearful of Catholicism and James's succession. It also meant that the London mob would not be able to mobilise in support of the Whigs. In his opening speech, Charles repeated his opposition to Exclusion and suggested, once again, that he would consider limitations to his brother's power. Shaftesbury ignored this offer and continued to press for Exclusion. Charles responded by dissolving parliament after just one week, without warning and after stationing 600 troops outside the building. The Whigs were forced to disperse, and Shaftesbury was arrested for treason and held in the Tower of London. Charles did not call parliament again during his reign as he had by now secured the necessary funds from Louis XIV.

ONLINE EXTRAS WWW
AQA

Test your understanding of the end of the Exclusion Crisis by completing Worksheet 17 at **www.hoddereducation.co.uk/accesstohistory/extras**

ONLINE EXTRAS WWW
Pearson Edexcel

Develop your analysis of the end of the Exclusion Crisis by completing Worksheet 17 at **www.hoddereducation.co.uk/accesstohistory/extras**

SUMMARY DIAGRAM

THE END OF THE CRISIS

Charles and James survived the Exclusion Crisis

↓

Second Exclusion bill defeated

↓

Oxford Parliament, 1681: final parliament in Charles's reign

Reasons for surviving Exclusion

1. Actions of the King
2. Lack of enthusiasm for Exclusion
3. The Whigs: weaknesses and divisions
4. Tory propaganda

5 Key debate

■ *Why did Exclusion fail?*

Charles not only survived the Exclusion Crisis, but as historian J.R. Jones (1961) has put it, he emerged 'as incontestably the strongest seventeenth-century monarch'. The hereditary succession was kept intact, and James became king in February 1685 when his brother died. The reasons for this survival have been subject to historical controversy and there are a number of interpretations that have been put forward to explain why a political decision that seemed inevitable to many at the height of the Popish Plot in 1678, fizzled out in 1681.

Traditional view: the actions of the King

For many years, historians tended to agree that Charles survived simply because he was able to use his prerogative powers to clamp down on the opposition and manage the situation. For example, when James suggested using the army to restore order, Charles ensured that his brother was swiftly removed from the political scene and sent abroad in order for the situation in England to calm. He was able to dismiss members of the Country party from Crown offices, including commands of the militia and local government. Through personal appearances in parliament, Charles was able to offer compromises, such as his assent to the Habeas Corpus Act in place of the first Exclusion bill and offers to restrict James's power when he became king. He was equally able to use these appearances to prorogue and dissolve parliament when opposition became particularly heated, and he made good use of delaying tactics.

Throughout all these events, however, Charles was in near-constant negotiations with the French, and it was the promise of French subsidies that gave him the confidence to dispense with parliament in 1681. His financial position had improved anyway, and by 1681 he was able to enjoy increased revenues from the continuing growth of trade. For the first time, the revenue of £1.2 million that he was promised in the Restoration Settlement was fulfilled.

INTERPRETATION QUESTION

Read Extracts 1–4. What are the different views put forward to explain why Exclusion failed in the years 1679–81?

ONLINE EXTRAS
AQA **WWW**

Get to grips with historical interpretations by completing Worksheet 18 at **www. hoddereducation.co.uk/ accesstohistory/extras**

EXTRACT 1

From J.R. Jones, *The First Whigs: The Politics of the Exclusion Crisis, 1678–1683*, Oxford University Press, 1961, p. 64.

In order to stifle the progress of the First Exclusion Bill, Charles prorogued parliament and dissolved it shortly afterwards. His action encouraged supporters to rally round the Crown, but the elections of August and September saw the Whigs strengthened, not weakened. When parliament did meet in October 1680 the Whig hold was stronger than ever. Unknown to the Whigs the turning-point in the crisis had already been passed. Having failed to significantly reduce their strength, the King preferred to become the client of France rather than the dependant of his own subjects. A secret agreement assured him of French support, and with this behind him he had no immediate need to call parliament at all.

Traditional view: lack of enthusiasm for Exclusion

It was also a long-held belief among historians that Exclusion was not successful because there was only limited appetite for it in the years following the Popish Plot. To many people, Exclusion threatened stability and hierarchy in society and there was a fear that if parliament altered the succession they might begin to tamper with other aspects of the law. Charles's advisers and supporters were generally loyal as a result. When Shaftesbury called on members of the Privy

Council to resign in November 1680, they refused to give up their positions. For the newer members in particular, this was their opportunity to forge a successful political career for themselves and they were not willing to lose a chance which might never again present itself.

This lack of enthusiasm was also evident in the waning of the Popish Plot. As time passed, it became increasingly clear that Oates's accusations did not amount to a serious threat. Local magistrates often failed to act against Catholics and the public mood for Exclusion was not always strong, even at the height of the anti-Catholic hysteria, as outlined by John Miller in Extract 2.

EXTRACT 2

From John Miller, *Popery and Politics in England: 1660–1688*, Cambridge University Press, 1973, p. 188.

There was not the same alienation of king and nation in 1678–81 as there had been in 1640–2 or as there was to be in 1688. Charles kept the support of a substantial section of the political nation and was able to exploit the Tory backlash for all it was worth. The Plot and the eventual confrontation over exclusion, though causally linked, were separated in time; the emotional excitement generated by the first had waned by the time of the second. The threat from Popery and arbitrary government seemed immediate in 1640–2 and in 1688; in 1679–81 it was only a possible threat, somewhere in the future. This lower level of intensity and of immediacy made the battles of the Exclusion Crisis more superficial than they might appear at first sight.

Revisionist view: weaknesses of the Whigs

In more recent years, an increasing number of historians have focused their research on the weaknesses of the Whigs. It was certainly difficult for the Whigs to establish themselves when parliament was dissolved and prorogued, and they also faced a lack of unity over who should succeed Charles. Some favoured Monmouth as the eldest son of Charles, whereas others preferred Mary as the eldest Protestant daughter of James. Both potential candidates had drawbacks: Monmouth was illegitimate, and Mary was married to a foreign prince. Shaftesbury's control was not always strong and as the crisis went on there was an increasing number of MPs who failed to vote for Exclusion despite Shaftesbury's intense canvassing of members.

EXTRACT 3

From Nicholas Fellows, *Charles II and James II*, Hodder & Stoughton, 1995, p. 80.

Throughout the period the Whigs faced a very difficult task. They had expected popular pressure to be sufficient to persuade Charles to give way. Once it became apparent that it was not, their position became much weaker. It was very difficult to maintain the momentum of the campaign when they appeared to be getting nowhere. When parliament was either dissolved or prorogued the Whigs found it hard to maintain the nation's interest, despite pamphlets, tours and pope-burning ceremonies. The Whig cause was further weakened by divisions within their own ranks. If James was to be excluded who should succeed? In the end Shaftesbury came down on the side of Charles's illegitimate son, Monmouth, but not all agreed with this choice. Charles had been able to exploit this and play upon the potential divisions within the opposition.

Revisionist view: Tory propaganda

More recently, Tim Harris has argued that the influence of Tory propaganda has been understated as historians have focused so much on the output of the Whig press. In fact, it has been suggested that Whig propaganda was actually ineffective, and that it served more as entertainment than a genuine call to action. Tory pamphlets and cartoons carried the slogan 'forty-one is here again' in reference to the crisis that immediately preceded the Civil War and acted as a reminder of the instability that might be caused if James was to be excluded. Tory propaganda was also able to portray Exclusion as particularly radical and presented James as a victim. After all, the Test Act had singled him out for punishment, and some Exclusionists even called for James to be hanged in the event that he tried to take the throne.

EXTRACT 4

From Tim Harris, *Restoration: Charles II and his Kingdoms*, Penguin, 2005, p. 345.

The crown and its Tory allies did not simply ride roughshod over public opinion; rather, they made a deliberate attempt to woo it, through a carefully crafted propaganda campaign. In the process, they sought to address public anxieties about the threat of popery and arbitrary government, insisting that the best way to avoid both was for people to resist the Whig challenge and rally behind the crown in defence of the traditional constitution in Church and state. And their efforts, we have been told, were successful. As the Exclusion Crisis progressed, there was a swing in public opinion to the Tories, which manifested itself in the form of loyal addresses and processions, as people sought to demonstrate their loyalty to the crown and the succession and their opposition to the Whigs and dissenters. By this account, persuasion rather than suppression was the key to the defeat of the Exclusionist challenge.

In reality, Charles and James survived Exclusion due to a combination of reasons. There is no doubt that propaganda on both sides, together with the long-held belief in English society that Catholics were a constant threat to stability, influenced popular opinion. The crisis was, however, played out in parliament and it was the leading MPs and members of Charles's government who had the most influence on the political decisions of the day. As long as the Whigs were divided over what a future succession should look like, they would never be able to defeat a king who had one objective to which he remained stubbornly loyal.

ONLINE EXTRAS
Pearson Edexcel WWW

Get to grips with historical interpretations by completing Worksheet 18 at www.hoddereducation.co.uk/accesstohistory/extras

CHAPTER SUMMARY

The Popish Plot was the culmination of decades of anti-Catholic suspicion and this helps to explain why stories of the Catholic threat spread so widely. The evidence of Oates and Tonge was eagerly received in parliament and at Court, as well as on the streets of London and elsewhere. Anti-Catholic sentiment increased to become a panic, resulting in the executions of 35 people, and this gave Shaftesbury and the Whigs the confidence to push for Exclusion. Through a combination of Whig weakness, skill at managing parliament and a lack of enthusiasm for Exclusion in some quarters, Charles and James were able to survive apparently unscathed. With French subsidies and an improved financial situation as a result of the growth of international trade (see Chapter 10), Charles could now embark on personal rule for the last four years of his reign. In these years, Charles acted in an increasingly absolutist manner and set the tone for the short reign of James from 1685 to 1688.

Refresher questions

Use these questions to remind yourself of the key material covered in this chapter.

1 What accusations were originally made by Titus Oates?

2 Who was Edmund Berry Godfrey and what was his role?

3 What was the role of William Bedloe?

4 What was the reaction to the Popish Plot in London?

5 Why were Edward Coleman's letters incriminating?

6 What happened to the Five Popish Lords?

7 What happened to the press in 1679?

8 What evidence is there of a lack of enthusiasm for Catholic recusancy laws?

9 Why did anti-Catholic feeling begin to diminish in 1679?

10 Why did the first Exclusion bill fail?

11 What was the Habeas Corpus Act?

12 Why did Oates's credibility decline in 1680?

13 How did Charles ensure that the second Exclusion bill was not passed?

14 Why did Exclusion fail, according to historians?

Question practice: AQA A level

Essay questions

1 How far do you agree that the Exclusion Crisis was the greatest challenge faced by Charles II in the years 1660–85?

EXAM HINT You need to analyse how serious the Exclusion Crisis was in comparison with other challenges faced by Charles II. A judgement could be stated in your opening paragraph, with the arguments in the essay flowing from this.

2 To what extent were Catholics tolerated by government and parliament in the years 1660–81?

EXAM HINT You will need to make sure that you do not describe, but focus on analysis, especially if you follow a chronological approach. Note the need for separate treatment of 'government' and 'parliament'.

3 How accurate is it to say that the threat of Catholicism was the most divisive issue for Charles II and parliament in the years 1660–81?

EXAM HINT The question is asking you to discuss the causes of division between king and parliament. Was it the threat of Catholicism? And were the issues constant throughout the period?

4 How far do you agree that the actions and attitudes of Charles II were responsible for his political survival in the years 1660–81?

EXAM HINT You need to assess how far it was Charles II that personally contributed to his political survival or whether other factors were more important, for example the fear of another civil war or foreign invasion.

Interpretation question

1 Using your understanding of the historical context, assess how convincing the arguments in Extracts 1 (page 88), 2 (page 89) and 3 (page 89) are in relation to the reasons for the failure of Exclusion in the years 1678–81.

EXAM HINT Analyse the content of each extract, identifying the main argument or arguments. Then use your contextual knowledge to assess how convincing the arguments in each extract are. There is no need for an overall judgement; treat it as three separate exercises on the same topic.

Question practice: Pearson Edexcel

Essay questions

1 To what extent were Catholics tolerated by government and parliament in the years 1660–81? [AS level]

EXAM HINT Analyse the different attitudes taken towards Catholics by the government and parliament, and explain the differences. Explain the reasons for parliament's hostility.

2 How accurate is it to say that the threat of Catholicism was the most divisive issue for Charles II and parliament in the years 1660–81? [A level]

EXAM HINT 'Most divisive' suggests that you should consider a number of factors which caused divisions between king and parliament, and make a case for the most divisive factor.

3 How far do you agree that the actions and attitudes of Charles II were responsible for his political survival in the years 1660–81? [A level]

EXAM HINT Assess the significance of Charles's political skills and set these against other key factors, such as fears of a return to civil conflict and the threats posed by the Dutch and the French.

CHAPTER 6

Charles II to James II, 1681–7

The seven years from the end of the Exclusion Crisis in 1681 to the Glorious Revolution of 1688 marked a period of Tory reaction, a renewed persecution of Dissenters and ultimately the promotion of the Catholic cause by James II. Charles's defeat of the Exclusion bill did not mean that the threat from the Whigs and Shaftesbury was removed, and he expended much energy in his final years ensuring that their danger was reduced. One individual who continued to act as a figurehead for the opposition was Monmouth, who remained popular and provided a challenge for his father, King Charles II. These events will be covered in the following sections:

◆ The Tory reaction, 1681–5

◆ James II: political settlement

◆ James II and Catholicism

KEY DATES				
1681	Purges of local office holders	**1685**	**Feb.**	Death of Charles II and accession of James II
1682	Shaftesbury fled England		**May**	Monmouth Rebellion
1683	Rye House Plot	**1686**		*Godden* v. *Hales*
1684	James restored to Privy Council in defiance of the Test Act	**1687**		James's first Declaration of Indulgence

1 The Tory reaction, 1681–5

■ *How successful was Charles in resisting political opposition during the final years of his reign?*

When Charles dissolved the Oxford Parliament in March 1681 he announced that he had every intention of calling another. At this point it was generally accepted that the Exclusion question would continue to run and that the Whigs had a reasonable chance of passing another Exclusion bill. Why, then, was Charles able to rule without parliament for nearly four years in contravention of the Triennial Act? Charles had three aims in 1681, which were generally in line with those he had followed earlier in his reign:

■ Ensuring his own survival without constitutional limitations.

■ Maintaining the hereditary succession that would give his brother the throne on his death.

■ To involve himself in parliamentary politics only when it could not be avoided or when an opportunity to increase royal power presented itself.

Royal government was still in a relatively weak financial position in 1681. In his final years Charles departed from the ambitious foreign policy of the 1670s because he understood that as long as he was reliant on parliament for funding, he would never have the power enjoyed by Louis XIV. His policy was ultimately dependent on that of his patron, Louis, and he was fortunate that in these years Louis did not embark on any new ventures that would require English assistance and consequently English money. This meant that Charles did not need to call parliament.

Attacks on the Whigs

Charles now stood a strong chance of defeating the Whigs, partly as the result of a swing of opinion against them and partly as a result of his own superior handling of the situation. In April 1681, William Scroggs – who had been a keen supporter of the Popish Plot allegations – was removed as Lord Chief Justice and the post was given to Francis Pemberton, a loyal Tory. Two weeks later, the legal reaction began with the trial of Edward Fitzharris.

Edward Fitzharris

The first victim of the Tory reaction was perhaps the most unexpected and surprising. Edward Fitzharris was born in Ireland and raised as a Catholic. He became a soldier and had to resign a military command as a result of the Test Act in 1673. He was accused of being the author of a **libel** against Charles II called *The True Englishman speaking in plain English, in a Letter from a Friend to a Friend*. This charged Charles with exercising arbitrary government and promoting the Catholic cause. Witnesses reported that Fitzharris was actually supportive of Catholic and French interests and had said he had written the pamphlet in order to frame the Whigs. However, he was found guilty and hanged on 1 July.

KEY TERM

Libel A written statement that is damaging to a person's reputation.

SOURCE QUESTION

Study Source A. In what ways might this document be designed to discredit the Whigs?

SOURCE A

From *The True Englishman speaking in plain English, in a Letter from a Friend to a Friend*. Supposedly written by Edward Fitzharris and distributed in 1681.

I thank you for the character of a Popish successor [James] which you sent me, wherein our fears are justly set out. But I am in greater fear of the present possessor [Charles]. Why do we frighten ourselves about the evil that is to come, not looking to that which is at hand? We would cut off the budding weeds, and let the poisonous root lie still. If James be conscious and guilty, Charles is so too. Believe me, these two brethren, they are in confederacy with the Pope and the French to introduce Popery and arbitrary government, as all their actions demonstrate. Let the English rise, and move as one man to self-defence, to open action. Blow the trumpet, stand on your guard, and withstand them, and since there can be no trust given to this couple of Popish brethren, nor no relief expected from a parliament; trust to your swords in defence of your lives, laws, religion and properties, like the stout Earl of Old, who told a King that if he could not be defended by Magna Carta, he would be relieved by Longa Spada [Long Sword].

Stephen College

The judicial campaign against the Whig supporters was soon in full swing. A London joiner named Stephen College was put on trial at the Old Bailey for riding to Oxford during parliament's brief sitting there, in an effort to start an uprising against Charles. The case was thrown out initially because the Whig sheriffs in London selected a sympathetic jury. It was then contended by the government that, as the acts complained of had taken place at Oxford, he should be tried there instead. His trial at Oxford was set for 17 August 1681. The case against him amounted to the following:

- He had acquired weapons worth about twice the value of his estate.
- He travelled to Oxford with the intention of seizing the King.
- When he arrived at Oxford he was armed with pistols, a helmet and armour.
- He had criticised the King in taverns and coffee houses.
- He was one of the accomplices of Fitzharris.

Stephen Dugdale, an informer who had already given evidence against many of those accused in the Popish Plot (see pages 72–7), now became a witness for the anti-Whig cause. He claimed that he had heard College accuse the King of promoting the Catholic cause and had received a supply of blue ribbon from College for distribution, with the words 'no popery, no slavery' written on it. College protested his innocence but eventually, at three o'clock in the morning, the jury announced a verdict of guilty. College was executed on 31 August.

SOURCE QUESTION

Study Source B. Why do you think Stephen Dugdale switched allegiances after giving evidence against those accused in the Popish Plot?

SOURCE B

From an account of the trial of Stephen College, from *The arraignment, trial and condemnation of Stephen College* (1681). In this section, Stephen Dugdale is examined as a witness. The text was approved for publication by the judges and printed in London to be sold commercially.

Judge: *What is the nature of your relationship with Mr College?*

Dugdale: *My Lord, I have been I think acquainted with Mr College two years or thereabouts. I have been several times in Mr College's company, and truly sometimes he has been mightily bent against Popery; he has sometimes uttered himself, that because the King did not prosecute the Papists as he thought sufficiently, that the King was a Papist himself, that he was as deep in the Plot as any Papist of them all, that he had a hand in Sir Edmund Berry Godfrey's death.*

Judge: *Who did tell you so?*

Dugdale: *Mr College did tell me that there was nothing to be expected from the King, but the introducing of Popery and arbitrary Government, this I believe Mr College will acknowledge to be true.*

Attorney General: *What did you know of his delivering any marks or signs for persons to be distinguished by?*

[continued on next page]

> Dugdale: *I had as much ribbon from him as came to forty shillings, with 'no Popery, no Slavery' written on it; and he gave it me to distribute among my friends in the country, that they might be known by other persons that would wear the same.*
>
> Judge: *Where was it to be distributed?*
>
> Dugdale: *Among those that I knew to be Dissenters in the country.*

Shaftesbury

Shaftesbury was sent to the Tower of London on a charge on treason on 2 July 1681. His papers were confiscated and on 24 November a special commission was issued for his trial. The London **grand jury** for the trial was selected by the Whig sheriffs and was therefore sympathetic to Shaftesbury. Chief Justice Pemberton was determined in his pursuit of Shaftesbury and reminded the jury that their role was not to be compassionate and that they should instead base their decision on the evidence presented to them.

The indictment against Shaftesbury was then read:

- He was accused of suggesting that if the King refused to pass an Exclusion bill at the Oxford Parliament, force would have to be used against him.
- He had said that the King was a man of no faith.
- He had advocated the re-establishment of a republic.

The grand jury threw out the charge against Shaftesbury and the decision was met with celebrations in London, demonstrating the continued popularity of the Whigs. When Charles fell ill in May 1682, Shaftesbury entered into discussions with Monmouth and others about what to do if the King died. It was ultimately decided that whether Charles survived or not, a rebellion should be organised. Shaftesbury became increasingly anxious to mount an uprising, but his fellow conspirators were not as eager. When it became clear that his plot was not going to come to fruition, he fled to the Netherlands, arriving in Amsterdam in December 1682 and dying a few months later.

Increase in royal power

During these years, Charles broke only one law: he failed to summon parliament as the terms of the Triennial Act demanded. However, he was able to increase royal power and reduce opposition without the need to spend large amounts of money or call a parliament.

Absolutism and local government

The Popish Plot and Exclusion Crisis had cemented the relationship between the Whigs and Protestant Dissenters, and the towns were the strongholds of both groups. In addition, town boroughs returned 80 per cent of members of parliament (MPs) to the House of Commons, many of whom had been hostile to Charles's policies in the past. Between 1681 and 1685, Charles mounted a campaign of renewing **borough charters**. They were revised and 51 new charters were issued between 1681 and 1685. The new charters put control of towns in the hands of the King's own nominees.

The corporation of the City of London was now controlled by Tory loyalists, and when petitions demanding the exclusion of James were presented to the corporation they were thrown out.

> ### SOURCE C
>
> From Gilbert Burnet's views on the remodelling of borough charters in his *History of My Own Time*, published in 1724.
>
> *The cities and boroughs of England were invited to demonstrate their loyalty, by surrendering up their charters, and taking new ones modelled as the court thought fit. It was much questioned, whether those surrenders were good in law or not. It was said that those who were in the corporations were not the proprietors nor masters of those rights. The matter goes beyond my skill in law to determine it; this is certain, that whatever may be said in law, there is no sort of theft more criminal than a body of men, whom their neighbours have trusted with their concerns, to steal away their charters and affix their seals to such a deed, betraying in that their trust and their oaths.*

Challenges to the orthodox view of local government reforms

The orthodox view that Charles completely destroyed the independence of towns has been challenged. This is because Charles did not always make significant changes to a charter once it had been surrendered, and he did not always remove well-respected people from office, even when they were his opponents. He took a personal interest in very few towns and left most of the work to his advisers. He did, however, pay special attention to London and York. He was particularly determined to ensure that London's charter was surrendered because he was conscious of how the loss of London ultimately led to the Civil Wars and his father's downfall. Charles ensured that leading positions in London were no longer filled by elections, and instead controlled the appointments of the **mayor** and **aldermen** himself.

Control of the judiciary

Justices of the peace (JPs) and members of the judiciary throughout the country who had previously persecuted Catholics were replaced with men prepared to persecute Dissenters. A list was found among Shaftesbury's papers of men in the localities who could be trusted to sit as judges and remain loyal to the Whig cause. Charles's advisers worked through the list and expelled each man named on the list.

In London, Charles managed to ensure that two of his supporters were elected as sheriffs in 1682. Since the sheriffs were responsible for the selection of juries, it would now be possible to guarantee that London juries would make decisions in favour of the Crown in political cases.

KEY TERMS

Borough charter A document granting a town certain privileges and allowing it to control some of its own affairs.

Mayor The head of a town or borough council.

Aldermen High-ranking members of a borough council.

SOURCE QUESTION

Study Source C. Burnet was associated with the Whigs. Who do you think the 'body of men' are that he refers to in the final sentence?

The Anglican Church

Charles abandoned his earlier policy of toleration for Protestant Dissenters and gave his full backing to the Anglicans. In return, the clergy were pleased to preach obedience to the monarchy. This unity between Church and king offered a real prospect of stability and settlement. It meant that when Charles failed to summon a parliament in 1684, as he was supposed to according to the terms of the Triennial Act, the leaders of the Church of England turned a blind eye and did not make any complaints. Charles had realised that his best hope of asserting his control of the country was by reaching an understanding with the most influential groups in society. This was reflected in a severe persecution of Nonconformists.

Attacks on Dissenters

In 1680, a letter was sent from the Privy Council to all corporations requiring them to put into force the 1661 Corporation Act (see page 21), which had effectively banned Dissenters from being involved in local government. This was followed, in September 1681, by an order from Charles requiring JPs to fully implement the laws and ensure that 'none of the dissenters be spared'. The association between the Whigs and Protestant Dissenters had now led to a comprehensive reaction against both.

There is much consensus among historians that this period marked the harshest persecution the Dissenters had experienced in the reign of Charles II, with Ronald Hutton (1989) writing that in the years from 1681 to 1685, 'the persecution was the most sustained of the reign and indeed, in history'. The Quaker William Penn noted that the English had protested against Catholic persecution in France but 'will not look at home upon greater cruelties'. The Conventicle Act was enforced with renewed vigour, and in Bristol meeting houses were destroyed in 1681 and crowds were allowed to take from them whatever they could salvage. The Baptist preacher John Miller had 400 sheep and other animals confiscated, as well as an entire year's worth of produce taken from his farm in Dorset. In the particularly harsh winter of 1683–4, over 100 Dissenters died in prison.

In its efforts to enforce the laws against all types of religious Nonconformity, the government attempted once again to make recusancy laws against Catholics work, but Protestant Dissenters were the main victims of persecution. Recusancy fines totalled £24,330 for the years 1681–5, which compares with £3403 for the years 1676–80. However, in Yorkshire, Warwickshire and Monmouthshire, as well as some other counties, the number of convictions for recusancy declined rapidly after 1681. In general, the areas that faced the biggest threat from Protestant Dissenters saw the most liberal use of the recusancy laws.

Table 6.1 Religious persecution, 1681–5

a) Total raised from recusancy fines	
1676–80	**1681–5**
£3403	£24,330

b) Conviction certificates for attending conventicles in London*				
1664–5	**1670**	**1674–5**	**1682–3**	**1684**
48	5	10	750	111

c) Percentage of London recusants identified as Protestant Dissenters		
1679	**1681**	**1683**
30%	42%	94%

d) Percentage of recusancy convictions outside London	
1678–9	**1682–3**
5%	66%

e) Percentage of convicted recusants in Norfolk confirmed as Catholic	
1676–9	**1684**
40–60%	6.5%

ONLINE EXTRAS AQA WWW

Develop your analysis of the aftermath of Exclusion by completing Worksheet 19 at **www.hoddereducation.co.uk/accesstohistory/extras**

ONLINE EXTRAS Pearson Edexcel WWW

Test your understanding of the significance of the Exclusion Crisis by completing Worksheet 19 at **www.hoddereducation.co.uk/accesstohistory/extras**

*Each conviction contained a number of names. The number of convictions in every other year of Charles's reign is zero.

The Rye House Plot, 1683

The Duke of Monmouth remained a figurehead for the Whig cause, and although he would not mount a personal challenge to the throne until the succession of James II in 1685, his supporters attempted a rising against Charles and James in 1683 that ultimately failed.

The appeal of Monmouth

Popular in London throughout the 1670s, Monmouth made no secret that he desired the exclusion of his uncle, James, from the throne. Although he was removed from his military command in 1679 and obliged to leave the country, he soon returned, and although Charles deprived him of all his civil and military offices, he maintained a high level of popularity.

It was probably at Shaftesbury's suggestion that Monmouth began to tour the country in order to appeal to popular sentiment. He visited Oxford and the western counties in 1680 and was greeted by large and excited crowds. His association with Shaftesbury, as well as other Whigs such as Stephen College, imposed a severe strain on his father, and he was removed from the chancellorship of Cambridge University in early 1682. He now spoke openly of rebellion, and he was well received on a tour of the northwest. In early 1683, he decided to tour the southeast, where his reception was poor. The new charters issued by Charles and the appointment of Tory officials meant that the sheriffs and justices who met Monmouth treated him coldly.

The Council of Six

With the exit of Shaftesbury from the political stage in England and any prospect of Charles tolerating the Whigs or Dissenters lost, the opposition became increasingly desperate. Two of the most eminent and principled opponents were **Algernon Sidney** and **William Russell**, who both canvassed other politicians for support.

This younger generation of Whig peers was represented by:

- William Howard, who had spent time in prison for treasonable correspondence with the enemy during the Third Anglo-Dutch War.

- John Hampden, who had spent time in exile and returned to England in 1682. He was well known for his radical political and religious leanings.

- Arthur Capel, Earl of Essex, who had held offices in Charles's government but had later allied himself with Shaftesbury.

Together, these five men, Russell, Sidney, Essex, Howard and Hampden, as well as Monmouth, became known as the Council of Six. From late 1682, they were in communication with a group of old Cromwellian soldiers who could assist them in an armed uprising. One of them, Richard Rumbold, lived at Rye House in Hertfordshire, 20 miles north of London.

Several people were closely involved with the planning of the plot. Rumbold agreed that his house and land could be used, and Green Ribbon Club members Robert West and Aaron Smith were involved in organising the logistics. The Council of Six, however, acted as figureheads and were not involved in the plot itself. Although some of the plotters favoured a role for James's daughter, Anne, in a new government, Monmouth was the figure who most plotters and supporters rallied around.

The failure of the plot

The plotters intended to conceal a force of men in the grounds of Rye House and ambush Charles and James as they passed by after returning from a horse race at Newmarket. The royal party's journey was delayed when a fire broke out in Newmarket on 22 March. Charles and James returned to London earlier than planned and the attack did not take place.

The Council of Six attracted several civilian radicals as well as the former soldiers with whom they had been communicating. What is certain is that they lacked leadership after Shaftesbury's political demise and death, and a wider circle became involved in the group. Josiah Keeling now emerged from obscurity on to the scene as one of those hired in London. A Baptist salt merchant, Keeling, like Oates, shared a story of a plot to murder the King and news soon reached the Privy Council in June. Keeling's testimony was used in many of the trials of the conspirators and it earned him a pardon.

SOURCE D

Playing cards depicting key figures in the Rye House Plot, from an anonymous artist.

SOURCE QUESTION

Study Source D. Do you think these playing cards were produced by a Whig or Tory supporter? Why?

The trials

Over the next few months, many people were implicated and twelve were ultimately executed for their involvement in the plot. The principal conspirators were relatively minor figures; however, the Privy Council made little distinction between these men and those who gave vague support (including MPs and Lords), viewing the plot as the perfect opportunity to arrest Whig leaders like Russell and Sidney.

- Thomas Walcott was the first to be tried. He had hosted the plotters at his house, and although he had the opportunity to escape, he preferred to write to the Secretary of State, Leoline Jenkins, with a full confession, in the hope that he would be pardoned. This was unsuccessful and he was hanged.

- The MP Thomas Armstrong fled to the Netherlands, but was captured and executed in London in 1684.

- Elizabeth Gaunt, who had helped some of the conspirators to escape abroad, was executed in October 1685.

- James Holloway had been tasked with securing Bristol after the execution of the King, and although he escaped to the Caribbean when the plot was discovered, he was returned to England and executed in 1684.

- Robert Baillie was a Scottish conspirator who had entered into communication with Russell and Monmouth. Although he was not involved in the plot directly, he was charged with treason and hanged in 1684.

- William Russell had attended meetings with some of the key conspirators, and despite his wife, Lady Russell, appealing personally to the King, Charles was insistent that Russell should be executed to protect the monarchy. He was beheaded in July 1683.

- Algernon Sidney was arrested shortly after the plot was revealed. He was found to have written a book that was critical of the King, and this was used as evidence against him. He was beheaded in December 1683.

Other conspirators were imprisoned and fined, including William Howard, who had acted as an informer at Russell's trial. Further conspirators and implicated men fled abroad, mostly to the Netherlands. Arthur Capel, Earl of Essex, killed himself in the Tower of London. Monmouth was obliged to remove himself from English politics entirely and went into exile at the court of William of Orange.

Assessment of the plot

Although the plot was a failure and there was never a genuine threat to the life of the King, Charles was able to use the fear created by it to remove his most vocal critics. The plot and subsequent trials have been viewed by some historians as the final stage in the crushing of the Whigs, following, as it did, Shaftesbury's political demise, the recall of borough charters and the attacks on their Nonconformist allies. The causes that the Whigs stood for – a more limited government and religious toleration – had not died out, however, and discontent with Stuart absolutism would soon be expressed in the Glorious Revolution of 1688 (see Chapter 7).

Final years

In May 1684, James was restored to the Privy Council and to his old office of Lord Admiral. He began legal action against Titus Oates for slander and several Catholic priests were released from prison. In the autumn of 1684, moves were made towards a more authoritarian and pro-Catholic policy. **George Jeffreys**, the recently appointed Lord Chief Justice, raised the matter of Catholic toleration in the Privy Council and justified this by stressing their loyalty in the Civil War.

KEY FIGURE

George Jeffreys (1645–89)

Jeffreys rose quickly through the ranks of the legal profession and although he was staunchly Protestant, found favour with James when he was Duke of York. He sat as a judge in the Popish Plot and Rye House Plot trials and condemned many conspirators to death in the aftermath of the Monmouth Rebellion, where he gained a reputation for brutality and ruthlessness. For this he acquired the nickname 'the Hanging Judge'.

Death of Charles

Charles died on 6 February 1685, aged 54, after an unexpected and short illness. The suddenness of his death led to suspicions that poison had been used against him, although this is unlikely. There is a general consensus among historians that he was received into the Catholic Church on his deathbed. He was buried at Westminster Abbey on 14 February.

Assessment of Charles's reign

Compared to his father and brother, Charles might appear to have been successful. However, assessing any Stuart monarch is difficult as the political backdrop to each of their reigns varied considerably. His successes and failures are summarised below.

Successes

- The fact that he kept his throne – in contrast with Charles I and James II – can be viewed as a success. In addition, he fought off the major challenge of the Exclusion Crisis from 1678 to 1681 and left the monarchy in a strong position in 1685.

- He had overseen the successful restoration of the Church of England. The Church preached obedience to the monarchy, as it had done during the reign of Charles I, and upheld the King's authority. Although he favoured toleration for most of his reign, the loyalty of the Church can be credited at least in part to Charles's good-natured relationship with the bishops.

- Finally, Charles left the treasury in a healthy state and Crown income reached the levels projected in 1660. After peace with the Dutch, spending was reduced and in 1685 England was neither at war nor entangled in a major alliance.

- Via Charles's reforms to borough charters, local government was more securely controlled from Westminster.

Failures

- It was virtually impossible for dissenting voices to be heard in the absence of a parliament and this stored up resentment that would be brought to the surface in the Glorious Revolution.

- Charles failed to heal the religious divisions that existed when he came to the throne. Although Dissenters were viewed favourably in the early years of his reign, the persecution after 1681 was particularly brutal.

- It could be argued that Charles lacked willpower and his natural idleness meant that he normally pursued the easiest course of action. This is reflected in his treatment of the succession problem, where he refused to investigate more creative solutions, such as bypassing James in favour of his daughters, to the ultimate detriment of the Stuart dynasty.

ONLINE EXTRAS WWW
AQA

Get to grips with the last years of Charles II's reign by completing Worksheet 20 at **www.hoddereducation. co.uk/accesstohistory/extras**

ONLINE EXTRAS WWW
Pearson Edexcel

Test your knowledge of the last years of Charles's reign by completing Worksheet 20 at **www.hoddereducation. co.uk/accesstohistory/extras**

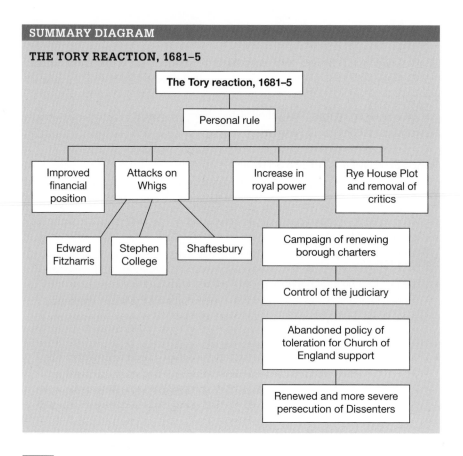

SUMMARY DIAGRAM

THE TORY REACTION, 1681–5

The later Stuarts and the Glorious Revolution summary diagram showing: The Tory reaction, 1681–5 leading to Personal rule, which branches to: Improved financial position; Attacks on Whigs (leading to Edward Fitzharris, Stephen College, Shaftesbury); Increase in royal power; Rye House Plot and removal of critics. Increase in royal power leads to Campaign of renewing borough charters, Control of the judiciary, Abandoned policy of toleration for Church of England support, and Renewed and more severe persecution of Dissenters.

2 | James II: political settlement

■ *How were James's beliefs about monarchy reflected in his policies and actions?*

James's political views were quite simple: he had a divine right to rule and he saw no room for sharing power or delegating it to others. He was not, however, interested in modelling himself entirely on Louis XIV, and had no desire to alter the constitution significantly. When comparing him to his brother, contemporaries were impressed with his moral qualities. Burnet declared that 'if it had not been for his popery, he would have been, if not a great, yet a good prince'. Despite his apparent strengths and good intentions, James was unable to weigh up what was and was not politically feasible. He was, therefore, open to manipulation by more intelligent men and was known to display a stubborn streak.

James's first speech to the Privy Council in February 1685 conveyed assurances that he would support and defend the Church of England and would not attempt to alter the law. The key appointments to the Council were all conferred on Anglicans and it seemed his government would remain faithful to the Church settlement of Charles II. James was, however, assisted more discreetly by a group of Catholics, consisting of the Duke of Norfolk, Lord Belasyse, Richard Talbot and Henry Jermyn.

1685 election

James began making arrangements for a new parliament almost immediately. In private, he explained to the French ambassador that he had decided to call a parliament so he could be granted revenue for life. In public, he stated that he was intent on healing the divisions created by the Exclusion Crisis and the Tory reaction.

The former Exclusionist **Robert Spencer**, the Earl of Sunderland, was placed in charge of organising the election. Letters were sent to Lord Lieutenants (responsible for the militia in each county), mayors and others with any local influence in order to ensure that, if any opponents of James did stand for election, a loyalist would be put up against them. The result was that, of the 513 MPs elected in 1685, 400 of these loyalists had never sat in parliament before. Of the 195 members representing boroughs with new charters, only nine Whigs were elected. James was pleased with the outcome of the election and said that he believed there were only 40 MPs on whom he could not rely.

Financial settlement

James's one and only parliament met on 19 May 1685. His speech to the new assembly paid close attention to the subject of his revenue, and he expressed disapproval of frequent parliaments and how they would only 'feed me from time to time by such proportions as they shall think convenient'. The Commons promptly voted him for life the revenue which Charles II had enjoyed. He was granted £1.5 million annually with an additional £400,000 a year for eight years to settle the debts accumulated by Charles. James also reminded parliament of the imminent threat of Monmouth and he was given further grants for the army and navy. With almost £2 million in income, he had become wealthier than all previous Stuart monarchs had been at the start of their reign.

Monmouth Rebellion

While in the Netherlands, Monmouth had busied himself with recruiting troops and he pawned many of his belongings to fund a fleet to bring him to England. On 11 June 1685, Monmouth landed at Lyme Regis in order to mount his claim to the throne with force. Lyme Regis was probably selected as his landing point because it was known that he was popular in the southwest. Much planning had gone into the rebellion, with further coordinated risings planned for Cheshire and London. Although an agent was sent ahead to rouse Monmouth's supporters in these areas, there was little enthusiasm for an armed uprising.

On 18 June, Monmouth arrived in Taunton and proclaimed himself king. His army of 7000 consisted mainly of peasants from Somerset and Dorset. If he had made it to Bristol, he might have had more hope of success as the city

KEY FIGURE

Robert Spencer (1645–89)

Sunderland served as a Secretary of State under both Charles II and James II and was Lord President of the Privy Council from 1685 to 1688. He had held a series of government posts in the 1670s and was a staunch opponent of French expansion.

was a stronghold of Whigs and Dissenters; however, Monmouth showed an uncharacteristic hesitation. He appears to have overestimated the strength of the royalist forces and his army was constantly being thinned by desertion. By the time he reached Bridgwater his army had been reduced to 3000 men.

Battle of Sedgemoor

On 5 July, Monmouth set out to mount a night attack on the royalist troops encamped on Sedgemoor. The attempt may well have succeeded as the royalist commander, Feversham, was notoriously ill-disciplined. However, Monmouth's deputy, Lord Grey, either disobeyed or misinterpreted his orders and attacked

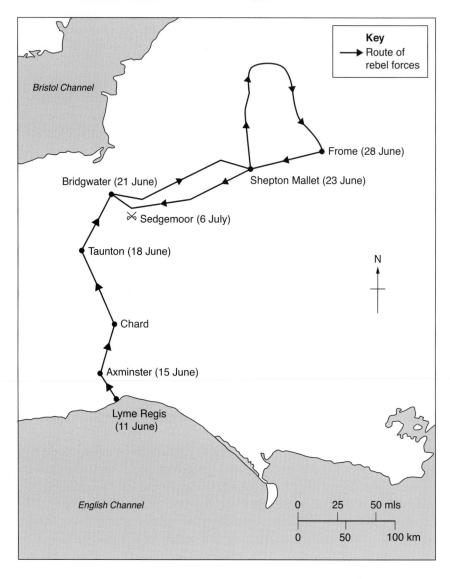

Figure 6.1 The progression of Monmouth's rebellion.

from the wrong side. This resulted in his cavalry struggling through a muddy ditch and his cannon were captured in the early morning of 6 July. Monmouth fled the battlefield, only to be captured shortly afterwards in disguise while sleeping in a ditch.

The Bloody Assizes

After Monmouth had declared his claim to the throne on arriving in England, parliament reacted by passing a **bill of attainder** against him so he could be executed immediately as a traitor without a trial. Despite appearing before James in person to make a plea for his life, the King – according to the contemporary James Wellwood – 'had no mind to pardon him', and he was beheaded on 15 July. Lord Grey was pardoned on the condition that he gave evidence against his accomplices.

Lord Chief Justice Jeffreys conducted a mopping-up operation in what became known as the 'Bloody Assizes'. Rebel soldiers were crowded into prisons in such large numbers that plague broke out among them. Trials began at Winchester in August, with Lady Alice Lisle the first to be tried for harbouring rebels. She was sentenced to death by burning, with Jeffreys stating that, 'had she been my own mother I would have found her guilty'. Burning was ultimately substituted for beheading as this befitted her social rank. She became the last woman in English history to be executed by beheading.

From Winchester, the commission proceeded to Salisbury, Dorchester, Exeter, Taunton, Wells and Bristol. In total, around 300 death sentences were handed down and approximately half were carried out. A further 800 rebels were sentenced to transportation to North America.

> **KEY TERM**
>
> **Bill of attainder** An Act of parliament confirming a decision to find someone guilty of a crime without the need for a trial.

> **ONLINE EXTRAS** www
> AQA
>
> Test your ability to compare the reign of James II with that of Charles II by completing Worksheet 21 at www.hoddereducation.co.uk/accesstohistory/extras

> **ONLINE EXTRAS** www
> Pearson Edexcel
>
> Ensure you have grasped the key features of the early reign of James II by completing Worksheet 21 at www.hoddereducation.co.uk/accesstohistory/extras

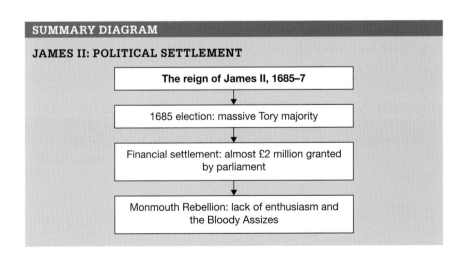

SUMMARY DIAGRAM

JAMES II: POLITICAL SETTLEMENT

The reign of James II, 1685–7
↓
1685 election: massive Tory majority
↓
Financial settlement: almost £2 million granted by parliament
↓
Monmouth Rebellion: lack of enthusiasm and the Bloody Assizes

3 James II and Catholicism

■ *Did James intend to reconvert the country to Catholicism?*

Louis XIV provided James with limited financial assistance in the early months of his reign, and in the aftermath of the Monmouth Rebellion, James's ministers approached the French for further subsidies. Louis replied that, as the rebellion had been crushed and as parliament had made generous grants, there was no requirement for a donation. James then resorted to pleading to Louis personally, telling him he had 'a French heart'; but Louis refused to change his position, telling James that the knowledge that God had assisted him in defeating Monmouth should be sufficient warrant for him to establish Catholicism in England. In total, James received just £125,000 (£14.6 million in today's money) from Louis – around one-tenth of what Charles received – in the course of his reign, compared with the £6 million granted by parliament.

Parliamentary opposition and the beginning of personal rule

James's parliament became one of the most sycophantic in English history due to his careful selection of MPs. There were, however, a small number of opponents who began to voice concerns with his government. In a speech to parliament in late 1685, James told the members that he planned to give commissions in the army to Catholics. This created a small nucleus of opposition around older parliamentarians Thomas Clarges, Thomas Meres and Edward Seymour. The increasing disquiet was indicated by a debate on a motion to provide more funding for the army. Clarges reminded the House that it had been prophesied in the Exclusion bill debates that 'a popish ruler would have a popish army'. The motion was rejected by 225 votes to 150.

The House of Lords was bolder still in its criticism. The opposition there was led by William Cavendish, Duke of Devonshire, and the Bishop of London, Henry Compton. They declared that if the army was officered by Catholics and if the Test Act was abandoned, the Church of England would be defenceless. Aware of this growing uneasiness, James prorogued parliament on 20 November. A series of further prorogations meant that parliament did not meet again during his reign.

Godden v. Hales

In April 1686, a Catholic army officer, Sir Edward Hales, was taken to court by his coachman, Arthur Godden, for not conforming to the Test Acts (see page 65). He appeared before the Rochester Assizes and was found guilty. Hales appealed and his case was heard before the Court of King's Bench. In reality, the legal action was prearranged by the government to prove that the King had the power to dispense with penal laws against Catholics. Hales argued that he possessed letters from the King that exempted him from taking the required oaths. The court had to decide whether the King could dispense with the Test Acts on an individual basis.

The judges voted 11–1 in favour of Hales, with the justification presented by Lord Chief Justice Herbert shown in Source E.

SOURCE E

The judgment of the court in the case of *Godden v. Hales*, 21 June 1686, quoted in Thomas Howell, *A Complete Collection of State Trials and Proceedings for High Treason and Other Crimes and Misdemeanors*, Longman & Co., 1815.

We think we may very well declare the opinion of the court to be that the King may dispense in this case; and the judges go upon these grounds:

1 The Kings of England are sovereign princes.
2 That the laws of England are the King's laws.
3 That therefore it is an inseparable prerogative in the Kings of England to dispense with penal laws in particular cases, and upon particular necessary reasons.
4 That of those reasons and those necessities the King himself is sole judge.
5 That this is not a trust invested in or granted to the King by the people, but the ancient remains of the sovereign power and prerogative of the Kings of England, which never yet was taken from them, nor can be.

SOURCE QUESTION

Study Source E. What are the potential consequences of the legal judgment made in the *Godden v. Hales* case?

Promotion of Catholicism

In the aftermath of *Godden v. Hales*, James began to introduce Catholics (and some Dissenters) into senior positions in the army and the universities. In July 1686, an Ecclesiastical Commission was established. This was based on the former religious Court of High Commission, which had been abolished in 1641, and James used it to punish those who were hostile to Catholicism. Clergy could be sanctioned and ultimately removed from their posts for disobeying James's edicts. Henry Compton was suspended as Bishop of London after he refused to discipline a minister who had preached against Catholicism.

In late 1686, James's increased confidence encouraged him to enhance the role of Catholics in public life:

- James provided the papal ambassador with a lavish reception at Whitehall Palace.
- In Scotland, the Marquis of Queensbury was dismissed as Royal Commissioner when the Scottish parliament failed to repeal the Test Acts. He and other high-profile Scottish officials were replaced with Catholics.
- James allowed the establishment of Catholic seminaries in London.
- Catholic-run printing presses in Oxford and London were funded by the King.
- Approximately half of royal judges were replaced with Catholics.

National and local government

Armed with impunity after *Godden* v. *Hales,* James appointed four Catholics to the Privy Council and created an inner cabinet composed of Edward Petre, Sunderland and Jeffreys. They began the formidable task of introducing Catholics into local government. Over 250 JPs were replaced with Catholics in 1686 and Catholics were commissioned into the county militia. The universities had Catholics imposed upon them, and in 1687, James insisted on the election of a Catholic master at Magdalen College, Oxford. He encountered fierce resistance, resulting in his decision to expel all the fellows of the college.

James and the Dissenters

By the end of 1686, James realised that the greatest obstacle to Catholic toleration was the Anglican Church, and as the Dissenters shared his hostility to the established Church, he judged that they would be a useful instrument in supporting his designs.

A renewed attack on borough charters began, this time led by Jeffreys. Whereas under Charles II towns had Dissenters removed from their councils, many were now reinstated, with over 2000 changes being made. Three questions were put to all JPs and members of corporations. These became the litmus test for employment in local government:

- Would they support the repeal of the Test Acts?
- Would they support a Declaration of Indulgence?
- If elected to parliament, would they pledge to give their votes only to members who answer positively to the first two questions?

James forged an unlikely friendship with the Quaker William Penn, who seemed to hold great influence over the King. Over 1000 Quakers were released from prison after a royal proclamation of March 1686 providing a general pardon to all who were in prison for religious reasons. The majority of Dissenters, however, remained suspicious about the prospect of an alliance with the Catholics. In order to appease them, and on the advice of Penn, James issued a Declaration of Indulgence in April 1687.

Declaration of Indulgence, 1687

James's first Declaration of Indulgence showed plainly that he was attempting to appeal to Dissenters as well as Catholics (see Source F, page 111). As with Charles's Declaration of 1672, it stated that the penal laws against non-Anglicans would no longer be enforced and James ultimately hoped that its terms would be adopted by parliament.

SOURCE F

An extract from the Declaration of Indulgence, April 1687, quoted in Andrew Browning, editor, *English Historical Documents, 1660–1714*, Eyre & Spottiswoode, 1953.

We will protect and maintain our archbishops, bishops and clergy, and all other subjects of the Church of England in the free exercise of their religion as by law established. It is our royal will that the execution of all penal laws for not coming to church, or not receiving the sacrament, or for any other nonconformity to the religion established, be immediately suspended. We do freely give them leave to meet and serve God in private houses or places purposely hired or built for that use. We do hereby give our free and ample pardon unto all nonconformists, recusants and other subjects for all crimes committed contrary to the penal laws formerly made relating to religion.

SOURCE QUESTION ?

Study Source F. Which aspects of the Declaration were designed to appeal to Protestant Dissenters?

Summary: James's position in 1687

With the benefit of hindsight, it is easy to view James in 1687 as a monarch out of touch with his subjects and doomed to the fate that would befall him in the Revolution of 1688. There is, of course, much truth in this, but in the campaign to win over the Dissenters he was enjoying some success and his fall was not necessarily predetermined. The Declaration of Indulgence meant that he could secure the services of people who would otherwise be disqualified. The Presbyterian Richard Baxter was released from prison and prominent Nonconformists were courted by James for their support.

Of course, James's character had not changed overnight and there was much evidence of this. He had already made it clear that his objective was to fill as many positions as possible with Catholics and there was now the genuine prospect that in a few years Protestants in England would no longer be among the governing classes. Religious toleration for Dissenters was, on the surface, a positive step, but England now had an army officered by Catholics, with a king who had both the moral and potential military support of Louis XIV.

ONLINE EXTRAS AQA www

Develop your analysis of James II and financial problems by completing Worksheet 22 at **www.hoddereducation.co.uk/accesstohistory/extras**

ONLINE EXTRAS Pearson Edexcel www

Get to grips with James II and financial problems by completing Worksheet 22 at **www.hoddereducation.co.uk/accesstohistory/extras**

SUMMARY DIAGRAM

JAMES II AND CATHOLICISM

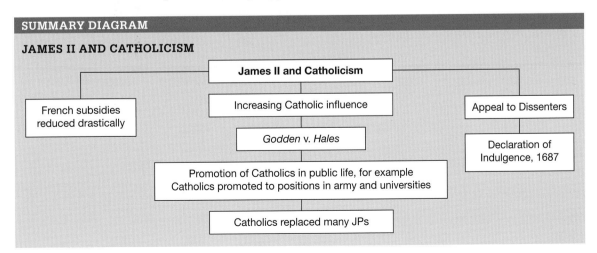

CHAPTER SUMMARY

After dissolving the Oxford Parliament in 1681, Charles did not call a parliament again for the rest of his reign. The period 1681–5 is defined by attacks on the Whigs who had attempted to exclude his brother from the throne. The threat from many of the Whig leaders, including Shaftesbury, was neutralised and Charles was able to reduce Whig power in local government. The continued threat to the monarchy from both Whigs and their Dissenter allies was brought home in the Rye House Plot. The first two years of James's reign were also marked by the threat of rebellion, although the Whig menace was diminished considerably after the failed Monmouth Rebellion. What differentiates the start of James's reign from his brother's is the generous financial settlement he was awarded in 1685. This meant that he was able to dispense with parliament after a short period of time.

Historians have put forward a variety of reasons to explain why the Stuart monarchy continued to face discontent in the 1680s. The explanation can be found in a combination of two reasons: the desire for royal absolutism from both kings and the increasing threat of Catholicism.

Refresher questions

Use these questions to remind yourself of the key material covered in this chapter.

1 What were Charles's aims in 1681?
2 What was Charles's financial position in 1681?
3 Why is the case of Edward Fitzharris important?
4 What happened to the Earl of Shaftesbury?
5 How and why did Charles remodel borough charters?
6 How were Dissenters attacked by the government in the years 1681–5?
7 Why did the Rye House Plot take place?
8 What were the consequences of the Rye House Plot?
9 How did James interfere with the 1685 election?
10 How generous was James's financial settlement and why?
11 Why did Monmouth feel that he was in a strong position to mount a rebellion in 1685?
12 Why did the Monmouth Rebellion fail?
13 Why was the outcome of *Godden* v. *Hales* important?
14 How did James promote Catholicism in public life?
15 Why did James attempt to form an alliance with the Dissenters?

Question practice: AQA

Essay questions

1 To what extent was the discontent faced by the Stuart monarchy in the years 1660–88 caused by a desire from Charles II and James II to become absolute monarchs? [A level]

EXAM HINT Analyse the causes – one of which will feature the perceived drive towards absolutism. Make sure you cover the whole period. You may find that causes are linked, for example fears of Catholicism linked to absolutism.

2 How successful were Charles II and James II in their aim to reduce opposition to their pro-Catholic policies in the years 1660–88? [A level]

EXAM HINT You may wish to cover the two reigns separately – the first reign registering successes and the second reign leading to failure. Or you may be able to link the two in arguments that cover the whole period, for example the characters of the monarchs.

Question practice: Pearson Edexcel

Essay questions

1 How successful were Charles II and James II in their aim to reduce opposition to their pro-Catholic policies in the years 1660–88? [AS level]

EXAM HINT You should note that Charles had some success in reducing opposition, whereas James's pro-Catholic policies were the main factor leading to his flight in 1688. Evaluate the extent of success and failure overall.

2 To what extent was the discontent faced by the Stuart monarchy in the years 1660–88 caused by a desire from Charles II and James II to become absolute monarchs? [A level]

EXAM HINT Link the threat of absolutism to Charles's foreign policy and to James's Catholic policies from 1685. Other reasons for discontent might include financial matters and parliament's persecution of dissent.

CHAPTER 7

How revolutionary was the Glorious Revolution, 1688–1701?

A coalition of Tories and Whigs moved against James II to invite William of Orange and his wife, Mary (the daughter of James), to take the throne in 1688. The Crown was secured in England with little disturbance, but William faced bloodier conflicts in Ireland and Scotland. William and Mary were presented with a Declaration of Rights by parliament, which became enshrined in law as the Bill of Rights. The Whig and Tory factions in parliament were solidified in these years, and the partisan nature of politics and increased frequency of elections have led to the period being known as the 'Rage of Party'. The issues that will be explored in this chapter are:

◆ Causes of the Glorious Revolution

◆ The Bill of Rights and political settlement

◆ The Revolution in Ireland and Scotland

◆ Monarchy and parliament

The key debate on page 133 of this chapter asks the question: How revolutionary was the Glorious Revolution?

KEY DATES

1688	**April**	James's second Declaration of Indulgence	**1693**	Glencoe Massacre
	June	Invitation sent to William of Orange to intervene	**1694**	Triennial Act
				Death of Mary II
	Dec.	Flight of James II	**1696**	The Association
1689		Bill of Rights	**1701**	Act of Settlement
		Claim of Right Act	**1702**	Death of William III
1690		Battle of the Boyne		

1 Causes of the Glorious Revolution

▪ *How did William and Mary become joint monarchs in December 1688?*

One way of measuring the success of James's goal of building an alliance against the Anglicans in 1687 and 1688 is the extent to which he achieved non-Anglican influence in local government. As part of his remodelling of local government, 64 per cent of the justices of the peace (JPs) selected in early 1687 were Catholics. In some counties, Catholics now formed a majority in local government. In Herefordshire, Lancashire, Monmouthshire and Flintshire, more than 50 per cent of JPs were Catholic.

The extent of Catholic influence by 1688

When James turned his attention to courting the Dissenters in order to bolster his anti-Anglican party, his government began assigning them to vacant posts.

- Most of the Catholics James desired for office were in place by the end of 1687, and between February and April 1688, 709 new JPs were appointed.

- This time, after the introduction of the 'three questions' (see page 110) to JPs assessing their preference for toleration, only fourteen per cent were Catholics and most were Dissenters.

- In Buckinghamshire, eight Catholics and nine Anglicans were appointed in 1688, compared to 21 Dissenters, none of whom had been appointed before.

- In total, 1714 JPs and Deputy Lieutenants were serving in England in 1688: 24 per cent were Catholic. As Catholics comprised little more than one per cent of the population, this would suggest that James had now pressed most of the available Catholics into his service.

Table 7.1 Catholics in local government, 1687–8

Date	Number of JPs appointed	Number of Catholics	Percentage who were Catholics
January 1687	455	290	64%
February–April 1688	709	99	14%

County in the southeast	Percentage of JPs identified as Catholic in 1688
Bedfordshire	7%
Berkshire	48%
Buckinghamshire	21%
Cambridgeshire	4%
Essex	16%
Hampshire	27%
Hertfordshire	3%
Kent	17%
Norfolk	22%
Oxfordshire	40%
Surrey	6%
Sussex	23%
Total JPs in 1688	**Percentage who were Catholics**
1197	19.9%
Total Deputy Lieutenants in 1688	**Percentage who were Catholics**
517	33.3%

Second Declaration of Indulgence

By filling local government positions with Catholics and Dissenters, James ultimately hoped to return another parliament that would be compliant and loyal. A further step towards this objective was his issuing of another Declaration of Indulgence in April 1688, with the same objective as the first, passed in 1687. It was hoped that its contents would be confirmed by parliament when it next met. On 4 May, before a parliament could be called, James issued an order that the Declaration be read out in every church in the country.

Trial of the Seven Bishops

On 18 May 1688, seven bishops, led by the Archbishop of Canterbury, William Sancroft, sent a petition to the King stating that they could not bring themselves to obey his order to read out the Declaration in their churches. They claimed that they could not 'in prudence, honour or conscience make themselves parties to it', and stated that as parliament had declared similar directives illegal in 1662, 1672 and 1685, their encouraging the spread of the Declaration would be against the law.

The seven bishops were tried for libel on 29 June. Arguing the case for the King, the Solicitor General contended that the bishops had no power to petition James out of parliament. Most of the presiding judges presented the opinion that there was no malicious intent in the petition, with one of them, John Powell, stating that 'I do not remember in any case in all our law, that there is any such dispensing power in the king'. One of the judges, the recently appointed (and Catholic) Richard Allibond, was fiercely critical of the bishops, claiming that 'it is the business of the government to manage matters relating to the government; it is the business of subjects to mind only their own properties and interests', and that 'such a petition is next door to treason'. On the conclusion of the case, the jury returned a verdict of not guilty. There were great celebrations on the streets of London and the bishops were presented as heroes in political pamphlets.

Birth of a male heir

In November 1687, it became publicly known that James's wife, Mary of Modena, was pregnant. As her other children had died in infancy and she had suffered several miscarriages, the possibility that she would give birth to a boy that would survive was slim. From the moment the news broke, however, there was much talk of what should happen if a male heir was to be born who would be raised a Catholic. When the boy, **James Francis Edward Stuart**, was born on 10 June 1688, the popular fear of a Catholic dynasty was intensified. Rumours immediately began to spread that Mary's baby was stillborn and a substitute had been smuggled into her chamber in a warming pan. This claim would soon be included in the list of justifications for invasion sent to William from his English supporters.

KEY FIGURE

James Francis Edward Stuart (1688–1766)

Known as the Old Pretender, for his efforts to win back the throne, James Francis spent the majority of his life in France. After James II's death in 1701 he took up his father's cause and mounted the failed Jacobite rising of 1715.

Invitation to William and Mary

The fear generated by the birth of a male heir, combined with the hope that followed the acquittal of the Seven Bishops, led to a political climate that made the Revolution of 1688 possible. From late 1687 and throughout 1688, private correspondence was being sent from England to William's Dutch supporters. Many of these communications concerned plans for an invasion of England and were written using elaborate codes. Immediately after the birth of James Francis, an invitation was sent to William by a group who later became known as the 'Immortal Seven': the Earl of Shrewsbury, Earl of Devonshire, Earl of Danby, Lord Lumley, Henry Compton, Edward Russell and Henry Sidney. Danby and Compton are generally considered to have been Tories, with the remaining five members of the group associated with the Whigs.

> ### SOURCE A
>
> **An extract from the invitation to William and Mary of Orange, June 1688.**
>
> *We have great reason to believe we shall be every day in a worse condition than we are, and less able to defend ourselves, and therefore we do earnestly wish we might be so happy as to find a remedy before it be too late for us to contribute to our own deliverance. Your Highness may be assured there are nineteen parts of twenty throughout the kingdom who are desirous of a change and who, we believe, would willingly contribute to it. We do upon very good grounds believe that their [James's] army would be very much divided among themselves, many of the officers being so discontented that they continue in their service only for a subsistence (besides that some of their minds are known already), and very many of the common soldiers do daily show such an aversion to the popish religion that there is the greatest probability imaginable of great numbers of deserters which could come from them should there be such an occasion; and amongst the seamen it is almost certain there is not one in ten who would do them any service in such a war.*

SOURCE QUESTION

Study Source A. How is this invitation designed to persuade William of Orange?

The Dutch invasion

Even at this late stage, the King might have saved his dynasty by a policy of moderation. However, as he was convinced that firmness would have saved his father, Charles I, so he was convinced that the same policy would save him.

- He removed two of the judges who presided over the Seven Bishops case, Powell and Holloway.

- On 13 July, a significant change was made to the oath of Privy Councillors. They were no longer expected to state that they would defend the king 'against all foreign princes, prelates, states or potentates [rulers]'.

- James also introduced a requirement for the names of all clergy who refused to read the Declaration of Indulgence to be sent to the Ecclesiastical Commission.

Although he was advised to moderate some of his policies by those close to him, the prospect of concessions came too late and, by the autumn, William's invasion plans were at an advanced stage.

After a series of delays occasioned by bad weather, William landed at Brixham, Torbay, with 54 ships and 14,000 troops on 5 November 1688. With an effective army at his disposal, James had every reason to believe that he could repel William's forces; however, he had failed to predict where William would land and his fleet of 52 ships were anchored on the Thames estuary.

William soon assembled his forces at Exeter; however, he was disappointed with the response of the local gentry. James, and a force about twice the size of William's, marched west from London and were at Salisbury by 19 November. The senior commanders of James's army hesitated and decided that their troops should retreat to London. This was followed by a series of high-profile desertions to William, including those of John Churchill (the future Duke of Marlborough) and the Duke of Grafton.

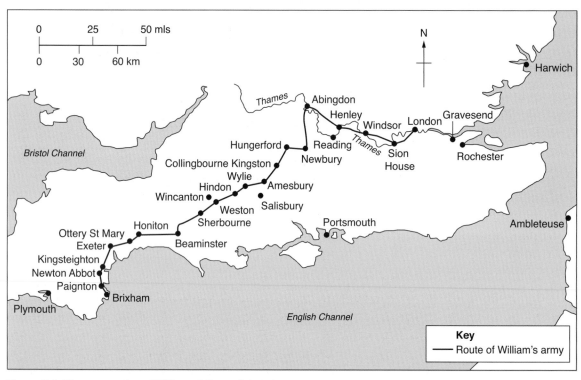

Figure 7.1 The progression of William of Orange's invasion.

The flight of James

William left Exeter on 21 November and met little opposition on his march to London. Having made the decision that his position was untenable, James left London on 11 December and boarded a vessel bound for France; however, he was held back by bad weather and relocated to Rochester. James wrote to William to request an audience, but William's response was to order his arrest. On 23 December, James finally left England and joined his wife and child at a residence provided for him by Louis XIV at Saint-Germain-en-Laye.

Why did James leave England when he still appeared to possess considerable military and political strengths?

■ The most obvious reason is that he feared that he would be deposed and may have even thought that his life was in danger. Like his father, he was a family man, and he was concerned for the safety of his wife and child.

■ He felt he had been forsaken by those in whom he had always had complete confidence – his generals and some of his chief ministers.

■ Neither his army nor his navy showed much enthusiasm for his cause.

■ What is certain is that he was sick in both body and mind and this impacted on his ability to think coherently. As the political system he believed to be infallible began to crack, James turned to God for an explanation. This led to a period of reflection and his thoughts around this time can be found in his correspondence. Had he offended God by keeping mistresses? Had he not been firm enough with his opponents? Had he provoked God's wrath as a result of his failure to achieve religious toleration?

ONLINE EXTRAS **WWW**
AQA

Test your knowledge of the causes of the Glorious Revolution by completing Worksheet 23 at **www. hoddereducation.co.uk/ accesstohistory/extras**

ONLINE EXTRAS **WWW**
Pearson Edexcel

Ensure you have grasped the causes of the Glorious Revolution by completing Worksheet 23 at **www. hoddereducation.co.uk/ accesstohistory/extras**

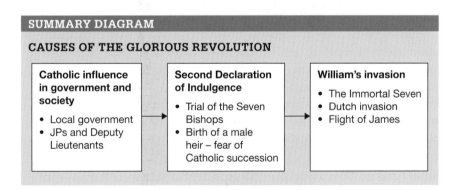

SUMMARY DIAGRAM

CAUSES OF THE GLORIOUS REVOLUTION

Catholic influence in government and society	Second Declaration of Indulgence	William's invasion
• Local government • JPs and Deputy Lieutenants	• Trial of the Seven Bishops • Birth of a male heir – fear of Catholic succession	• The Immortal Seven • Dutch invasion • Flight of James

2 The Bill of Rights and political settlement

■ *Did the Bill of Rights benefit Crown or parliament?*

On 23 December, the day James left for France, William summoned all persons who had served in any of Charles II's parliaments to meet on 26 December, along with the mayor and aldermen of London. This assembly asked William to summon a Convention Parliament, which met on 22 January 1689. The election of the Convention Parliament resulted in the return of a House of Commons in which the majority were old Whig opponents of Stuart rule, although there were a number of Tories who, although alienated by the conduct of James, were not prepared to give their blessing to a break in the hereditary succession.

On 29 January, parliament passed a resolution stating that a Catholic king was inconsistent with a Protestant state, which was approved with virtually no debate. Lord Falkland was the first member to propose that before they filled the throne, parliament should decide exactly what powers were to be conferred on the new ruler. A committee was established to formulate these constitutional proposals and on 2 February, it produced the first draft of what would become the Declaration of Rights.

Declaration of Rights

The Declaration provided an explanation for recent events and highlighted the wrongs committed by James. It included thirteen clauses intended to limit the power of the Crown in the future (Source B). The Declaration was scrutinised by the Lords and they rejected by 55 votes to 41 a reference that stated that the throne had been left vacant. This led to a period of debate over the nature of the Revolution. The Whigs argued that the invitation to William was justified because James had left the throne vacant. Many members of the Lords maintained that occupation of the throne was hereditary and that Mary, as the daughter of James, should inherit the throne with William as **regent**, thus placing full sovereign power in Mary's hands.

The deadlock was broken by William himself. He had always made it clear that he only ever intended to rule as a king and now told parliament that he would return to Holland if he was not given full regal power. Mary provided backing to William by sending a letter to senior Lords stating that she would only occupy the throne with her husband as king.

KEY TERM

Regent A person appointed to administer a government in place of the legitimate ruler, normally when the monarch is incapacitated or too young to rule alone.

SOURCE B

The thirteen clauses of the Declaration of Rights intended to limit the power of the Crown, 1689.

1 That the pretended power of suspending the laws or the execution of laws by regal authority without consent of Parliament is illegal;

2 That the pretended power of dispensing with laws or the execution of laws by regal authority, as it hath been assumed and exercised of late, is illegal;

3 That the commission for erecting the late Court of Commissioners for Ecclesiastical Causes, and all other commissions and courts of like nature, are illegal and pernicious;

4 That levying money for or to the use of the Crown by pretence of prerogative, without grant of Parliament, for longer time, or in other manner than the same is or shall be granted, is illegal;

5 That it is the right of the subjects to petition the king, and all commitments and prosecutions for such petitioning are illegal;

6 That the raising or keeping a standing army within the kingdom in time of peace, unless it be with consent of Parliament, is against law;

7 That the subjects which are Protestants may have arms for their defence suitable to their conditions and as allowed by law;

8 That election of members of Parliament ought to be free;

9 That the freedom of speech and debates or proceedings in Parliament ought not to be impeached or questioned in any court or place out of Parliament;

10 That excessive bail ought not to be required, nor excessive fines imposed, nor cruel and unusual punishments inflicted;

11 That jurors ought to be duly impanelled [enlisted] and returned, and jurors which pass upon men in trials for high treason ought to be freeholders [property owners];

12 That all grants and promises of fines and forfeitures of particular persons before conviction are illegal and void;

13 And that for redress of all grievances, and for the amending, strengthening and preserving of the laws, Parliaments ought to be held frequently.

SOURCE QUESTION

Study Source B. Which clauses in the Declaration of Rights are aimed at protecting the rights of
a) parliament and
b) ordinary citizens?

Bill of Rights

Many of the clauses of the Declaration of Rights were enshrined in law as the Bill of Rights, which received the royal assent from William in December 1689. A number of other Acts complemented the Bill of Rights, with the Crown and Parliament Recognition Act confirming all Acts passed by the Convention Parliament. In Scotland, corresponding legislation was passed under the Claim of Right Act (1689).

The Declaration of Rights was read out to both William and Mary at the same time as the offer of the Crown, and again at their coronation ceremony. It became one of the most significant constitutional documents in English history and established in law many of the principles that had been sought by the Whigs and their predecessors since the Restoration in 1660. According to the Bill of Rights, parliaments had to be held frequently and elections were to be 'free', meaning those entitled to vote should be able to make free choices without interference from the Crown. The great political issue of the day – the dispensing power of the king – was explicitly prohibited. It could be argued, however, that the final document was a watered-down version of the Declaration of Rights, and opportunities to further restrict the royal prerogative were missed. Clauses that did not make it into the Bill of Rights included:

- A proposal to unite all Protestants under a national Church that would include both Presbyterians and Anglicans.
- Measures to monitor the behaviour of judges more closely.
- Prohibiting the buying and selling of public offices.

Apart from the clauses found in Source B (see page 121) – many of which can be interpreted as reactions to the recent behaviour of James – there was no attempt to define the extent of royal power. Many of the monarch's rights were left untouched, including:

- The right to choose his own ministers.
- The power to appoint bishops and create peers.

> **SOURCE QUESTION**
>
> Study Source C. What is the significance of the monarchy being shared between William and Mary?

SOURCE C

The Protestants' Joy, from an engraving of the coronation of William III and Mary II. Woodcut from a popular English ballad-sheet.

- The power to summon, prorogue and dissolve parliament.
- The right to veto (block) legislation.
- The **prerogative of mercy**.
- The power to declare war and peace.

Some historians have played down the importance of the Bill of Rights because of the fact that it lacked any mention of democracy, the extension of the voting franchise or the furthering of economic opportunities for the common people. However, there was a great deal included that related to the legal rights of the subject. These are rights to which we are now so accustomed that they are taken for granted, such as the right to petition the government without fear of reprisals and freedom from judicial torture.

Mutiny Acts

In addition to the Bill of Rights, a Mutiny Act was passed in March 1689. This ensured that the monarch could not court-martial soldiers at will, without the consent of parliament. However, it provided William with the power to impose the death penalty for desertion and was seen as necessary after the Scottish soldiers of Lord Dumbarton's regiment had mutinied out of loyalty to James after the Revolution. They were re-formed when their commander left with James for the Continent, and resented the appointment of a foreigner, the **Duke of Schomberg**, as their colonel-in-chief.

As each Act was valid for only one year, the King had no choice but to turn to parliament regularly for approval if he wanted to maintain a disciplined army. Parliament renewed the Mutiny Act regularly until 1879, so it was theoretically possible for the Crown's right to punish mutineers to be revoked if parliament so wished.

The Act did not provide any guarantee, however, for the regular summoning of parliament. Indeed, the first series of Mutiny Acts came to an end with the conclusion of the Nine Years' War in 1697 (see page 144), which William was closely involved with, and was not renewed again until 1701. In this three-year lapse, the Crown's military power was not adversely affected.

> **KEY TERM**
>
> **Prerogative of mercy**
> The power of the monarch to grant royal pardons to convicted criminals.

> **KEY FIGURE**
>
> **Frederick Schomberg (1615–90)**
> Schomberg was a professional soldier who was born in Germany and fought for both Sweden and France in the Thirty Years' War. He continued in French service for many years. As a Protestant he was forced to leave France after Louis XIV revoked the Edict of Nantes (1685), which had given protection to Protestants. He soon joined William on his expedition to England in 1688 as second-in-command. He was killed at the Battle of the Boyne in 1690.

> **ONLINE EXTRAS** WWW
> AQA
> Test your understanding of the political settlement by completing Worksheet 24 at **www.hoddereducation. co.uk/accesstohistory/extras**

> **ONLINE EXTRAS** WWW
> Pearson Edexcel
> Develop your understanding of the political settlement by completing Worksheet 24 at **www.hoddereducation. co.uk/accesstohistory/extras**

SUMMARY DIAGRAM

THE BILL OF RIGHTS AND POLITICAL SETTLEMENT

Convention Parliament
- Declaration of Rights
- Bill of Rights
- Mutiny Acts

3 The Revolution in Ireland and Scotland

■ *How did the Glorious Revolution impact Ireland and Scotland?*

Historians have highlighted the fact that the Revolution in Ireland and Scotland was more divisive and violent than it was in England. As soon as he arrived in France, James began plotting his return to the throne and he possessed significant support in both countries. His Jacobite followers were involved in important confrontations with the supporters of William, with mixed results.

Ireland

Towards the end of his reign, James filled the judiciary, the army and the borough authorities in Ireland with Catholics, as he had done in England. This led to a steady migration of Protestants from Ireland to England. The stage was being set for one of the most tragic episodes in Irish history.

On 15 February 1689, James left France for Ireland in an attempt to win back the crown, accompanied by a force of French soldiers. By the end of February, around 100,000 Irish Catholics had armed themselves and were prepared to fight for the former king's cause. The small Protestant communities that did remain were obliged to capitulate and much Protestant property was stolen and destroyed. James reached Dublin on 24 March and met the Irish parliament. In the wake of the anti-Protestant action, of 69 Protestant peers, only five turned up and no representatives appeared from the strongly Protestant boroughs of Ulster. James proceeded to dispossess many Protestant landholders of their property without any compensation. Many skirmishes, sieges and pitched battles soon took place across Ireland:

■ The siege of Londonderry began in April 1689. The city had harboured militant Protestants and James directed his attention to it with a view to starving its residents into surrender. Thousands perished in the 100-day siege and a combination of miscommunication and incompetence among the English commanders tasked with protecting the city, resulted in long delays before relief could be sought.

■ The north of Ireland was ultimately saved for the Protestant cause after William Wolseley, although outnumbered, defeated a detachment of James's army at Newtown Butler, near Enniskillen, in July 1689.

■ In August 1689, Schomberg sailed for Ireland with 10,000 of William's men. Schomberg insisted on encamping this relatively modest army for a needlessly long time when they could have been pursuing James. The autumn rains soon came and with inadequate clothing and shelter, William's troops, according to one contemporary, began to 'die like rotten sheep'. About half of their number perished in these conditions.

Battle of the Boyne

In early 1690, William decided to go in person to Ireland to retrieve what was becoming a dire situation. He landed at Carrickfergus on 14 June with an army of 35,000 men. Approximately half of this force was made up of English troops, whose loyalty and competence were questionable. The other half was made up of Danes, Dutch, Germans and some French Huguenots. In contrast, James's army was smaller and composed mainly of Irish and French troops, assisted by a lesser number of his English supporters.

William's army advanced south to the River Boyne, the only serious barrier on the coast road between Belfast and Dublin. He arrived on 30 June and attacked James's army, which had already secured a more favourable position, the following day. William's forces dominated and James, with the remnants of his army, fled from the battle and succeeded in reaching Dublin; 1600 Jacobite troops were killed, wounded or taken prisoner. William's losses were around one-third of James's, with Schomberg the most high-profile victim: after riding across the river to encourage his cavalry, he was mortally wounded by a shot to the neck.

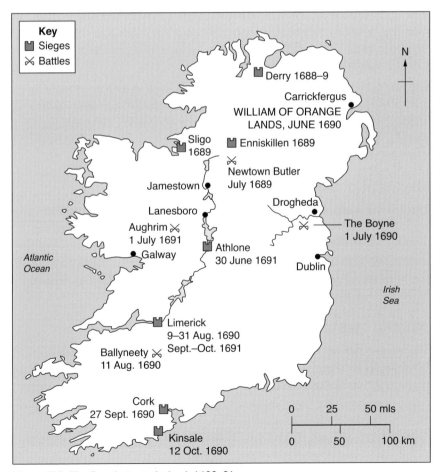

Figure 7.2 The Revolution in Ireland, 1688–91.

Aftermath of the Battle of the Boyne

The battle was followed by a general retreat of the Jacobites and James soon returned to France. Several Irish strongholds remained, however, including Limerick, Cork and Athlone. William targeted Limerick in August 1690, although he returned to England before he could complete the siege. In September, Cork was besieged by William's forces and was captured within a few days. This was followed shortly afterwards by the capture of Kinsale. After a pause in hostilities, Athlone was taken by William's supporters in June 1691. The French general who had been tasked with protecting Athlone, the **Marquis de St Ruth**, retreated to Aughrim, where he was defeated and killed on 1 July.

The remnants of James's army, numbering around 15,000 men, retreated to Limerick, where they made their last stand. The city eventually surrendered on 3 October 1691.

Scotland

When William arrived in England, he was accompanied by several Scotsmen who had migrated to Holland after fleeing James's rule. Among them were the clergymen Gilbert Burnet, who became Bishop of Salisbury, and William Carstares, who became chaplain to the new king. They were joined by nobles, statesmen and soldiers. By the time he became king, William was more familiar with Scottish affairs than with English.

The alarm felt in England after the birth of James's son in 1688 was shared by most Scottish people. William presented himself to the Scots as their liberator, and his message was well received in the southern lowlands. The Catholic chapel at Holyrood Palace was destroyed and the Jesuits were expelled by the Scottish Privy Council.

The Claim of Right Act, 1689

The Scottish parliament met shortly after William's arrival in England and agreed to a Claim of Right. This was similar to the Declaration of Rights, but went further in its language. It asserted that James had attempted to change the constitution from a limited monarchy to 'an absolute despotic power'. It accused him of turning Protestant churches into Catholic meeting places and imposing his own nominees on town councils.

Jacobite resistance

The Scottish **clan** leaders were concerned primarily to secure their estates. Traditionally, the highlanders had been among the most faithful of Stuart supporters, and this presented a significant challenge for William. In March 1689, James appointed John Graham, Viscount Dundee, as commander-in-chief of his Scottish forces. In July, the commander of William's forces in Scotland, Hugh Mackay, intercepted Dundee at Killiecrankie. Although Dundee was killed at the ensuing battle, the Jacobites achieved a resounding victory. Of a force of 3000 soldiers, Mackay lost more than 1500.

Despite their triumph at Killiecrankie, Dundee's Scottish troops were left without a leader. On 21 August, the two sides met again at the town of Dunkeld. This turned out to be the decisive battle of this short war. With little more than 1000 men, William's forces repelled as many as 5000 Jacobites in close-quarter fighting in the streets around Dunkeld Cathedral. James had lost the confidence of the highland clans, on whom his control of Scotland would have to rest. William's control of Scottish politics was now virtually complete.

The Glencoe Massacre

After their defeat at Dunkeld, the highlanders loyal to James were no longer a threat on the battlefield, but they continued to pose a danger. As trouble was anticipated from this region, Mackay established a fort at Inverlochy that was later named Fort William. In 1691, a policy of bribing local chieftains for their loyalty was attempted, and all clan leaders were ordered to take the oath of allegiance to the Crown by 1 January 1692.

One of the clans that was traditionally resistant to English rule was the MacDonalds. The chief of the Glencoe MacDonalds was forced to delay taking the oath until 6 January after harsh winter weather delayed his journey to Inverary to swear it in front of a sheriff. This delay encouraged his enemies – in both Westminster and the lowlands of Scotland – in their desire to exterminate a community that they regarded as troublesome and disloyal. A warrant was issued from the Secretary of State for Scotland, Sir John Dalrymple, for soldiers to march against those who failed to take the oath or had taken it late.

In late January, approximately 100 men from the Earl of Argyll's Regiment of Foot arrived at Glencoe, ostensibly to be quartered there. Argyll was from the clan Campbell, who had a long-standing feud with the MacDonalds and were known to support the government in order to advance their interests. They stayed for several days and on 13 February, they began massacring the local population. Nearly 40 people, including women and children, were killed. Little was known of the incident for some time, but as news began to spread, outrage increased and the Jacobites were able to exploit it for propaganda purposes. The Scottish parliament conducted an inquiry and found that those who were late in taking the oath had been expected to be given mercy. William was exonerated from having ordered the massacre, but he showed indifference to the demand that those responsible should be punished.

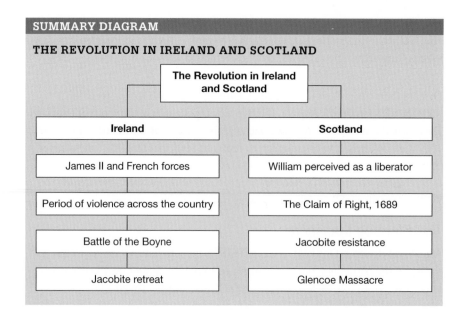

SUMMARY DIAGRAM

THE REVOLUTION IN IRELAND AND SCOTLAND

The Revolution in Ireland and Scotland

Ireland	Scotland
James II and French forces	William perceived as a liberator
Period of violence across the country	The Claim of Right, 1689
Battle of the Boyne	Jacobite resistance
Jacobite retreat	Glencoe Massacre

4 Monarchy and parliament

■ *How far was parliamentary sovereignty achieved as a consequence of the Glorious Revolution?*

The Revolution of 1688–9 is remembered as the dividing line between two periods in the history of **sovereignty** in Britain. The period before the Revolution – although monarchical power had diminished after the execution of Charles I – was a time when there was no guarantee for the summoning of parliament. In the period after the Revolution, the importance of parliament was assured, although the monarch was still in possession of significant prerogative powers that meant parliamentary sovereignty was not yet realised.

In spite of the Bill of Rights, many of the monarch's powers remained. It must be remembered that in the seventeenth century the royal prerogative was viewed by many as something essentially good. This is because it did not injure the rights of the subject and it was widely held that the powers of the monarch were ordained by God. However, Stuart monarchs had abused the royal prerogative too many times and an enhanced role for parliament was felt necessary in order to avoid reoccurrences of this.

The Whig Junto

As he was not familiar with the English political system, William struggled to understand the concept of political parties and was keen to appoint advisers who could transcend political differences. Danby, who had been so active in the government of Charles II before his downfall, was appointed Lord President of the Council. Charles Montagu, the future Earl of Halifax, who had been careful not to commit wholly to either the Whig or Tory factions, was made Lord Privy Seal. In the first two years of his reign, William focused on selecting a balance of Whigs and Tories to key posts in his government, although during his absence in Ireland in 1690 he left loyal Court Tories in charge.

A group of Whig rebels known as the 'Whig Junto' rose to prominence between 1692 and 1693. They favoured a strong executive and supported William's ongoing conflict with Louis XIV in the Nine Years' War (see page 144). Although William did not favour all members personally, by 1694 they dominated government. Their membership included:

■ Charles Montagu, who became Chancellor of the Exchequer in reward for having devised the establishment of the Bank of England (see page 148).

■ John Somers, who was made Lord Keeper. He had defended the Seven Bishops at their trial and had been Solicitor General and Attorney General under William, becoming a close adviser.

■ Edward Russell, who became First Lord of the Admiralty. He was one of the Immortal Seven who invited William to become king in 1688 and had assisted in planning his invasion.

■ Thomas Wharton, who was Comptroller of the Household under William. This role was normally associated with management of the royal household, but under Wharton the office became a senior government position.

The group held considerable influence in government between 1694 and 1699, but as its members began to be given peerages or fell out of favour at the Royal Court, their influence in the Commons began to wane. Despite their influence in the Commons, their success in the Lords was limited.

Triennial Act, 1694

The 1664 Triennial Act had stated that parliament was to meet at least every three years, although there was no legal mechanism to enforce it (see page 15). Charles II had violated the Triennial Act and parliament feared it was likely that James would do the same. It was a priority for parliament, therefore, to ensure that it would be summoned regularly. As early as 1689, a bill was drafted to ensure that ten months after a dissolution, elections should be held automatically if the monarch failed to summon a new parliament. This radical bill was dropped when William prorogued parliament in January 1690.

A further attempted Triennial bill was vetoed by William in 1693, but finally, in 1694, a Triennial Act received the royal assent. It stated that parliament must be summoned at least once every three years, and a new proviso was added: that no parliament should last longer than three years.

The Rage of Party

William kept to his word and parliament was summoned regularly. The longest intermission between parliaments during his reign was a period of ten months. Contemporaries hailed the Act as the beginning of a golden age in politics, and the next few years have been coined the 'Rage of Party' by historians, as the party divisions between Whig and Tory became more defined and impassioned. After 1694, voting in the Commons was conducted largely along party lines, with 86 per cent of members of parliament (MPs) voting strictly for one or other of the two parties for most of the time. The partisan nature of politics is evidenced by the relatively large number of constituencies that were contested by more than one candidate, which had been unusual earlier in the century (see Table 7.2, below). Because parliaments now had a definite maximum life, there was undoubtedly a greater amount of management and preparation in the constituencies, leading to an increase in political knowledge and interest among the population.

Soon, some sections of the political nation began to criticise the increasing frequency of elections:

- Some felt that more frequent elections endangered traditional gentry influence in the localities, as outsiders became more likely to intervene.

- As elections became more frequent, more money had to be spent on them. This caused resentment in the constituencies, as taxes were increased before elections were held.

- MPs felt less stability because they were aware that they could easily be removed from their position at the next election. This resulted in an increasing number of ambitious politicians attempting to be appointed to positions at the Royal Court, as promotion and success were more likely there. In this sense, the Triennial Act actually strengthened the hand of the monarchy rather than parliament.

Table 7.2 General elections in England, 1689–1701

Year	Whig MPs	Tory MPs	Percentage of constituencies contested
1689 (Convention Parliament)	319	232	28%
1690	241	243	38%
1695	257	203	31%
1698	246	208	45%
January 1701	219	249	38%
November 1701	248	240	34%

The Association, 1696

The election of November 1695 was the first to be held after the passing of the Triennial Act. This resulted in a House of Commons comprising 257 Whigs and 203 Tories. In February 1696, a Jacobite conspiracy to assassinate the King was discovered. The Whigs proposed a loyal 'Association' – effectively an oath of allegiance to the King – to be taken by MPs. The Association was passed by 364 votes to 89, demonstrating William's strong position.

However, anti-government feeling was strong in some areas, with relatively large numbers of MPs in parts of the midlands and Wales refusing to sign the Association.

William's use of the royal veto

William vetoed five parliamentary bills, four of which covered wide-ranging and important areas of legislation:

- a bill clarifying the salaries and tenure of judges (1692)
- an early version of the Triennial Act (1693)
- a bill for free and impartial proceedings in parliament (1694)
- a bill for regulating elections (1696).

William's use of the veto demonstrates the continued importance of the royal prerogative, which was criticised by contemporaries. In 1694, a motion was tabled in parliament accusing William of being ignorant of the English constitution in his behaviour. He narrowly survived an associated vote on the motion by a slender majority. This criticism does appear to have had an impact on William, as he did not use the veto after 1696.

The Act of Settlement, 1701

The Whig Junto began to disintegrate in 1698. The election of that year was one of the most fiercely partisan in the Stuart era, with 45 per cent of constituencies being contested by more than one candidate. A gulf had grown between 'Junto Whigs', who supported the small group that was directing policy, and the 'Country Whigs', who were suspicious of a growing executive. The Country opposition were able to secure a bill that restricted the size of the army in England to 7000 and William's request to retain his Dutch guard was refused. Montagu was demoted within the Privy Council and Russell was forced to resign his office in the Admiralty.

At the dawn of the eighteenth century, parliament now turned its attention to two issues:

- As Mary had died in 1694 and William was suffering ill health, the future of the succession became the great political topic of the day.
- The Bill of Rights had left a number of constitutional questions unanswered and parliament hoped to clarify these through a new bill.

The Act of Settlement was subsequently given the royal assent in 1701 and stated that, in order to bypass potential Catholic heirs to the throne, the succession would be vested in the House of Hanover, a German royal dynasty, after the reign of Queen Anne (the second Protestant daughter of James II). The House of Hanover was linked to the Stuarts through Sophia, a granddaughter of James I (see the Stuart succession diagram on page 83). As William, Mary and Anne had no surviving children, Sophia qualified as the closest Protestant heir. She married Ernst Augustus, Elector of Hanover, and died before she could inherit the throne, thus passing the succession to her son, who became George I of England, Scotland and Ireland in 1714.

The terms of the Act of Settlement

The key elements of the Act of Settlement can be summarised as follows:

- Catholics, and those married to Catholics, were barred from the succession and all future monarchs were required to be members of the Church of England.

- Judges could no longer be dismissed by the monarch without the consent of parliament.

- Royal pardons were to be declared void in cases of impeachment. This was included in the Act as the Tories hoped to impeach some of William's Whig advisers.

- All government matters were to be conducted only in Privy Council meetings. This clause was included because parliament wanted to be made aware of who was advising William and deciding on policies.

- No person who held office under the monarch was to be an MP. This clause was included to avoid excessive royal influence over the House of Commons.

- After the death of William and his immediate successor, Queen Anne, no future foreign monarch would be allowed to involve England in war on behalf of another country.

Impact of the Act of Settlement

As well as providing for a smooth succession, the Act enabled a number of legislative proposals first discussed in 1688–9 to reach the statute book. The Act has been viewed by some historians as a reaction to the policies of William, rather than simply an attempt to resurrect some of the reforming zeal of 1689. The clause concerning the religion of the monarch reflected concerns over William's Dutch Calvinism as much as a fear of Catholicism.

A fear of absolutism and a desire to rein in the monarchy are clear throughout the Act. The proviso that no future foreign monarch was allowed to enter England into a war to defend another country served as a clear response to the potential threat of William. William had entered England into the expensive Nine Years' War (see page 144). However, William remained in a strong position as several of the clauses only came into effect after his death.

ONLINE EXTRAS
AQA
WWW

Ensure you have grasped the key features of monarchy and parliament by completing Worksheet 25 at **www.hoddereducation.co.uk/accesstohistory/extras**

ONLINE EXTRAS
Pearson Edexcel
WWW

Test your knowledge of monarchy and parliament by completing Worksheet 25 at **www.hoddereducation.co.uk/accesstohistory/extras**

SUMMARY DIAGRAM

MONARCHY AND PARLIAMENT

Whig Junto	Triennial Act	Extent of royal power	Act of Settlement, 1701
• Support for strong executive • Decline from 1698	• Parliament to meet every three years • Parliaments limited to three years • Increase in political engagement • Rage of Party	• The Association • Use of royal veto • Maintenance of prerogative	• Protestant succession • No future foreign monarch to enter England into war to defend another country

5 | Key debate

■ *How revolutionary was the Glorious Revolution?*

Historians have developed contrasting views about the impact of the Bill of Rights, Act of Settlement and the wider political settlement in the years 1689–1702. The key question they have wrestled with pertains to whether the Glorious Revolution led to a modern, limited monarchy or whether the powers of the monarch remained relatively intact.

The Whig view: restoration of an ancient constitution

The 'Rage of Party' initiated after the Revolution cemented Whig and Tory allegiances and led to a period of Whig domination of politics that lasted into the early eighteenth century. This continued under Robert Walpole, who became prime minister in 1721, and Whig writers began to produce retrospective works that both celebrated and justified the actions of 1688–9. The crux of the Whig argument was that the Revolution simply restored an 'ancient constitution' that had long been established in England, and that many of the liberties referred to in the Bill of Rights – such as protection from arbitrary imprisonment and restrictions on the monarch collecting taxes without parliamentary consent – were already in existence. James had attempted to subvert the existing constitution and the Revolution was the political nation's method of achieving a return to the principles on which government had always been based. The Whig view was put forward most notably by Thomas Macaulay in the mid-nineteenth century.

Some modern historians have built on the Whig interpretation to present the Revolution as changing little except the line of succession. John Morrill (1991) called it a 'sensible revolution' that was essentially conservative and did little to encourage new rifts in the English political system.

EXTRACT 1

From Thomas Macaulay, *The History of England from the Accession of James II*, Longman's & Green, 1848, pp. 673–5.

The continental revolutions of the eighteenth and nineteenth centuries took place in countries where all trace of the limited monarchy of the middle ages had long been effaced [destroyed]. The right of the prince to make laws and to levy money had, during many generations, been undisputed. His subjects held their personal liberty by no other tenure than his pleasure.

These calamities our Revolution averted. It was a revolution strictly defensive, and had prescription and legitimacy on its side. Here, and here only, a limited monarchy of the thirteenth century had come down unimpaired to the seventeenth century. Our parliamentary institutions were in full vigour. The main principles of our government were excellent. They were not, indeed, formally and exactly set

---

INTERPRETATION QUESTION ❓

Read Extracts 1–3. What are the different views put forward to explain whether the Glorious Revolution was revolutionary or not?

ONLINE EXTRAS WWW
AQA

Get to grips with historical interpretations by completing Worksheet 26 at **www.hoddereducation.co.uk/accesstohistory/extras**

forth in a single written instrument; but they were to be found scattered over our ancient and noble statutes; and, what was of far greater moment, they had been engraved on the hearts of Englishmen during four hundred years. That, without the consent of the representatives of the nation, no legislative act could be passed, no tax imposed, no regular soldiery kept up, that no man could be imprisoned, even for a day, by the arbitrary will of the sovereign, that no tool of power could plead the royal command as a justification for violating any right of the humblest subject, were held, both by Whigs and Tories, to be fundamental laws of the realm. A realm of which these were the fundamental laws stood in no need of a new constitution.

Marxist view: power maintained in the hands of the elites

Marxist historians, most notably Christopher Hill, have tended to downplay the Revolution in favour of the events of the 1640s. They argue that the real revolutionary events took place between 1640 and 1649, when the traditional relationship between landlords and tenants broke down and the ruling elites were undermined and replaced with a bourgeois gentry. According to the Marxists, the events of 1688–9 were simply a manifestation of the new power relations in England and only solidified the existing settlement that had been created with the execution of Charles I. The evidence the Marxists put forward to support this view includes the fact that William had to rule in collaboration with the existing ruling classes, as he had no other base of support in England.

EXTRACT 2

From Christopher Hill, *The Century of Revolution 1603–1714*, Routledge, 1969, pp. 237–9.

The revolution of 1688 saw a restoration of power to the traditional ruling class, the Shire gentry, and town merchants, as well as a change of sovereigns. Borough charters were restored. The militia was returned to safe hands, and was used henceforth chiefly against any threat from the lower classes.

The revolution demonstrated the ultimate solidarity of the propertied class. Whigs and Tories disagreed sharply about whether James had abdicated or not, whether the throne should be declared vacant, whether Mary alone or William and Mary jointly should be asked to fill it, or declared to have filled it. But these differences were patched up, and the Declaration of Rights simply stated both positions and left it to individuals to resolve the contradictions as they pleased. One reason for this solid front was the behaviour of James and William. The latter, so far from remaining inscrutably in the background, made it perfectly clear that he was determined to have the title of King. But a second reason for agreement was men's recollections of what had happened forty-five years earlier, when unity of the propertied classes had been broken.

Revisionist view: violent and divisive revolution

In recent years, historians have tended to qualify the Whig and Marxist interpretations and have focused on two issues:

- The restrictions made to the powers of the monarch have been interpreted as the beginnings of a modern **constitutional monarchy**, as explored by John Miller in Extract 3 (see below). Parliament established the contractual nature of royal government in the Act of Settlement, which attempted to restrict the prerogative powers of William's Hanoverian heirs. Political parties began to take shape. However, this system did enable William to control parliament to an extent. His willingness to discard one party in favour of the other effectively helped him to control both parties and reduced parliamentary independence.

- Steve Pincus (2009) and Edward Vallance (2006) present the Revolution as one that was popular, violent and divisive. This is particularly true when events in Ireland and Scotland are taken into account. Pincus has described the events as the 'first modern revolution'.

> **KEY TERM**
>
> **Constitutional monarchy** A system of government where the power of a monarch is limited by a constitution.

EXTRACT 3

From John Miller, *The Stuarts*, Hambledon Continuum, 2006, p. 242.

The Revolution had effectively removed the threat from the royal prerogative. Kings had to rule as Parliament expected. The Triennial Act of 1694 laid down that there had to be a general election at least every three years. This was intended to deny ministers the time to build up a substantial 'court party' in the Commons. In fact the danger was never quite as great as it appeared. William, Anne and their managers did not want either party to win sweeping electoral victories. An evenly balanced House of Commons was easier to manage than a heavily partisan one and allowed the monarch more scope to appoint moderates and neutrals to office. Within the 'crown', the monarch exercised less and less personal power as ministers ruled in his or her name. These ministers derived their power over the monarch from their ability to push government bills (especially money bills) through Parliament, but also from the support that they enjoyed in the wider society.

Summary

Events after 1688 have been reinterpreted to characterise them as violent and radical rather than peaceful, and the constitutional settlement certainly confirmed that divine right monarchy was no more. The Bill of Rights is still a cornerstone of the British constitution and it set into law concepts of freedom of speech, free elections and parliamentary taxation. The judiciary became independent of the Crown and no longer served 'at the king's pleasure'.

Despite much recent scholarship focusing on the radical nature of the political settlement, there is some truth in the argument that the Revolution helped to maintain the Crown's existing prerogatives. Parliament was still only an

> **ONLINE EXTRAS** WWW
> Pearson Edexcel
>
> Practise your analysis of historical interpretations by completing Worksheet 26 at **www.hoddereducation. co.uk/accesstohistory/extras**

advisory body and the office of prime minister did not emerge until Robert Walpole informally took the title alongside the already established office of First Lord of the Treasury in 1721, although even Walpole was reluctant to accept this title. In 1741, when under attack for his style of government, he said in the Commons, 'I unequivocally deny that I am sole and prime minister'. The monarch was still pre-eminent in the political system, parliament continued to represent just two per cent of the population and the electorate was relatively small.

What was created as a consequence of the Glorious Revolution can best be described as the foundations for a constitutional monarchy. Parliament had a leading role in deciding who the next monarch would be and its members could suspend the Mutiny Act at any time in order to restrict the monarch's control of the army. The Bill of Rights and Act of Settlement were not an end product, but were fundamental building blocks of a modern, limited constitution.

CHAPTER SUMMARY

Within 100 years of the Glorious Revolution, parliament had become the chief decision-maker in the political system, controlling taxation and public spending, deciding many matters of foreign policy and meeting more regularly than ever before. All of this can be traced back to the revolutionary events of 1688–9. The increasingly absolutist behaviour of James and his promotion of Catholics alienated almost every section of the political nation and paved the way for William and Mary's arrival in England. In the wake of decades of division and strife, the Declaration of Rights settled a number of issues of sovereignty and the rights of parliament; however, many of the monarch's prerogative powers remained untouched. Although a political settlement was achieved relatively easily in England, Ireland and Scotland saw violence and division as James's supporters mounted fierce resistance to the new regime.

As William was unfamiliar with English politics and constrained by the Bill of Rights, he resorted to ruling with the Whig Junto, which assisted him in controlling parliament in order to achieve his aims. Finally, two Acts of great constitutional importance were passed under William: the Triennial Act and Act of Settlement. Like the Bill of Rights, they both paved the way for increased parliamentary authority; however, they did little to diminish William's significant prerogative powers.

Refresher questions

Use these questions to remind yourself of the key material covered in this chapter.

1 In what ways did James II attempt to increase Catholic influence in government and society?

2 Why is the trial of the Seven Bishops significant?

3 Why was Mary of Modena's pregnancy important?

4 What was the role of the Immortal Seven?

5 Why did James flee for France in December 1688?

6 What were the most significant clauses of the Declaration of Rights?

7 Which prerogative powers did William retain?

8 What is the significance of the Mutiny Acts?

9 Why did Ireland and Scotland witness more violence than England in response to the political settlement?

10 How did the Whig Junto assist William?

11 What did the Association of 1696 demonstrate about the balance of power between monarch and parliament?

12 What is the significance of William's use of the royal veto?

13 What were the main terms of the Act of Settlement?

14 In what ways did the Act of Settlement attempt to restrict the powers of the monarchy?

Question practice: AQA A level

Essay questions

1 To what extent were monarchs successful in managing parliament in the years 1672–1702?

EXAM HINT This covers three reigns, and you will need to decide if you are going to deal with each separately. If you do follow this approach, introduce your overall conclusion in your introduction so that what follows is part of the argument and avoids the danger of becoming narrative.

2 How far do you agree that parliament's power was significantly increased in the years 1678–1702?

EXAM HINT It is important to avoid a descriptive chronological approach. Think about the powers of parliament and the ways in which they increased (for example, over finance, over the succession), but in other respects did not (for example, foreign policy).

Interpretation question

1 Using your understanding of the historical context, assess how convincing the arguments in Extracts 1 (page 133), 2 (page 134) and 3 (page 135) are in relation to the impact of the Glorious Revolution in the years 1688–1702.

EXAM HINT Analyse the argument or arguments in each extract and use your contextual knowledge to assess how convincing each one is. Do not attempt an overall judgement – just a conclusion on each one. Do not introduce arguments that deal with provenance – especially tempting in Extract 1.

Question practice: Pearson Edexcel A level

Interpretation question

1 In the light of the interpretations in Extracts 1 (page 133) and 3 (page 135), how convincing do you find the view that the Glorious Revolution transformed the relationship between Crown and parliament?

EXAM HINT Examine the content of Extract 1 (limited monarchy already existed) and Extract 3 (1688 began a gradual transition to limited monarchy). Then deploy your own knowledge to reach a judgement on 'transformation'.

CHAPTER 8

The Glorious Revolution, 1688–1701: religious and financial reform

As well as the political settlement, a religious and financial settlement was established after the Glorious Revolution. On his arrival in England, William was faced with division in the Church of England and was concerned with following a middle path between toleration and uniformity. The Toleration Act of 1689 gave a measure of religious freedom to Protestant Dissenters; however, in order to be appointed to most government positions, office holders were expected to take Anglican Communion. The financial settlement was certainly revolutionary: the Bank of England was founded in 1694, government finance was entirely restructured in order to fund William's foreign policy objectives, and government expenditure was scrutinised closely for the first time. This chapter explores these issues under the following headings:

◆ The Toleration Act

◆ The Nine Years' War and government finance

◆ The establishment of the Bank of England

◆ Parliamentary scrutiny of government finance

KEY DATES

1688	Start of the Nine Years' War	**1694**	Bank of England founded
1689	Toleration Act	**1697**	End of the Nine Years' War
1690	Public Accounts Act	**1698**	Civil List established

1 The Toleration Act

■ *How far was religious toleration achieved for Protestant Dissenters?*

After the Restoration in 1660 there had been several attempts by Charles II to grant toleration to Protestant Dissenters. However, since the Exclusion Crisis of 1679–81, and later in the reign of James II, the Dissenters had been cast aside by both monarchs in favour of Catholics. The arrival of William III gave renewed hope to Dissenters, and the Convention Parliament discussed two bills that concerned religious toleration:

■ A comprehension bill was the more ambitious of the two. Its intention was to relax the recusancy laws that prevented Nonconformists from attending parish churches and modify some of the rituals in the Church (such as kneeling at the altar). In effect, it would have altered the principles of the Church of England in order to accommodate Dissenters. The bill was abandoned by parliament in April 1689 and did not become law. The argument had prevailed that, as **convocation** was about to be summoned, this great religious issue should be discussed there instead.

KEY TERM

Convocation A formal assembly of bishops and clergy that meets to consider matters of Church policy.

- A toleration bill was suggested by William after he had urged the removal of the sacramental test for public office holders. This would have meant repealing the Test Act that required all office holders to take Anglican Communion. The suggestion was met with fierce resistance from the bishops in the Lords and many of the pro-Anglican members of the Commons, so William suggested a Toleration Act as a compromise.

The content of the Toleration Act

The Toleration Act did not abolish any of the existing laws against Protestant Dissenters (specifically the Acts of the Clarendon Code), but declared that they should not be enforced against those who fulfilled certain conditions. These conditions included:

- An oath of allegiance to William and Mary, which was expected to be taken by all laymen.
- The standard oath against transubstantiation already taken in the Church of England, which was to be taken by Dissenters.
- Dissenting ministers were expected to subscribe to the **Thirty-nine Articles**.
- The Act gave special dispensations for certain dissenting groups: as the Quakers refused to take oaths, they were allowed to declare, rather than swear, that they denied the Pope's authority.
- Some recognition of the status of dissenting ministers was to be found in their exemption from local office and from serving on juries. These were the same exemptions enjoyed by Anglican priests.

Continued restrictions on Dissenters

In addition, there were still restrictions on what Dissenters could do:

- Dissenters were not allowed to lock the doors of their meeting houses. If they locked their doors, they would be found to have broken the law and their meeting house would lose its licence.
- Dissenters, like everyone else, were expected to continue to pay tithes and other local religious taxes. They could still be prosecuted for non-payment in the ecclesiastical courts, overseen by bishops of the Church of England.
- Dissenters were exempted from punishment only if they accepted the 1678 Test Act. This meant that they could not enter public employment without swearing loyalty to the Anglican Church.
- The Act excluded Catholics, **non-Trinitarians** and Jews. These groups comprised a small fraction of the population; however, some high-profile non-Trinitarians, such as **Isaac Newton**, were forced to conceal their religious views in order to find employment. As a professor at Trinity College, Cambridge, Newton would have been forced to leave the university if he made his beliefs public. He unequivocally subscribed to the articles of the Church of England when he took public office in 1689, 1696 and 1699, and probably did so with deep reservations.

KEY TERMS

Thirty-nine Articles
A document from 1571 that set out the doctrines of the Church of England.

Non-Trinitarians
Christians who do not believe in the doctrine of the Trinity; the notion that divinity exists within God, Jesus and the Holy Spirit equally.

KEY FIGURE

Isaac Newton (1642–1727)
One of the most influential scientists of all time, Newton was a mathematician, astronomer, physicist and theologian. Although he is known primarily for his contribution to scientific thought, Newton wrote extensively on religion and the Bible.

- As the Test Act was not repealed, non-Anglicans could not sit in parliament or hold public office. Those who did not swear allegiance to the Anglican Church could not attend university, work in the legal profession or practise medicine.

SOURCE A

Extract from the Toleration Act (1689), quoted in Andrew Browning, editor, *English Historical Documents, 1660–1714*, Eyre & Spottiswoode, 1953.

There are certain dissenters from the Church of England, who scruple the taking of any oath; be it enacted by the authority aforesaid, that every such person shall make and subscribe the aforesaid declaration, and also this declaration:

'I do sincerely promise and solemnly declare before God and the world, that I will be true and faithful to King William and Queen Mary; and I do solemnly profess and declare, that I do from my heart abhor, detest, and renounce, as impious and heretical, that damnable doctrine and position, that princes excommunicated or deprived by the Pope, or any authority of the See of Rome, may be deposed or murdered by their subjects, or any other whatsoever. And I do declare, that no foreign prince, person, prelate, state, or potentate, hath or ought to have, any power, jurisdiction, superiority, pre-eminence, or authority ecclesiastical or spiritual within this realm.'

And shall subscribe a profession of their Christian belief in these words:

'I profess faith in God the Father, and in Jesus Christ His eternal Son, the true God, and in the Holy Spirit, one God blessed for evermore, and do acknowledge the Holy Scriptures of the Old and New Testament to be given by divine inspiration.'

SOURCE QUESTION

Study Source A. Why do you think people were expected to declare their loyalty to William and Mary as part of the Toleration Act?

Impact of the Toleration Act

Meeting places could be registered with a bishop, an archdeacon or the judges at the **court of quarter sessions**. In most areas there appear to have been few applications to the ecclesiastical authorities for the registering of meeting places before the second half of the eighteenth century. This has been explained by historians in terms of the reluctance of Dissenters to apply to a bishop so soon after the end of severe religious persecution. Many more applications were made to the quarter sessions, with over 2500 dissenting places of worship licensed between 1691 and 1710. The Act certainly made it easier for Dissenters to worship freely and, by 1714, there were around 400,000 Dissenters in England (approximately eight per cent of the total population).

Despite the emphasis frequently placed by historians on the anti-Catholic nature of the Revolution, in reality, Catholics had little to fear from William III's government, as he had effectively guaranteed their safety by entering into an alliance with a number of Catholic powers against the French in the League of Augsburg in 1686. Some contemporaries even commented that Catholics were really the group that gained the most from the Revolution. The influential Whig bishop, Gilbert Burnet, wrote that 'I am none of those that damn all Papists; for I have known many good and religious men among them', and the

---

KEY TERM

Court of quarter sessions A criminal court held four times a year empowered to try all but the most serious offences and hear appeals.

Bishop of Lichfield, William Lloyd, stated that Catholics 'are more at ease under King William than under any Protestant king since the Reformation'. When Frenchman Henri Misson commented on the state of England in the 1690s, he noted that, despite legal limitations, Catholics appeared to be enjoying universal toleration. William used his royal authority to influence judges and curb Church interference in the lives of Catholics and dissenting sects not covered by the Act.

Impact on dissenting clergy

In the years immediately after the passing of the Toleration Act, there were echoes of the short-lived implementation of Charles II's Declaration of Indulgence in 1672. As in 1672, Nonconformist ministers registered their existing meeting houses and made applications for new ones, and there was a sense of optimism among many of them. On the day the Toleration Act was passed, Phillip Henry, a minister from north Wales, wrote in his diary that he 'saw much of God in the carry on of the work of this day'. Oliver Heywood wrote of 1689 as 'the wonderful year when all of a sudden a bright sun appeared out of the East'. However, Dissenters who had been made similar promises on a number of occasions since 1660 were cautious. Many would have preferred inclusion within the Church of England to toleration of their own meeting places outside it.

Although the power of the ecclesiastical courts had declined, senior figures within the Church of England were still able to use their influence to single out Nonconformist ministers in order to bypass the Toleration Act. Richard Frankland, who had founded a Dissenting Academy in north Yorkshire in 1670, was hounded by the Anglican clergy whose parishes surrounded him. They wrote to the Archbishop of Canterbury, John Tillotson, in 1692, in an effort to close down the academy. Frankland's academy had its licence withdrawn, ostensibly because it was not required in the district, but in reality because of long-standing Anglican opposition.

Although comprehension of Nonconformists into the Church of England was not achieved under William, a relatively large number of gentry who held Presbyterian beliefs used their patronage rights to appoint clergy of their choosing to vacant posts.

SOURCE QUESTION

Study Source B. Why do you think Henry described the impact of the Toleration Act as only a 'resurrection in some measure'?

SOURCE B

Extract from the diary of Phillip Henry, a minister from north Wales, 24 May 1689.

The condition of many ministers and people hath been, in outward appearance, a dead condition. The words of the Act of Uniformity are that they shall be as if naturally dead; but, blessed be God, there hath been a resurrection in some measure, a coming out of the grave again, of which, whoever was the instrument, the Lord Jesus himself hath been the principal agent.

Conclusion: was the Church transformed after the Glorious Revolution?

Despite the introduction of the Toleration Act, the vast majority of people ultimately maintained loyalty to the Anglican Church. It was in William's interest to gain the approval of the Anglican Church establishment and he respected a number of their wishes. The rejection of inclusion within the Church of England for Presbyterians and other Dissenters was welcomed. The prayer book was modified in 1690 to introduce a new annual service of thanksgiving on 5 November. William ordered that the thanksgiving service celebrate both the deliverance from Guy Fawkes in 1605 and his own 'happy arrival' and the 'Deliverance of our Church and Nation' on the same date in 1688.

In the two years following the Revolution many vacancies for parish priests and bishops occurred. Most of these were filled by moderate Anglicans, many of whom would be classified as Tories. The historian J.P. Kenyon (1990) has asserted that 'the Church of England continued to be associated with the divine right of kings in its most extreme form'. This has been explained by the fact that the Church occupied a middle ground between the denominations on either side (Puritan and Catholic) that were defined by resistance and upheaval. For this reason, a large number of Whigs and Tories subscribed to, and acted to strengthen, the doctrines of the Anglican Church.

Before her death in 1694, however, Queen Mary proved to be a vital patron to more radical clergymen. She noted in her memoirs that 'filling the bishoprics was the only thing of business I concerned myself in' while William was in England. She had strong low-church preferences in religious matters and openly attended both Anglican and Presbyterian churches. She was influential in ensuring that some of the bishops appointed in the years 1689–94 reflected her religious views.

> **ONLINE EXTRAS** **WWW**
> AQA
>
> Develop your analysis of the Toleration Act by completing Worksheet 27 at **www.hoddereducation.co.uk/accesstohistory/extras**

> **ONLINE EXTRAS** **WWW**
> Pearson Edexcel
>
> Test your understanding of the Toleration Act by completing Worksheet 27 at **www.hoddereducation.co.uk/accesstohistory/extras**

SUMMARY DIAGRAM

THE TOLERATION ACT

```
                    Religion and the
                    Toleration Act

   Laws against Protestant Dissenters     Continued to be some restrictions
   suspended if they met certain                   on Dissenters
            conditions
                                          Negative impact on dissenting
                                                     clergy

                                            Continued Anglican dominance
```

2 The Nine Years' War and government finance

■ *What were the economic demands of the Nine Years' War (1688–97)?*

War in Europe began on 14 September 1688, when Louis XIV dispatched his forces to the middle Rhine before his enemies in the region were able to mobilise. Two years earlier, in 1686, these enemies had formed a federation known as the League of Augsburg. The league included both Catholic and Protestant members, and many of the members' territories bordered France: the Spanish Habsburg territories, the Dutch Republic, the Kingdom of Sweden, the Duchy of Savoy and various territories within the Holy Roman Empire. These members shared the common objective of limiting the territorial expansion of France.

This defensive league was interpreted by Louis XIV to be a hostile coalition and he cited its existence as a pretext for resorting to arms. Louis declared war on the Dutch only after William's invasion of England, and thus William's new kingdom was brought into the war. The French-backed Jacobite risings in Ireland and Scotland (discussed on pages 124–8) have been interpreted as an extension of the Nine Years' War.

British involvement in the war

The League of Augsburg possessed a joint total force of 60,000 men in 1688, commanded by William's nominee, Prince George Waldeck. This number increased to over 100,000 by the end of 1689 and William became the League's figurehead and driving force. A treaty between the members was soon concluded that committed England to providing 50 warships. England's formal involvement in the war was justified by William with the following reasons:

KEY TERM

Privateers Privately owned armed ships with government authority to capture foreign merchant vessels.

■ Louis had encroached on the British Newfoundland fisheries.

■ He had invaded the English Caribbean Islands and French **privateers** had attacked English ships.

■ Heavy duties had been imposed on English imports into France.

■ English Protestants had been persecuted in France.

These accusations were based on fact, but even taken together they would hardly justify war in normal circumstances. In reality, England's motives in declaring war on France were to preserve the Revolution settlement, limit James II's chances of mounting an attack on England and support William's Dutch army.

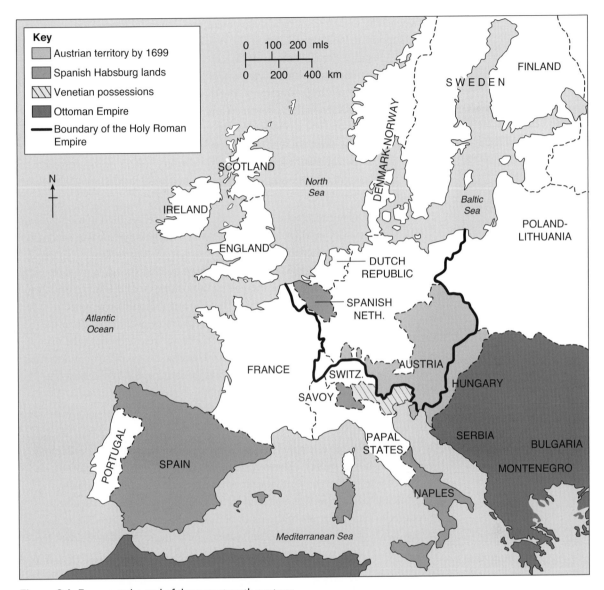

Figure 8.1 Europe at the end of the seventeenth century.

Extent of British involvement

The Tories in parliament argued that the English contribution to the war should be limited to the sea and not involve a land army. However, William was concerned only with increasing the number of troops who could fight on the Continent. During the course of the war, the number of British troops in his service increased from 8000 to 90,000, at a cost of around £2.7 million a year.

Between 1689 and 1692, British involvement was generally limited to providing naval support to William's Dutch army. While William was on campaign in Ireland, a decisive French victory off Beachy Head in July 1690 caused national panic and a genuine fear that an invasion of England was imminent. Thanks to an active shipbuilding programme, the disparity between the English and French fleets was subsequently reversed and by 1692 the English were in a far stronger position. The House of Commons voted for £570,000 towards 27 **men-of-war**, a new shipyard was constructed in Plymouth and a dry dock was installed in the naval base at Portsmouth. In February 1692, a newly designed mortar was brought into service, which fired a shell of 30 lbs (14 kg), 40 times an hour.

The Battle of La Hogue, off the coast of northern France, resulted in a conclusive Anglo-Dutch victory in May 1692, and the remaining years of the war saw major land battles as well as a continuation of the sea war. William entered into peace talks with the French in 1696 and although these quickly stalled, both sides were bankrupt by 1697. William faced increasing opposition from the Tories and non-Junto Whigs in parliament who argued that the army should be reduced in size. Peace talks resumed and with both England and France wary of war and the French suffering an economic crisis, a settlement was reached under the terms of the Treaty of Ryswick in September 1697. The French agreed to abandon their claims to land in Germany and Holland, and Louis accepted William as the legitimate king of England.

Financing the war

By October 1691, the estimates for the army and navy presented to parliament were more than £4 million. These costs meant that William would have to find more money than any previous monarch to fund the war. Ultimately, a significant part of this was financed by long-term borrowing, particularly through the establishment of the Bank of England (see pages 148–50), as well as new (and sometimes controversial) taxes. The policy of funding the war by traditional taxation was beginning to be abandoned.

Traditional taxation

By the late seventeenth century, the main source of revenue consisted of two indirect taxes: Customs and Excise. The Customs were charged as a flat fee on all woollen cloth exported and a levy of five per cent on imports and exports, according to their value in the **Book of Rates** (1660). In 1686–7, the yield from Customs exceeded £640,000, but the disruption of war caused a decline in revenue until 1697.

The Excise was a combination of taxes paid to the king either for life or granted from time to time by parliament. The Excise was mainly paid on beer, ale and vinegar. In the course of William's reign, it yielded slightly more than the Customs. As the Excise was levied on items that were considered necessities, it became a dependable source of revenue.

KEY TERMS

Man-of-war A heavily armed warship.

Book of Rates
A document that listed how much tax was due to be paid on all items that could be imported into, and exported from, England.

Other taxes

Other methods of raising revenue used by William included:

■ A Land Tax, charged typically at twenty per cent and raising £1.6 million per year, was imposed in 1690 and renewed in 1691. Catholics were expected to pay double. The tax helped to raise around one-third of the required funds for the war.

■ In 1695, the Marriage Duty Act introduced taxes on christenings, marriages and burials. Although the basic rate for those of low status was just a few pence, nobles were expected to pay the considerable sum of £30 for a baptism and £50 for marriages and burials. All births (not just those christened in the Church of England) were to be registered with parish officials for a fee of sixpence (2.5p). This enabled the authorities to collect money from those baptised by dissenting ministers. The Act was unpopular and was described by the member of parliament (MP) Charles Davenant as a 'fine upon the marriage-bed – a very grievous burden upon the poorer sort whose numbers compose the strength and wealth of any nation'. The Act was found to be unenforceable and in 1696 it raised just £50,000.

■ A Window Tax was imposed in 1696. This was a property tax levied on the number of windows in a house. Like the Marriage Duty Act, it was designed to impose tax on a progressive basis and payments were paid relative to the wealth of the taxpayer. Each house paid a flat rate of two shillings (10p), with houses with above ten windows paying an additional four shillings and houses with more than 20 windows paying a further eight shillings. It was introduced too late to have a significant impact on war financing, but later became an important source of income for the government and was not abolished until 1851.

■ On several occasions between 1689 and 1698 a Poll Tax was levied. This was a tax on every adult and was paid relative to the taxpayer's rank or profession. At the lower end of the scale, labourers were expected to pay a flat rate of sixpence and at the top, those who were in receipt of government salaries paid one shilling in the pound. The tax was unpopular because it was based on rank rather than income. It was also administered by local commissioners appointed by the Privy Council, many of whom were corrupt in their collection of the tax and overlooked their friends and families.

■ Other taxes that were introduced or increased included: a tax on stamped paper, licences of **hackney coaches**, tobacco pipes, salt and coal.

> **KEY TERM**
>
> **Hackney coaches**
> Horse-drawn carriages hired to carry passengers in London.

The total raised through taxation in the years 1689–1702 was more than £58 million, with £40 million of this raised during the war years of 1689–97. The government's success in collecting these taxes varied considerably, with some northern districts succeeding in reducing their Land Tax commitments, while it became very difficult to collect the Poll Tax in the southwest due to some intense opposition. Ultimately, William had to turn to long-term borrowing to make up the shortfall.

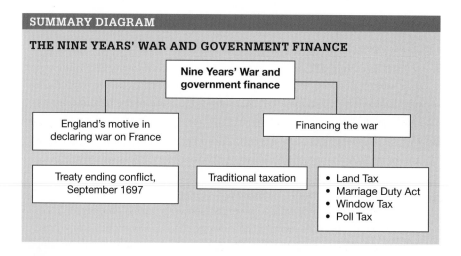

SUMMARY DIAGRAM

THE NINE YEARS' WAR AND GOVERNMENT FINANCE

3 The establishment of the Bank of England

■ *To what extent did English involvement in the Nine Years' War (1688–97) lead to a revolution in government finance?*

Because the Nine Years' War required a level of funding that had never been witnessed before in England, William needed to use other new methods of raising revenue. He did this by turning to long-term borrowing.

Long-term borrowing

Participation in the Nine Years' War cost William, on average, around £5.4 million per year. It may have been possible to fund this from taxation; however, other financial commitments meant that this was never enough. Around £1.2 million per year was required for the maintenance of civil administration and William inherited a debt of £2 million from James II's government. The value of silver coinage had also depreciated by nearly 40 per cent between 1672 and 1696, which led to significant losses for the government. All of this resulted in a shortfall of more than £14 million by 1697. A system of long-term borrowing was thus initiated whereby large sums of money could be raised by William on credit and paid back over a number of years from the proceeds of taxes.

The Million Loan, 1693

In 1693, a **tontine loan** of £1 million was sought from investors. The investors received ten per cent interest until 1700 and after this a share in a fund, which was divided between them as each member died. When only seven were left, the fund was closed and these investors received what remained. Some historians have interpreted the Million Loan as an important turning point in the economic history of Britain as it helped to create a national debt, which has increased in size ever since.

The Million Lottery, 1694

The Million Lottery was another device that was intended to fund the war and involved the government paying investors back over a long period. Investors were invited to purchase 100,000 lottery tickets for £10 each, 2500 of which were 'fortune tickets' that entitled the recipient to a cash prize. The investors also received interest on their investment at the generous rate of fourteen per cent, funded from taxes on salt.

The Malt Lottery, 1697

The success of the Million Lottery was tempered by the failure of the Malt Lottery of 1697. The interest rate for this lottery was lowered to just six per cent, which led to a reduced take-up from investors and only £17,000 was raised for the government from an anticipated £1.4 million. Nevertheless, the lottery model proved popular and privately organised lotteries soon became widespread. In some cases, tickets could be purchased for a penny, and the popularity of private lotteries had a negative impact on the income the government received from state lotteries. William reacted by passing an Act declaring private lotteries illegal in 1699.

Table 8.1 Some of the major sources of government revenue, 1689–1702

Name	Method	Date	Total revenue	Notes
The Excise	Tax	1689–1702	£13,500,000	
The Customs	Tax	1689–1702	£13,000,000	
Poll Tax	Tax	1689–98	£2,000,000	
Land Tax	Tax	1690–1702	£19,000,000	Over £12,000,000 of this total was raised in the war years (1690–7)
Million Loan	Loan	1693	£1,000,000	
Establishment of Bank of England	Loan	1694	£1,200,000	
Million Lottery	State lottery	1694	£1,000,000	
Loan repaid from the proceeds of marriage taxes	Loan	1695	£650,000	The tax produced just £54,000, resulting in the lenders losing most of their investment
Extension of the Bank of England's privileges	Loan	1696	£5,000,000	The members of the Bank of England had their privileges renewed until 1710 in exchange for a loan of £5,000,000
Malt Lottery	State lottery	1697	£17,000	Of 140,000 £10 tickets, only 1763 were sold. Unsold tickets were used by the government as cash to pay for pensions and annuities
Establishment of the 'new' East India Company	Loan	1698	£2,000,000	Investors were incorporated into the East India Company

The Bank of England

Of all the institutions and devices established to fund the war, the Bank of England had the greatest long-term impact. In April 1694, Charles Montagu, as Chancellor of the Exchequer, proposed a bill intended to raise a loan of £1.5 million and establish a national bank. The bill was opposed in the Lords as it was seen to be conferring additional privileges (in the form of money) on the monarch, but was eventually passed by 43 votes to 31. It became known as the Tonnage Act and it stipulated that investors paying into the loan were to be incorporated into the Bank of England – effectively becoming shareholders – and paid back at an interest rate of eight per cent from taxes on imports, as well as additional duties on beer and vinegar.

Investors in the Bank were given the authority to deal in bills of exchange. The bills were essentially paper money and were offered by the Bank as notes of £100. In return, investors received a guarantee that they would be paid through Excise duties. The Bank of England became a vital component of William's wartime administration, as a large number of investors could be attracted to deposit small amounts to be lent to the government at short notice. However, this system was only made possible because it had the backing of an Act of Parliament. The Bank gradually took over affairs related to military funding and opened a branch in Holland from which to attract investors. Confidence in the Bank of England increased significantly after William's death, when more emphasis was placed on long-term investment, and government borrowing was increased to over £2.5 million per year in the decade after 1701.

Despite its successes, long-term lending accounted for less than half of the money borrowed during the Nine Years' War and William had to rely on short-term loans and taxation for the majority.

ONLINE EXTRAS
AQA WWW

Test your knowledge of the Nine Years' War by completing Worksheet 28 at **www.hoddereducation. co.uk/accesstohistory/extras**

ONLINE EXTRAS
Pearson Edexcel WWW

Get to grips with the Nine Years' War by completing Worksheet 28 at **www. hoddereducation.co.uk/ accesstohistory/extras**

? SOURCE QUESTION

Study Source C. Why does Defoe believe that the Bank of England was founded at a convenient time for the English nation?

SOURCE C

From Daniel Defoe, *An Essay on Projects* (1697). Most famous as the author of the novel *Robinson Crusoe*, Defoe wrote over 500 titles, including commentaries on the state of the economy. He was a Dissenter and supporter of William and Mary.

I believe it [the Bank of England] is a very good fund, a very useful one, and a very profitable one. It has been useful to the Government, and it is profitable to the proprietors; and the establishing it at such a juncture, when our enemies were making great boasts of our poverty and want, was a particular glory to our nation and the City in particular.

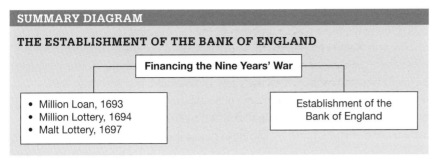

4 Parliamentary scrutiny of government finance

■ *How effective was parliament in scrutinising government finance in the years 1689–1702?*

The huge sums of money being spent on war led to concerns among backbench MPs and, as a consequence, the Public Accounts Act was passed in 1690. This led to the formation of a Public Accounts Commission in 1691, tasked with examining government expenditure.

Public Accounts Commission

The commission was a forerunner to modern-day parliamentary select committees. It was made up of MPs and had the power to interrogate ministers and call for papers from government to be read and consulted in order to establish whether money had been spent inappropriately. The commissioners published reports that frequently exposed corruption and waste at William's court. The commissions were organised along the following lines:

■ Nine commissioners were voted to their positions via a ballot of MPs.

■ The commission was renewed each year.

■ Members were paid an annual salary of £500 and were ultimately responsible to parliament rather than the king.

■ Their work was carried out with unprecedented attention to detail. Meetings and interviews took place daily.

■ After they had conducted their investigations and interviewed relevant officials, the commissioners produced reports outlining their findings. These were sent to the Privy Council and shared with parliament.

Parliament was now able to examine in detail the estimates of income and expenditure put forward by the Privy Council in a way that had rarely been permitted before. The examination of the estimates became an intrinsic part of the parliamentary timetable, establishing the rights of MPs to scrutinise and even reduce prospective government expenditure. The announcement of the estimates became an opposition's opportunity to exploit or even bargain over. One of the most vocal supporters of the right to scrutinise government finance was **Robert Harley**, who was perhaps the most active member of the commission. Although he had always been associated with the Country Whigs, he later distanced himself from the party factions and, in a speech in 1693, declared, 'I think the senseless name of parties hath almost ruined us'. He was instead concerned with ensuring that all MPs could work together to hold the actions of the Privy Council to account.

William III was generally content with adopting the suggestions of the commission for its first five years and it was ultimately successful in compelling him to reassess the size of the army and navy.

The political impact of increased financial scrutiny

- As the Commons became more confident in scrutinising government estimates and supply, regular sessions of parliament, as well as long daily sittings, became a necessity.

- The government's need to find the approval of the House before their estimates could be ratified meant that those members who could sway the House through the force of their oratory or personality became vital to William. Management of the Commons through bribery in the former style of Danby was no longer sufficient.

- As a consequence, it required parliamentary and political skills, deployed regularly in the House, to make a name for oneself and receive the approval of William. A new route to power had opened up: the parliamentary route.

- A strong rapport grew between Whig members of the Public Accounts Commission, such as Robert Harley and Paul Foley, and their Tory colleagues, including Sir Thomas Clarges and Sir Benjamin Newland.

- High-profile members of the House, such as the Speaker, Sir John Trevor, were expelled for financial malpractice. In Trevor's case, he was found to have been taking bribes and he was replaced with a leading member of the commission, Paul Foley.

Limits of the Public Accounts Commission

In the second half of the 1690s, the commission lost some of its momentum and was increasingly used to attack unfavoured ministers rather than fulfilling its original purpose of holding the government to account for its financial decisions. In addition, from its inception, court officials regularly obstructed the work of the commission by withholding papers or refusing to answer questions.

The most noteworthy example of this obstruction came in the case of the Secretary to the Treasury, William Jephson. He had been responsible for paying over £100,000 per year out of public revenues for 'Secret Service' money paid directly on the order of the King without public record. The commission feared that much of this money was being used to pay royal favourites or to bribe MPs. Jephson died in June 1691 and over the next six months, the commission tried desperately to recover his secret accounts by pleading with his employers at the Treasury. All the commission received in return were partial answers, none of which explained where the money had gone. In the end, the commission was able to account for payments to only eighteen MPs, totalling £27,000, a fraction of the £243,000 in secret money distributed by Jephson. The MP Sir John Thompson captured the mood at the time when he said, 'I stand amazed that, in the best times and governments, things should be in such darkness'.

William blocked any further commissions from 1697 and later attempts to renew the commission were unsuccessful.

The Civil List Act

While the Nine Years' War was financed through a combination of taxation and borrowing, an adequate funding settlement to cover day-to-day government expenditure was still not formalised after the Revolution. On the accession of William and Mary in 1689, parliament voted £600,000 specifically for their civil expenses, beginning a custom that led to the passing of the Civil List Act in 1698. The Act assigned £700,000 per year from duties on wine 'for the service of his Majesty's household and other uses', with any surplus granted only with the consent of parliament.

This funding was allocated to meet the expenses of William's government, including the salaries of civil servants and judges, as well as the expenditure of the royal household. This meant that all military and naval expenditure, in times of peace and war, was ultimately the responsibility of parliament. Monarch and parliament were expected to meet regularly in order to renew the civil list.

Scrutiny of military expenditure

In the years that government policy was controlled by the Whig Junto after 1692, it was difficult for parliament to secure reductions to British involvement in the Nine Years' War. As the war ended and the Whig Junto began to disintegrate, the Country opposition were able to secure votes limiting the amount of parliamentary finance offered to William. A vote, spearheaded by Robert Harley, was passed in 1697 that limited William to sustaining an army of just 10,000 men through government grants. In addition, the Irish army was reduced to 12,000 and both armies were restricted to recruiting only native troops. This ensured that Dutch regiments could not serve in England. The Bill of Rights had made the maintenance of a professional armed force in peacetime dependent on the approval of parliament; however, this had not been an issue during the war years. William wished to maintain an army of at least 30,000 during the ensuing peace, but parliament was able to use the powers it had claimed in 1689 to secure the reduction. In 1698, the army was reduced again to 7000.

In 1698 and 1699, William engaged in a struggle with the radical Whig press and a coalition of MPs over the size and funding for a peacetime army. It ultimately became the issue in English politics in which William became the most involved, and was the closest king and parliament came to a genuine contest in the later part of his reign. His Dutch army was kept at 45,500.

Conclusion: how far did William's involvement in the Nine Years' War lead to a financial revolution?

Historians disagree about how far the 1690s represent a financial revolution, but there is a general consensus that government finance and scrutiny was transformed in these years. To what extent was this the result of British involvement in the Nine Years' War?

The Nine Years' War as a financial revolution

As we have seen, the Nine Years' War was extremely costly. More than £5 million per year was required to fund British involvement in the years 1689–97. Thus, there was a need to restructure government finance and the long-term borrowing and lotteries of the 1690s were necessary to keep the government afloat. However, state lotteries had existed since 1567 and were already popular. Private lotteries – those that provided no funding for the government – were widespread in the 1690s. The people taking part in these lotteries were socially diverse, which is at odds with the view traditionally presented by historians that the financial revolution was dominated by the landed elites.

The experiments in long-term borrowing have been described by the historian P.G.M. Dickson (1967) as being marked by 'haste, carelessness and episodic failure', and it is true that they were not all entirely successful. What the war did do, however, was to establish a permanent, funded debt. By the end of William's reign, the national debt stood at almost £17 million.

Growing power of parliament

ONLINE EXTRAS **WWW**
AQA
Learn how to write effective introductions by completing Worksheet 29 at **www. hoddereducation.co.uk/ accesstohistory/extras**

It could be argued that it was not the Nine Years' War that caused a revolution in government finances, but the increased power of parliament in the years following the Glorious Revolution. After the Bill of Rights set out the rights of parliament in 1689, ambitious MPs moved to limit the monarch's free hand over spending, and with the establishment of the Public Accounts Commission, government spending was scrutinised as never before and corruption was thoroughly investigated.

Improved trading conditions

It should be noted that the success of long-term borrowing was not guaranteed. Some of William's projects, such as the Malt Lottery, were failures and it was only improved trading conditions and the growth of the English empire (see pages 186–91) that gave investors the confidence to lend to William. Investors were normally paid interest on their loans from government tax revenue and as international trade boomed, receipts from the Customs and other levies increased.

Had a revolution in government finance already taken place?

Although William borrowed more than any previous monarch and created a significant national debt to pay for the war, the practice of the government borrowing large sums of money from private individuals and companies was nothing new. Charles II had done just this when he relied heavily on the goldsmith bankers to fund his government in the 1660s.

ONLINE EXTRAS WWW
AQA

Test your knowledge of the consequences of the Glorious Revolution by completing Worksheet 30 at **www. hoddereducation.co.uk/ accesstohistory/extras**

ONLINE EXTRAS WWW
Pearson Edexcel

Test your understanding of parliament's power after the Glorious Revolution by completing Worksheet 30 at **www.hoddereducation. co.uk/accesstohistory/extras**

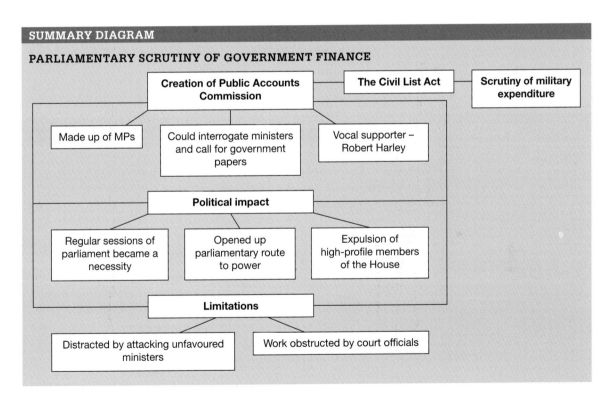

SUMMARY DIAGRAM

PARLIAMENTARY SCRUTINY OF GOVERNMENT FINANCE

- Creation of Public Accounts Commission
  - Made up of MPs
  - Could interrogate ministers and call for government papers
- The Civil List Act
  - Vocal supporter – Robert Harley
- Scrutiny of military expenditure

- Political impact
  - Regular sessions of parliament became a necessity
  - Opened up parliamentary route to power
  - Expulsion of high-profile members of the House

- Limitations
  - Distracted by attacking unfavoured ministers
  - Work obstructed by court officials

CHAPTER SUMMARY

The debate concerning religious toleration had been ever-present in the later Stuart era and the years following the Glorious Revolution were no exception. Although the Church of England itself remained virtually unaltered, toleration for those outside it was achieved, to an extent, with the passing of the Toleration Act. Dissenters were to be left alone if they fulfilled certain conditions (although many continued to be hounded by the authorities), and they were expected to continue paying tithes, could be prosecuted in ecclesiastical courts and were compelled to take the Test Act in order to hold public office.

British involvement in the Nine Years' War resulted in a need for huge amounts of money to pay for William's military needs. Traditional methods of taxation were initially supplemented by a Land Tax and various other new taxes that were of mixed success. With the establishment of the Bank of England and several schemes to borrow money from investors, William was able to adequately fund the war until 1697, although a national debt of £16.7 million was created. Parliamentary scrutiny of William's spending became a key issue, and as well as the establishment of the Civil List in 1698, the Public Accounts Commission led to an enhanced role for parliament in dictating where government income was spent.

Refresher questions

Use these questions to remind yourself of the key material covered in this chapter.

1 Why was the question of religious toleration regarded as so important in 1689?

2 What conditions were placed on Dissenters in order for them to achieve toleration?

3 In what ways did Dissenters continue to face restrictions after the passing of the Toleration Act?

4 What was the impact of the Toleration Act on dissenting clergy?

5 In what ways was Anglicanism still dominant after the Glorious Revolution?

6 Why did England become involved in the Nine Years' War?

7 What is the difference between Customs and Excise taxes?

8 What was the Land Tax and why was it important during the Nine Years' War?

9 What were the main features of the Million Loan and the Million Lottery?

10 Why can the Malt Lottery be considered a failure?

11 What were the main features of the Bank of England?

12 What was the Public Accounts Commission?

13 What were the limits to the success of the Public Accounts Commission?

14 What was the political impact of increased scrutiny of government finance?

15 What was the Civil List?

16 In what ways was military spending scrutinised by parliament?

Question practice: AQA A level

Essay question

1 To what extent was religious toleration achieved in the years 1678–1702?

EXAM HINT It is important that you analyse the extent to which religious toleration was achieved and do not present a descriptive version of events. This may be best done by looking at different religious groups across the period and assessing how each one fared.

Question practice: Pearson Edexcel A level

Interpretation question

1 In the light of the interpretations in Extracts 1 and 2, how convincing do you find the view that the Toleration Act of 1689 was effective in granting freedoms to Dissenters?

EXAM HINT Extract 1 states that toleration was achieved, while Extract 2 notes the continued operation of the Test and Corporation Acts. Use your own knowledge to reach a conclusion on the effectiveness of the Toleration Act.

EXTRACT 1

From G.N. Clark, *The Later Stuarts, 1660–1714*, Clarendon Press, 1963, p. 149.

The Anglicans are not to be blamed for the failure of the attempt at comprehension. The plan was, in any case, not tactfully brought forward. Before any clerical authority had been consulted, the houses of parliament were engaged in discussions about kneeling at the sacrament. The bill failed the pass the commons.

The nonconformists had to be content with another act, called the Toleration Act. This allowed protestant nonconformists who believed in the Trinity to have their own places of worship, provided they met with unlocked doors and certified the place of meeting to the bishop, the archdeacon, or quarter-sessions. They were allowed to have their own teachers and preachers, if these took certain oaths and declarations to which none of them had in fact any objection. The act, although it maintained the Restoration system of excluding the nonconformists from public affairs, may be taken as marking the point from which nonconformist life and thought were free to develop without interference by authority. There was another step towards toleration which has sometimes been given too much prominence in historians of freedom of thought. The Licensing Act of the Restoration, which had already been in abeyance for one short period in Charles II's time, ran out in 1694 and was not renewed. There was no strong desire to renew it: parliamentary opinion had ceased to regard ecclesiastical and administrative censorship as a guarantee for the public peace.

EXTRACT 2

From G.V. Bennett, 'Conflict in the Church' in G. Holmes, editor, *Britain after the Glorious Revolution, 1689–1714*, Macmillan, 1969, pp. 161–2.

The most delicate question of the year 1689 was that of the degree of toleration to be allowed to the dissenters. Its solution was strangely unsatisfactory. Two bills were introduced into the House of Lords: one for comprehension, the other for toleration. The two were designed to go together. On 14 March both bills received a second reading. But two days later King William made a grievous error. Without testing the opinion of his Tory ministers, he appeared in the House of Lords and proposed the abolition of the Test and Corporation Acts. Anglican anger and alarm were difficult to keep within bounds. Not only was the King's proposal overwhelmingly defeated, but the Comprehension bill itself was lost, and the Toleration bill alone went on to become law. No mention was made of permission for dissenting education; and nonconformists still laboured under the disabilities of the Test and Corporation Acts. The Toleration Act specifically laid it down that the old laws about attendance at church on a Sunday still applied to those who did not resort to a licensed meeting-house.

The result was that the meaning of the Toleration Act was always in doubt. Although the clergy professed to stand by its strict provisions, it was interpreted quite differently by the government and by the great majority of ordinary lay-people.

CHAPTER 9

Stuart society

In addition to the profound political and religious events that took place between 1660 and 1702, society itself experienced some dramatic changes. With a rising population came increasing urbanisation, as more people moved to towns in order to find work. This increased population, combined with political and economic uncertainty, led to an increase in poverty, and the Elizabethan Poor Laws were modified in an attempt to counter this. In contrast, members of the gentry flourished, enjoying the benefits of their involvement in politics and international trade. With the Restoration came important changes in the lives of women, although their role in public life continued to be severely restricted. These issues will be covered in this chapter under the following sections:

◆ Population trends

◆ Aristocracy, gentry, merchants and professionals

◆ Women and the poor

KEY DATES			
1650	The end of the 'long sixteenth century' period of population growth	**1665**	Beginning of the Great Plague
		1666	Great Fire of London
1662	Settlement Act	**1702**	Population reached 5.1 million

1 Population trends

■ *What was the impact of changing population trends in the late seventeenth century?*

Seventeenth-century British society and its economy have been described by historians in several contrasting ways:

■ a time of prosperity

■ a century of stagnation

■ a century of prolonged economic depression

■ an age of recession after an expanding sixteenth century

■ and, most commonly, a period of crisis associated with revolutionary political events.

This variety of interpretations has stemmed in part from the different criteria applied by historians when attempting to measure when changes in economy and society took place. Historians have long talked about the 'long sixteenth century' as a time of expansion and population growth beginning in 1520 and ending in 1650. Most historians agree that the second half of the seventeenth century was different in almost every respect from the first half.

The period up to 1650 saw a continuation of the average population increase of around 0.5 per cent per year that had begun in 1520. In this period the population of England had almost doubled. With an increasing population consuming the country's resources, prices and rents increased and wages remained static.

After 1650, **fertility rates** reached a low point and did not begin to rise again until 1680. The easing of population pressure as a result of decreased fertility ended the upward spiral of inflation and with a smaller labour force, employers offered higher wages. For those in employment, therefore, real incomes rose and the standard of living improved.

Demographics

Recent **demographic** projections based on parish records suggest that there were around 5.25 million people living in England and Wales in 1650, an increase from 4 million in 1600. The decline in growth after 1650 resulted in a population of 4.87 million in 1684 and an increase to 5.1 million by 1702. These projections

Table 9.1 Gregory King's estimate of population in England and Wales, 1688

Rank	Number of families (husband, wife and children)	Number of persons
Lords	186	6,920
Baronets	800	12,800
Knights	600	7,800
Esquires	3,000	30,000
Gentlemen	12,000	96,000
Persons in offices	10,000	70,000
Merchants	10,000	64,000
Persons in the law	10,000	70,000
Clergymen	10,000	52,000
Freeholders	180,000	980,000
Farmers	150,000	750,000
Persons in sciences and liberal arts	16,000	80,000
Shopkeepers and tradesmen	40,000	180,000
Artisans and handicrafts	60,000	240,000
Naval officers	5,000	20,000
Military officers	4,000	16,000
Common seamen	50,000	150,000
Labourers	364,000	1,275,000
Cottagers and paupers	400,000	1,300,000
Common soldiers	35,000	70,000
Vagrants	–	30,000
Total	**1,360,586**	**5,500,520**

are lower than the estimate of 5.5 million offered by the statistician **Gregory King** in 1688, although his approximations for the proportion of each group in society are broadly accurate (see Table 9.1, page 160).

Medical knowledge and midwifery practices were improving only very slowly and average life expectancy was around 35 years from birth. This figure resulted from the high levels of mortality among infants and children. King's most accurate and detailed study was of his hometown of Lichfield, and his findings here reflect wider trends in life expectancy (see Table 9.2 below). Just twelve per cent of the population were over the age of 50 when King carried out his survey in 1695 and 37 per cent were below the age of fifteen.

Impact of disease and mortality on population trends

The end of the period of population growth coincided with the restoration of the monarchy as well as a series of outbreaks of plague. The Great Plague of 1665–6 killed 69,000 people in London, up from 33,000 and 41,000 in the previous outbreaks of 1603 and 1625. When plague broke out, it affected towns much more acutely than the countryside. For example, when plague broke out

KEY FIGURE

Gregory King (1648–1712)

King is remembered as one of the first economic statisticians and held various positions in the civil service. He had access to the results of most government demographic surveys of the period and used this to make intelligent inferences about the total population in his writings.

Table 9.2 The ages of the population of Lichfield, 1695

Age (years)	Bachelors	Spinsters	Husbands	Wives	Widowers	Widows	Total
<5	167	201	–	–	–	–	368
5–10	227	183	–	–	–	–	410
10–15	156	127	–	–	–	–	283
15–20	136	170	–	1	–	–	307
20–25	44	125	15	22	–	–	206
25–30	49	72	38	69	1	3	232
30–35	9	25	68	81	7	5	195
35–40	6	22	105	87	7	29	256
40–45	1	3	52	43	4	16	119
45–50	1	1	66	46	6	13	133
50–55	1	2	21	22	3	12	61
55–60	4	–	37	38	8	25	112
60–65	2	1	17	23	3	22	68
65–70	–	1	21	10	8	41	81
70–75	–	–	2	1	2	9	14
75–80	1	–	–	–	4	5	10
80–85	–	–	–	–	1	2	3
85–90	–	–	–	–	1	1	2
90–95	–	–	–	–	–	–	0
>95	–	–	–	–	–	1	1
Total	804	933	442	443	55	184	2861

Source: D.V. Glass, Gregory King and the population of England and Wales at the end of the seventeenth century. *The Eugenics Review*, pp. 170–83, 1946.

in the West Riding of Yorkshire in 1644–5, the cloth-making centre of Leeds lost about one-third of its population. In the crowded dockyard town of Chatham, 900 people died out of a population of 3000 in 1665–6. In contrast, much of rural Kent remained virtually unaffected, despite its proximity to London. It should be noted that populations were usually able to recover relatively quickly after bouts of plague. In the parish of Eyam, Derbyshire, children who died in the plague were replaced within ten years by the surviving adult population having more children. When older members of a family died, the younger members often gained an earlier opportunity to marry and consequently had, on average, a larger number of children than they would have done otherwise.

Infectious diseases spread widely after 1660. Variously described by contemporaries as 'agues' or 'sweating sickness', these included influenza and malaria, and there was a large concentration of cases in the years 1678–80. Smallpox and typhus were endemic in London and other large towns in the period.

Historians have found that the spread of plague and other infectious diseases was linked to the condition of the harvest. Studies of the condition of skeletons in plague cemeteries have revealed that the disease was not indiscriminate and that people who were already malnourished were more likely to become infected. The mid-seventeenth century saw a series of bad harvests caused by catastrophic weather conditions, although this was the last of the most serious harvest failures. There were failures again in 1661, 1693 and 1697, although none appears to have had a major impact on mortality rates.

Fertility rates

Levels of fertility varied depending on the social status of individuals and where they lived:

- One group that bucked the trend of slowing population growth was the gentry elite, who continued to expand regardless of where they lived. Because the gentry had a higher standard of living, elite women could marry earlier and subsequently had more surviving children.
- Those living in the countryside were more likely to live longer and have more surviving children than those living in towns.
- Greater employment opportunities in towns resulted in a higher birth rate, as marriages generally took place earlier. However, the higher incidences of urban disease meant that fewer children survived to adulthood.
- Historians have discovered that at times when death rates were high, fertility rates were also high. This is because average ages for marriage tend to be lower at times of increased mortality.

Migration

Towns offering employment prospects were very attractive to migrants, and they were integral in contributing to growth. The population expansion experienced by London in the seventeenth century required at least 8000 new migrants per year throughout the seventeenth century in order to sustain these employment opportunities. As the number of deaths exceeded births in towns, large numbers of young migrants were needed to maintain growth.

- Economic migrants arrived from the **Low Countries**. Many were skilled weavers and settled in East Anglia (the economic impact of these migrants is discussed on pages 182–3). They were resented by local workers at first as they were given privileged access to resources; however, the innovative techniques and skills they brought with them ultimately had a positive impact on the indigenous workers. Fundamentally, the number of economic migrants from abroad was far too small to make any difference to rural and urban social structures.

- Internal migration was much more common than immigration. The traditional view that people lived their entire lives within a few miles of their place of birth has been questioned by historians in recent years. Cloth-worker migrants made up as much as 35 per cent of the population of Norwich, which became the second largest city in England. In Colchester, those employed in the textile industry rose from 26.4 per cent in 1619 to 40 per cent in 1699, in large part because of internal migration.

- Migration to find work was common, with up to 50 per cent of people moving within 20 miles of their birthplace at some point in their lives. Long-distance migration was more common among people at the upper and lower ends of the social scale. The very richest families possessed the resources to be able to move to London in order to take advantage of its many attractions, and the very poorest and the unemployed had no choice but to travel long distances to find work.

Towns

Wealth was concentrated in the south and east of England, in areas that possessed the most fertile **arable land**. This is also where the most prosperous towns were located. Away from the south and east, the towns that expanded most in the later seventeenth century tended to be ports or industrial centres, and their success was associated with the increased economic prosperity that came from a boom in international trade.

More people and more money in the booming towns led to increased prestige for local officials and the governing class, which in turn led to the construction of new public buildings, churches and grand town houses. In contrast, smaller market towns changed very little since they were unable to attract economic migrants in the same way as London and the industrial centres.

Ports

Port towns like Bristol (population 20,000 in 1670) and Liverpool (population 5000) were centres for the processing of goods imported from abroad. Liverpool also benefited from an influx of London merchants after the plague and Great Fire of London (see page 29). The ports in the west gradually developed at the

KEY TERMS

Low Countries The coastal lowland region of northwest Europe, consisting of modern-day Belgium, the Netherlands, Luxembourg and parts of northern France.

Arable land Land suited to growing crops.

expense of those on the east coast, thereby relieving congestion on the Thames and diminishing the significance of older ports such as Boston and King's Lynn. Newcastle, on the northeast coast, was able to survive this change because it was a centre for the coal extraction industry.

? SOURCE QUESTION

Study Source A. What did Liverpool and London appear to have in common, according to Fiennes?

SOURCE A

From *The Journeys of Celia Fiennes, 1685–1698*. Fiennes was from a gentry family and never married, giving her the freedom to travel widely. She visited every county in England and wrote a memoir recording her journeys.

Liverpool is built on the river Mersey. It is mostly newly built houses of brick and stone after the London fashion: the first original was a few fishermen's houses. It has now grown into a large fine town and but a parish and one Church, though there be 24 streets in it. There is a little chapel and there are a great many Dissenters in the town; it is a very rich trading town, the houses of brick and stone built high and even; there is an abundance of persons you see very well dressed and of good fashion. The streets are fair and long. It is London in miniature as much as ever I saw anything. There is a very pretty exchange. It stands on 8 pillars, over which is a very handsome town hall.

Mortality rates in towns

Disease spread easily in towns, in part because of the large numbers of migrants travelling from town to town who brought with them diseases from elsewhere. The dense population of towns combined with poor public hygiene increased the danger of serious epidemics. Parishes that had once been the centre of the domestic system of cloth production were amalgamated to make new industrial towns, such as Birmingham and Manchester. Some of the older towns saw very little population growth as their traditional industries went into decline. Across all towns, it has been calculated that populations could decrease by 25 per cent over a three-year period if they were affected by disease and food shortages.

London

In the middle of the seventeenth century, the population of London surpassed 400,000 for the first time. It was more than ten times larger than the next largest town and this rapid expansion experienced by London necessitated a need for 400 per cent more grain between 1600 and 1680. By 1700, nine per cent of England's total population lived in the capital, up from 2.25 per cent in 1520. London was ideally placed to power the later Stuart economy as it was at the heart of the road and shipping network and could support the increasing demand for goods.

Historians have pointed to the fact that London's economic prosperity grew as a result of several developments that happened to coincide:

■ The banking and insurance industries were based in London and were able to grow because of relatively safe trading conditions in the late seventeenth century.

ONLINE EXTRAS
Pearson Edexcel **WWW**

Get to grips with population trends by completing Worksheet 31 at **www. hoddereducation.co.uk/ accesstohistory/extras**

- London was the centre of the legal system and with an increasing number of gentry and merchants, more legal services were required.

- Investment in transport helped London to grow. The Thames, unlike many other rivers, was dredged and widened, and was navigable for most of its length. The system of turnpike roads (see page 181) initiated from 1663 was initially based around London.

- Skilled and educated workers were more likely to move to London as it offered more than simple **subsistence work**.

- The number of markets in London meant that it was the focal point for economic activity in the southeast. The national prices of livestock, grain and cloth were dictated by the London market after the Restoration.

SUMMARY DIAGRAM

POPULATION TRENDS

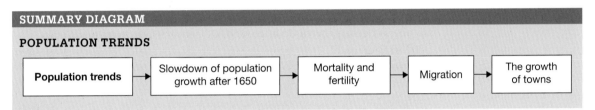

2 Aristocracy, gentry, merchants and professionals

- *What changes came about in the fortunes of the upper classes?*

The aristocracy had lost many of their privileges during the Civil Wars and Republic, in particular their right to sit in the House of Lords when it was temporarily closed down in 1649. In addition, many of those nobles who had supported the royalists in the 1640s had much of their property confiscated. In the reign of Charles II, however, their rights were frequently affirmed, and in some cases extended:

- Their houses could not be searched for arms without a warrant from the monarch.

- Lords in hereditary offices were not obliged to take the Test Act against Catholicism and transubstantiation imposed in 1673.

- They could not be charged in the courts for minor misdemeanours.

- As a witness, a lord gave evidence not on his oath, but on his honour, because all peers were of 'known integrity'.

- Anyone slandering a lord could be punished in the pillory and with the loss of his ears.

- When indicted for a criminal offence, lords were allowed to claim the right to be tried by their peers (their fellow lords). This normally meant that they were acquitted and consequently, after the Restoration, several lords were found not guilty of serious crimes such as murder and manslaughter.

Despite Charles's emphasis on maintaining a hierarchical society, the dividing line between nobility and gentry became increasingly difficult to define. It was possible for a member of the gentry to be wealthier and wield more influence than a noble. The nobility had also been subject to an economic decline during the reign of Elizabeth I, which was showing no sign of stopping. Inflation undoubtedly had a role in this, as did the high levels of spending expected from an aristocratic family. The overheads of noble landowners were high. They were expected to maintain servants and stables, provide hospitality to neighbours and embark on expensive visits to the Royal Court. The wealth to pay for all this was locked up in properties that were expensive to maintain and difficult to sell.

Gentry

Between the early Tudor period and the middle of the seventeenth century, the numbers of gentry increased by around 300 per cent. They were made up of 3000 'greater' and 12,000 'lesser' gentry. The greater gentry tended to have more extensive business interests and family connections outside their county than the lesser gentry and had more in common with the minor titled nobility. They controlled an immense amount of land and wealth by 1700.

The gentry had benefited greatly from the closure of the monasteries in 1540 and by buying up many of the former Church lands, although by 1600 the numbers of gentry exceeded the available supply of land, which slowed their expansion somewhat. Before the Reformation, around 35 per cent of land was held by the king or Church, but by 1700 this had fallen to just ten per cent. The nobility's share of land throughout this period remained static at twenty per cent. The gentry's share of land was as high as 45 per cent in 1700. Some held property in only one parish, while others owned several estates and manors, with the richest and most influential gentry effectively controlling the politics of an entire county. This was especially the case in counties such as Cheshire where there were few resident peers. Here, the Booth family was one of the richest in the county, and Sir George Booth used his influence in the northwest to muster support for Charles II in 1660 and was subsequently rewarded with a peerage after the Restoration.

Not all gentry families flourished after the Restoration. As the gentry grew in numbers and wealth there was a great demand for new titles to mark their enhanced status. Tudor monarchs had been careful not to confer too many new titles, but both Charles I and Charles II were generous in their patronage. In 1611, the new hereditary title of baronet was created, which could be purchased by any family that could prove they had had a coat of arms for three generations and could afford the fee of £1095 (later falling to £220). Between 1640 and 1688, the number of baronets increased from 400 to 800. This led to an 'inflation of honours' among the gentry, whereby knighthoods and other titles lost their significance.

After 1660, many of the lesser gentry had to sell up because they could not meet the costs of improving their estates to keep up with the greater gentry. This impacted most significantly on the gentry who had fought for the royalists in the Civil Wars and had become impoverished after having their estates confiscated. By the end of the century, the market for land was very restricted and it became difficult for the younger sons of the gentry or new entrants to acquire estates.

The pseudo-gentry

Many of the men involved in professional occupations (see page 168) could be classified as the pseudo-gentry. These were men who were from gentry families, but could not afford a country estate. They tended to move to London and became lawyers, financers, civil servants and merchants. Historians have referred to this group as the 'landless gentry' because, although they possessed enough wealth to lead the same leisured lifestyle as the elites, they tended to live in smaller properties in towns.

Merchants

The boom in international trade and the stabilisation of the economy after the Restoration led to increased opportunities for merchants. In the later seventeenth century, they can be placed into two categories:

- *Merchant tradesmen.* This group were already long established by the time of the Restoration and were generally involved in the manufacture of goods (normally textiles) and their subsequent transportation and sale. Their lives were relatively itinerant and it was common for merchant tradesmen to be questioned by constables and justices of the peace (JPs) to ensure that they were not vagrants. They benefited from a consumer boom after 1650 that had resulted from improved trading conditions, and some opened shops and factories.

- *International merchants.* These merchants, who were generally based in London, were involved in trading with the colonies of North America and the Far East. Many had connections with the East India Company (see pages 189–90) and other international trading organisations. Some were the younger sons of the gentry.

The number of merchants grew from 34,000 to 64,000 between 1580 and 1688, and those involved in international trade benefited from the growth of London and other port towns, such as Bristol and Liverpool. It was possible for merchants to acquire a level of wealth that matched members of the gentry and some married into elite landholding families. In London, a small but extremely wealthy class of merchants developed. Many of them entered public office as aldermen and mayors and some received knighthoods for their commercial success and public service. Although acquiring large estates in the countryside was becoming more difficult, the ultimate aspiration of many London merchants was to join the ranks of the gentry and provide their children with a scholarly education.

The professional classes

A process of specialised urban employment led to the development of modern professions. Previously, the most notable and recognised profession had been that of the clergy:

- Physicians were given higher status by their incorporation into a Royal College (1663). Aspiring doctors now had to satisfy and be certified by the Bishop of London, who was assisted by a panel of experts.

- Lawyers were members of one of the oldest learned professions. Many of the younger sons of gentry families were admitted to the **Inns of Court** to train in the law. As many as 90 per cent of students admitted in the later Stuart period were from gentry and noble families.

- As the wealth and living standards of the gentry and merchants increased, there was a new demand for new buildings and a generation of master architects became extremely successful in the 1660s and 1670s.

The Royal Society and the development of intellectual understanding

With an increasing number of gentry and merchants having the opportunity to pursue leisurely interests and Charles II's personal interest in science, the Restoration became a period of increased activity for intellectuals and scientists. The Royal Society was founded in 1660 and received a royal charter from the King. Its aim was to encourage the development and use of science for the benefit of humanity.

The Royal Society was responsible for the publication of the first scientific journal, *Philosophical Transactions*, which began in 1665. For the first time, a critically reviewed publication became widely accessible and the articles included in it acted as a stimulus for wider debate and challenge. It had an international appeal and thinkers from across Europe were able to engage with, and respond to, the research being carried out by members of the society.

Many of its early members were **polymaths** who had an interest in a wide variety of subjects. They included:

- Robert Boyle (1627–91), who is regarded as one of the founders of modern chemistry, but who also wrote widely on religion, biology and physics.

- John Wilkins (1614–72), a clergyman who became Bishop of Chester. As a founding member of the society, Wilkins was instrumental in formulating one of its guiding principles: that the society would be open to religious Nonconformists. This was in contrast to Oxford and Cambridge Universities, which were dominated by Anglicans.

KEY TERMS

Inns of Court The four legal societies given the right to confer the title of barrister on law students.

Polymath Someone who possesses significant knowledge about a wide variety of subjects.

ONLINE EXTRAS Pearson Edexcel **WWW**

Test your understanding of aristocracy, gentry, merchants and professionals by completing Worksheet 32 at **www.hoddereducation. co.uk/accesstohistory/extras**

- Perhaps its most famous member was Isaac Newton (1642–1727), who conducted much research including notable work on gravity, light, acoustics and colour. Both Newton and Boyle, as well as other members of the society, fruitlessly practised alchemy (the attempt to turn base metals into gold) in addition to their scientific work. Newton also became obsessed with finding hidden codes in the Bible and believed strongly in **numerology**.

- John Locke (1632–1704) followed the tradition established by Francis Bacon of practising **inductive reasoning**. He is noteworthy for his promotion of what is now known as empiricism, the idea that the mind is blank at birth and is filled through experience alone.

SUMMARY DIAGRAM

ARISTOCRACY, GENTRY, MERCHANTS AND PROFESSIONALS

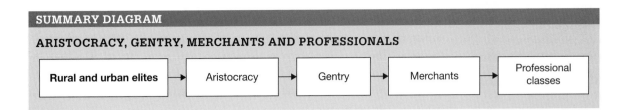

Rural and urban elites → Aristocracy → Gentry → Merchants → Professional classes

---

3 Women and the poor

- *Did the condition of women and the poor improve in the later Stuart era?*

Two groups who had progressed little in the early Stuart period were women and the poor. Some progress was made in the lives of both of these groups, but their fortunes were still mixed, at best.

The poor

Although population growth had slowed by the time of the Restoration, competition for work led to an increase in poverty. By the 1670s, around one-third of people were reliant on basic subsistence work and were at risk of ruin if they experienced a bad harvest or a period of unemployment. The poor can be divided into two groups:

- The settled poor were those who were established in one parish and did not relocate in order to beg or find work. They made up around one-quarter of the population.

- The vagrant poor were those who wandered from parish to parish in order to beg or find employment. Gregory King estimated that there were 30,000 vagrants in 1688, which was around 0.6 per cent of the population.

Elizabethan legislation had laid the foundations of a system of poor relief in an Act of 1601 and important additions were made in the Poor Relief Act of 1662 (known as the Settlement Act). The 1601 Act treated vagrants as criminals and made provisions for those unable to work through disability or age. Parish officials, called overseers of the poor, were charged with the collection of poor relief taxes and were responsible for deciding who was entitled to poor relief. Begging for food was permitted only in a person's home parish. Vagrants could be sent to a **poorhouse**, whipped or expelled from a parish if they were found to be begging.

The Settlement Act, 1662

The Settlement Act stated that individuals who arrived in a parish and rented property worth less than £10 were liable to be sent back to their former place of settlement if they appeared likely to become a burden on the parish by claiming poor relief. Their former place of settlement was defined as the last place that the individual had lived for at least 40 days. In order for these individuals to claim poor relief, 'Settlement certificates' were introduced that helped to prove where a person's home parish was.

The new Act was justified on the grounds that there had been a spike in the number of vagrants to 80,000 since the turmoil of the Civil Wars in the 1640s, and it was claimed that vagrants had become adept at moving parishes until they had exhausted all the local resources they could, before moving on once more. The Act also introduced rewards of two shillings (10p) to anyone apprehending a vagrant or beggar.

There is much evidence to suggest that the generosity of the overseers of the poor varied considerably from parish to parish. Some parishes were fortunate enough to be well served by charitable trusts and **almshouses**, while others were at the mercy of unscrupulous JPs and overseers. The 1662 Act provided £4000 for the construction of a large poorhouse in London, but by 1669 it was rumoured that parts of it had been turned into an alehouse and that its funds had been embezzled to such an extent that the poor were being maintained by the private charity of London merchants rather than from poor relief taxes. Poor relief was still the most common topic of petitions presented to the quarter sessions after 1662. The petitions show that even people who appeared to meet the criteria for the receipt of poor relief were being denied it and, in many cases, had to obtain the support of local dignitaries or their minister to stand any chance of receiving help (as was the case in Source C, page 171).

KEY TERMS

Poorhouse Also known as a workhouse, an institution funded by parish taxes to provide accommodation for the poor.

Almshouse A house supported by charity to provide for the poorest and most vulnerable.

SOURCE QUESTION

Study Sources B and C. What appear to be the limits of the 1662 Settlement Act?

SOURCE B

The petition of John Gleave of Handford to the Cheshire Quarter Sessions, March 1678, quoted in Sharon Howard, editor, *Petitions to the Cheshire Quarter Sessions*, from *British History Online* (available at **www.british-history.ac.uk/petitions/cheshire/1678**).

The humble petition of John Gleave of Handford in the county of Chester, labourer.

Your petitioner, having a wife and three small children and his wife great [pregnant]

Chapter 9 Stuart society

again, is destitute of a habitation, having no place to live in. And they have lain in the lane [street] several nights to the great hazard and danger of his wife and children's lives, therefore your petitioner humbly prays your order to the overseers of the poor of Handford to provide some place for him. Your petitioner will ever pray for your honours.

[The petition was rejected by the judges.]

SOURCE C

The petition of Elizabeth Sadler of Hartford to the Cheshire Quarter Sessions, April 1678, quoted in Sharon Howard, editor, *Petitions to the Cheshire Quarter Sessions*, from *British History Online* (available at **www.british-history.ac.uk/petitions/cheshire/1678**).

The humble petition of Elizabeth Sadler of Hartford, spinster.

Your petitioner is a very weak and poor woman and by reason of a long and lingering sickness and many bodily infirmities, is altogether unable to maintain herself by her hand-labourers (as formerly she had done), without being chargeable to any [parish].

Your petitioner having nothing of her own to subsist on, nor having had any relief from the overseers of the poor of Hartford, nor being able to go abroad to seek her relief, is likely to starve for want, unless her necessitous condition be considered and relieved by this noble bench.

May it therefore please your honours that the overseers for the poor of Hartford shall afford and pay something weekly to your petitioner, to prevent her perishing. And your petitioner will ever pray for your honours.

Charity

The relative failure of both legislation and parish authorities to cope with the problem of poverty led to an increase in private charity and philanthropy. The London businessman Thomas Firmin began employing the poor in cloth-making from 1665 and opened a factory employing 1700 people. Children as young as three were taught to read and spin. Similar operations were active in Norwich, Bristol and Newcastle.

Had the lives of the poor improved by 1702?

Despite the variable success of poor relief at a local level, absolute destitution was virtually eradicated by the end of the seventeenth century. The number of people facing general hardship, however, increased in the period. There was still no remedy for the impact of seasonal underemployment, and illness and accidents regularly resulted in families facing temporary difficulties. Generally, wealthier members of a parish were content to pay the poor rates because it provided them with security and distinguished them from the poor. Because the system was organised at a parish level, it never became impersonal because the officials distributing the relief knew most of the recipients. In general, the parish authorities were sympathetic and were as generous as they could be with the money they received.

Women

While the Interregnum provided women with some new opportunities, such as the introduction of civil marriage (outside the Church of England) and an enhanced role in some of the more radical religious sects, the Restoration has generally been considered as a return to tradition and social order. The Act for the Relief of Maimed Soldiers (1662) introduced payments for the families of injured soldiers who had faithfully served Charles II and his father in the Civil Wars. The provision this made for war widows was far short of what had been provided under Cromwell, and in 1664 the Privy Council received a petition from 162 women, 'to save them from perishing, as the Act of Parliament had not provided for them'. Despite the return to traditional social structures, there were a number of developments in the role and rights of women after 1660.

Opportunities for women after 1660

Charles II became notorious for the large number of mistresses he kept. The potential rewards for joining his inner circle were huge. Court mistresses could earn enormous political influence, titles and honours for their children, as well as financial security. Women were still defined by their marital status, being classified as a maid (before marriage), wife or widow. However, in the later seventeenth century the term 'spinster' (meaning an unmarried woman) began to appear. The fact that some women did not marry at all is significant, although these women, who often lived on the fringes of their communities, were most likely to be accused of witchcraft. The Witchcraft Act, which imposed the death penalty for sorcery and consulting evil spirits, was not repealed until 1736, and witch trials were still common at the end of the Stuart era.

Financial opportunities

While women were married, they had very limited property rights, and were not allowed to enter into any contracts or make a will without the permission of their husbands. Unmarried women and widows, however, could earn their own money and own property. Before the Great Fire of London in September 1666, six of the 22 businesses on Pudding Lane (where the fire broke out) were owned by women. In the centre of Leicester in the 1660s there was an area called the 'women's market'.

Women participated in the investment opportunities that presented themselves in the later seventeenth century. Women comprised 37 per cent of the purchasers of tickets in the first private lottery of the 1690s, although in 1685 women held no more than four per cent of East India Company stock. Between 1660 and 1702, women were eight times more likely to invest in lotteries than in loans to the Crown and companies. The disproportionate involvement of women in lotteries is reflective of the fact that women who had very few opportunities to enrich themselves attempted to provide for themselves with a chance of independent wealth.

Women and religion

The 1650s had seen a flurry of radical religious activity that appeared to promise a more comfortable existence for women. One of the most radical of the sects, the Diggers, had advocated compulsory education for all, and the Quakers (see page 10) even opened schools to educate girls. While they were initially progressive in their acceptance of women, the Quakers reversed their stance by 1700 and prevented women from preaching in all but the most exceptional circumstances and increasingly began to hold separate meetings for men and women. Some women had become preachers in the 1640s and 1650s; however, the Church of England was still centuries away from allowing female voices to be heard. The restoration of the Anglican Church and the *Book of Common Prayer* in 1660 saw a woman's role in church revert to what it had been for centuries: subservient and obedient.

Women in the theatre

With the reopening of the theatres after the Restoration and Charles II's enthusiasm for the inclusion of women in performances, they were permitted to act on stage after 1660. Previously, female roles had been played by young boys. Perhaps the most famous actress of the era was **Nell Gwyn**, who became a mistress to Charles II from around 1670.

> **KEY FIGURE**
>
> **Nell Gwyn (1650–87)**
>
> Gwyn's origins are mysterious, but it is known that her father died in a debtors' prison and she moved with her mother to London, where she began acting at around thirteen or fourteen years of age. She performed a variety of roles including servants, courtiers and witty females. Gwyn conducted a long affair with Charles II and had two sons by him, who were both given peerages.

> **SOURCE QUESTION**
>
> Study Source D. How significant was the decision to allow women to act on stage after the Restoration?

SOURCE D

Portrait of Nell Gwyn, from the studio of Peter Lely, *c*.1675.

The Restoration was also the first era to see women become professional playwrights. Anne Finch (1661–1720) was a courtier and poet who also wrote plays in the 1680s. She wrote openly about what she saw as the moral duty of women to better themselves. **Aphra Behn** was one of the first women who could be classified as a professional playwright as she earned a living from writing. Although Behn became the most prolific female writer of the Restoration era, she was not the first to be published. In 1663, Katherine Phillips (1631–64) produced a translation of Pierre Corneille's tragedy *Pompey* for a popular performance in London.

Women in work

The slowing of population growth and the expansion of the economy offered greater opportunities for single women to find work. However, the hardening of negative male attitudes towards women after the restoration of traditional institutions, and the restrictions on education after 1660, made it very difficult for poorer women to obtain any formal education. As women could not access skilled training, they came to be regarded as a cheap source of labour. The kind of work taken up by women was monotonous and included spinning, knitting and basic agricultural work. Spinners could expect to earn two pence a day and women received four pence a day for agricultural work.

With growing prosperity among the upper classes came a renewed demand for domestic servants, and these jobs were filled almost exclusively by young women and girls. At the beginning of the century most servants were married men and women, although after 1660 it became fashionable to keep a large number of servants, and adolescent girls provided a cheap labour force. The expansion of this kind of employment has been viewed by historians as evidence of the worsening status of women, as it reinforced the idea that housework was the only appropriate type of female work.

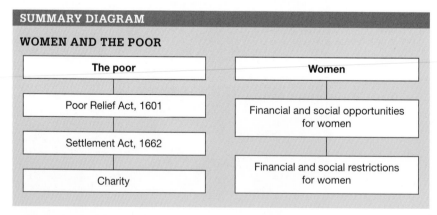

SUMMARY DIAGRAM

WOMEN AND THE POOR

The poor	Women
Poor Relief Act, 1601	Financial and social opportunities for women
Settlement Act, 1662	Financial and social restrictions for women
Charity	

CHAPTER SUMMARY

After many years of population growth and economic expansion, the period following the Restoration was marked by a slowdown of population and an increase in both wages and living standards. The population bounced back to the levels of the 1650s by the early eighteenth century, although there was no significant change to life expectancy. London continued to expand rapidly, despite the national slowdown in population growth, and this required a large number of migrants. Towns across England expanded more rapidly than the rate of population growth after 1650. A new class of urban merchants developed who owed their success to their involvement in international trading companies. Despite the success of the merchants, the aristocracy and gentry retained the most political power and status in society.

The political rights of women changed little after the Restoration, but the place of women in elite society was altered somewhat. Women could act on stage and it became more common for them to be published as playwrights and poets. The financial rights of women did not change, and they were still reliant on their husbands and fathers, although the number of independent, unmarried women did increase. By the time of the Restoration a basic system of poor relief existed, and this was modified in the 1662 Settlement Act.

Refresher questions

Use these questions to remind yourself of the key material covered in this chapter.

1 In what ways did population trends change after 1650?

2 What happened to the population of England in the seventeenth century as a whole?

3 What was the impact of disease and mortality on population trends?

4 Why did migration increase after 1660?

5 Why did towns grow in the southeast?

6 Why did ports flourish in the west of England?

7 Why were mortality rates high in towns?

8 Why did London grow after 1660?

9 In what ways were the nobility given privileged status after the Restoration?

10 What were the economic restrictions on the nobility?

11 What were the political and economic strengths of the gentry?

12 Why did the growth of the gentry begin to slow?

13 Who were the pseudo-gentry?

14 Why were merchants so successful in the late seventeenth century?

15 Why was there an increase in the number of professionals?

16 Why was the Settlement Act inadequate?

17 In what ways did women experience improved opportunities?

18 In what ways did women continue to face restrictions?

Question practice: Pearson Edexcel AS level

Essay questions

1 How far do you agree that opportunities for women improved in the years 1625–88?

EXAM HINT There were significant opportunities for women during the Civil War period but the Restoration brought back the traditional order of pre-Civil War times.

2 To what extent was migration responsible for fluctuating population trends in the years 1625–88?

EXAM HINT Examine the significance of Protestant migration from Europe to escape religious persecution. Other factors might include the high death rate during the Civil War and the plagues of the 1660s, and the trend towards later marriages.

3 How accurate is it to say that the lives of the poor improved in the years 1625–88?

EXAM HINT While the growing economy did help the poor overall, and Charles I's Books of Orders organised poor relief in parishes, rising unemployment resulted in an increase in homeless beggars and vagrants.

4 To what extent did the structure of society change in the years 1625–88?

EXAM HINT The period saw the gradual decline of the nobility and the rise of the commercial and merchant classes. Consider also the rise of an educated gentry class whose wealth depended on non-landed income.

CHAPTER 10

The Stuart economy

The economy of England was in a depressed state until the early 1650s and then began to improve rapidly. This is despite the fact that the structure of the economy had changed little since the Tudor era. With a slowdown of population growth came the end of the rapid inflation experienced in the first half of the seventeenth century and, as a result, employment opportunities and the standard of living for most people improved. In addition, London became the centre of a world market and a hub for a new breed of bankers and merchants. The themes that will be discussed in this chapter are:

◆ Agriculture

◆ The cloth trade

◆ Banking and international trade

KEY DATES

1659	The first cheque was drawn
1660	The second Navigation Act passed
1663	Turnpike Act

1674	Peace with the Dutch after loss of the Third Anglo-Dutch War
1675	Publication of the first road atlas
1688	Lloyd's coffee house opened

1 Agriculture

■ *What changes came about to agricultural techniques and transport infrastructure in the later Stuart period?*

With around 90 per cent of people employed in agriculture and a population that had been steadily growing in the early Stuart period, the efficiency of agricultural production was foremost in the minds of farmers and landowners. Agricultural practices had changed very little since medieval times but in the seventeenth century, farmers were forced to diversify and innovate in order to meet demand.

Enclosure

The enclosure of land – whereby several smaller holdings were consolidated into larger farms – had been popular in the sixteenth century. Many landlords found that it was more profitable to produce wool, rather than crops, and land was thus converted from arable to pasture to maximise the number of sheep that could be sustained on one farm. Enclosure continued in the early Stuart period, but by 1660 the lower price of wool helped to restore the balance between pasture and arable. The enclosures of the later seventeenth century, therefore, had been dictated mainly by the suitability and most profitable utilisation of natural resources. In many of the counties of the southeast, the soil and climate were more suited to the growing of wheat and rye, and some very large enclosed farms were created as a result. In the north, enclosures continued to take place to create large cattle and sheep farms.

By 1660, the counties wholly or partially enclosed included Essex, Kent, Hereford, Middlesex, Somerset and Durham, and despite significant anti-enclosure rioting earlier in the century and the loss of 7 million acres of **common land** since 1500, the amount of violence had decreased markedly. Some counties bucked this trend. In Leicestershire, enclosure was only just beginning to gather pace and there was significant disquiet, particularly among small farmers who experienced a decline in profits. In other counties where enclosure was not widespread, the **open-field system** continued to dominate and some of these counties were very successful centres of agricultural innovation. They included Northamptonshire, Oxfordshire, Cambridgeshire, Lincolnshire and Bedfordshire.

Land reclamation

The reclamation of marshy land, particularly in the Fens of East Anglia, helped to increase the amount of agricultural land available. Around 300,000 acres were drained and reclaimed in parts of Norfolk, Suffolk, Cambridgeshire and Northamptonshire. In Lincolnshire, around 25,000 acres were reclaimed for arable farming, enabling the county to make up for some of the prosperity lost as a result of a declining wool trade. Reclaimed land was almost invariably enclosed.

Attempts had been made to drain parts of the region in the early Stuart period, but it was the Dutchman **Cornelius Vermuyden**, with the assistance of 4000 Dutch drainage experts, who finally achieved this vast undertaking after 1650. Wind and water mills were used to pump water and mud from both rivers and marshland. Canals and drainage channels were dug by hand by the Dutch engineers and local labourers to divert water into rivers and the sea. Contemporaries noted that the reclaimed land had become particularly fertile. The diarist John Evelyn visited Norfolk in 1670 and noted that weeds grew as high as a man on horseback. In Source A (below), Jonas Moore, who worked on the draining of the Fens, gives a glowing description of the impact of land reclamation.

KEY TERMS

Common land Land that can be used by all residents of a parish to graze animals and collect firewood.

Open-field system The traditional medieval system of farming. Land was divided into strips and managed by tenants or peasants, with areas set aside for common grazing.

KEY FIGURE

Cornelius Vermuyden (1595–1677)

After training in the Netherlands as an engineer, Vermuyden moved to England and worked on several projects on the River Thames. He came to the attention of Charles I and from the 1630s the majority of his work involved the drainage of land in East Anglia.

? SOURCE QUESTION

Study Source A. What benefits did Moore believe that land reclamation had brought to East Anglia?

SOURCE A

From Jonas Moore, *History of the Great Level of the Fens*, 1685. Moore was a mathematician and surveyor who was closely involved in the draining of the Fens.

I sing floods muzzled and the ocean tamed,
Luxurious rivers governed and reclaimed
Water with banks confined as in a gaol
'Til kinder sluices let them go on bail

Streams curbed with bridles, taught to obey
And run as straight as if they saw their way.

When these fair fields are ploughed, then cast with me
How large, how fat the livings here must be.
Thrive backwards and too dearly purchase wit,
Leave off these lotteries, and here take your lot,
The profit's certain, and with ease 'tis got.

Agricultural techniques

With an increasing population significantly more food was required.
Landowners experimented and introduced innovative new techniques in
order to increase their yield. Nutritious and nitrogen-rich plants such as
sainfoin, clover and **lucerne** were mixed with grasses in order to replenish soil
and provide more food for livestock. This kind of experimentation required
investment, and consequently it was on the larger enclosed farms that this
normally took place. Other improvements advocated by writers of the period
included:

- Charring surface soil and scattering ash as a fertiliser.

- Seeds were usually soaked before sowing in order to secure greater fertility
  and protect them from animals.

- The use of turnips, particularly a frost-resistant variety from the Netherlands,
  became more widespread. They helped to provide winter food for cattle and
  acted as a **cleaning crop**.

- Potatoes were planted in some areas, although the English disliked them
  so much that a contemporary recipe book dedicated to their use advocated
  cooking them with rich herbs and spices to disguise their flavour.

> **KEY TERMS**
>
> **Sainfoin** A drought-resistant grazing crop.
>
> **Lucerne** A grazing crop, which converts large amounts of nitrogen from the air to enrich soil.
>
> **Cleaning crop** Any crop suited to growing in place of weeds in order to 'clean' the soil.

Table 10.1 Land use in 1500 and 1700 (millions of acres)

Land use	1500	1700
Arable	9.0	11.0
Wheat	1.8	1.4
Rye	0.2	0.9
Barley	1.5	1.9
Oats	1.3	1.2
Beans/peas	1.2	1.3
Turnips	0	0.4
Clover	0	0.5
Potatoes	0	0.1
Pasture	4.0	9.0
Common land	20.0	13.0

- Crops that aided industry were grown in larger numbers. These included flax for the manufacture of linen, hemp for rope-making and hops for brewing beer.
- In the 1660s, large four-wheeled farm wagons began to replace two-wheeled carts. This change was necessary to cope with greater harvests. By the 1690s, twenty per cent of farmers in Oxfordshire used wagons, which would increase to 34 per cent in the 1720s.

Water meadows

Although water meadows had been used since the early sixteenth century, their use expanded rapidly in the late seventeenth century. They worked by diverting water from rivers or streams to fields, using a network of gates and dams. This irrigation dampened the soil all year round, reducing the chance of frost in early spring and encouraging grass to grow earlier in the year. This ensured that animals were well fed for longer, and the success of this system is reflected in an increased number of working and non-working animals. For example, the number of working horses doubled between 1600 and 1700.

Market gardens

The huge demand for food for London and other large towns resulted in increased investment in infrastructure in order to transport agricultural produce. In addition, market gardens began to develop in the immediate vicinity of London, in places like Fulham and Whitechapel. As they were located close to such a large population centre, they were able to provide food that was fresher than it would otherwise have been.

Limits to agricultural change

The improvements in agricultural techniques were sometimes openly derided. Tenants were not always in favour of agricultural improvements since they might provide a pretext for increased rent. In the Commons in 1673, a landlord declared that he had no interest in them because by increasing production they lowered prices. Farmers after 1660 were urged to export grain overseas so that prices in England would rise as less grain would be available. After 1673, farmers received financial incentives for doing so. This effort to maintain prices proved to be in vain, as prices fell steadily between 1660 and 1750.

Reclaimed land became more prone to flooding as the level of the land was lowered, and by 1700 flooding became commonplace. Despite an increase in large farms, the open-field system continued to provide considerable yields in some areas that did not witness extensive enclosures. Small tenants suffered as a result of enclosure and they could not afford to diversify and experiment in the same way as the owners of larger specialised farms. At the expense of small tenants, the number of wage-dependent agricultural labourers grew. They were invariably employed on the estates of large landowners, meaning that this kind of employment was relatively secure. Around 240,000 of these labourers, however, also had to work in the cloth industry in order to maintain an adequate income.

Improvements to infrastructure

With the growth of national markets for agricultural produce and manufactured goods, improvements were required to road and water transport. Some of these were undertaken by county officials, but much of the money to fund these schemes was provided by merchants and country gentry who saw opportunities to make a profit.

Water transport

The London market thrived in part because of the abundance of agricultural land to the west. Transporting goods on the River Thames was the most efficient way of reaching the London market and the river was dredged and widened in order to facilitate this. In the Fenland counties that had witnessed much of the marsh drainage, rivers were deepened and straightened and artificial banks were created. Elsewhere, fifteen Acts of parliament under Charles II and William III made provisions for the cleaning of rivers, with local taxes levied to pay for the work.

Road transport

Traditionally, roads had been the responsibility of local parishes and most were in a poor state of repair in the first half of the seventeenth century. The exceptions to this were the routes that followed the old Roman roads, which were passable by cart throughout the year. The **Turnpike** Act was passed in 1663, allowing for the creation of new toll roads. The first road to be turnpiked by the Act was the Great North Road from Hertfordshire to Huntingdonshire. The money collected in tolls helped to pay for the upkeep of these roads and they were invaluable in linking major market towns. Their spread in the later Stuart period was limited, however, and none yet existed outside the southeast.

The development of the stagecoach was also important for communication, and the first coaches from London to Bristol appeared in 1657. John Ogilby's *Britannia* (1675) served as England's first road atlas. Designed to be used by merchants, it provided detailed directions from London to the major ports and market towns. Older roads that were essential for trade were repaired via Acts of parliament and additional county taxes were normally levied for the period that the work was carried out.

> **KEY TERM**
>
> **Turnpike** A gate or barrier that prevented passage on a road until a toll had been paid.

SOURCE B

An Act for making navigable the Rivers of Wye and Lugg in the county of Hereford, 1695. This was one of several Acts of parliament designed to benefit trade by widening and cleaning rivers.

The free and open navigation upon the Rivers Wye and Lugg and the streams falling into them may be a great increase of public trade and beneficial to ease the conveyance of timber for the supply of His Majesty's navy. From the city of Hereford to the city of Bristol there should be boats fitted for passengers as well as merchandise weekly to go to and again between the said cities … The sum to be

SOURCE QUESTION

Study Sources B and C (page 182). Why do you think the government was willing to invest significant amounts of money in transport schemes in the later Stuart period?

taxed on the said county shall not exceed the sum of three hundred and seventy pounds [per month] … with the payment for demolishing weirs [structures designed to alter the flow of a river], mills and iron-works and clearing the said rivers from all obstructions that may hinder the passage of barges and boats.

SOURCE C

An Act for repairing the highway between Reigate in the county of Surrey and Crawley in the county of Sussex, 1696.

The lanes herein mentioned are in a ruinous and dangerous state, and several parishes are unable themselves to repair them. [The road provides] great trade and commerce to the county of Sussex and is almost impassable for above three miles in length, insomuch that it has become dangerous to all persons that pass those ways. It may be enacted that several persons may be appointed as surveyors … to consider the defects and the best method that can be used for repairing the lanes. The surveyors are empowered to appoint such persons to come and work in the said places as they think reasonable and they shall pay such labourers according to the usual rate of the country.

ONLINE EXTRAS
Pearson Edexcel **WWW**

Ensure you have grasped the key features of agricultural change by completing Worksheet 34 at **www. hoddereducation.co.uk/ accesstohistory/extras**

SUMMARY DIAGRAM

AGRICULTURE

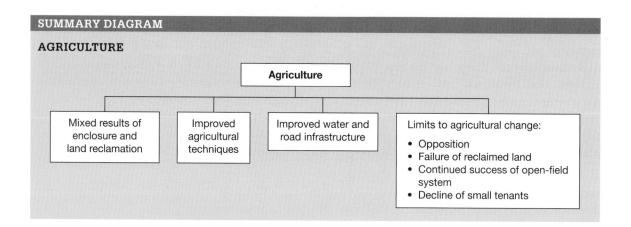

2 The cloth trade

■ *How successful was the cloth industry in the later Stuart period?*

The cloth trade had been responsible for the growth of the English economy in the medieval period and, like agriculture, the basic system of production had changed very little in the Tudor and early Stuart period.

The domestic system and the New Draperies

Most parts of England contributed to the cloth industry in some way. Cloth had a long tradition of being worked as a **cottage industry**. By the seventeenth century, there was a variety of occupations that had been created by the working of wool. Spinners made the yarn, weavers wove the cloth, **fullers** thickened and felted it, and dyers coloured the final product. Much of the work that took place in people's homes involved spinning and weaving and was an integral part of the so-called putting-out system. This involved merchants buying the raw wool, supplying it to cottage workers to weave and then selling the final product after paying the workers for their labour.

Each region supplied a distinctive type of product, and earlier in the seventeenth century, several varieties, known as the New Draperies, were introduced. These were particularly fine and resembled the textiles found in the Low Countries. The arrival of Dutch weavers in East Anglia during a time of crisis for the cloth industry in the sixteenth century assisted the industry. The new arrivals were able to teach local workers to produce new types of cloth. English apprentices learned new skills and techniques and the New Draperies rejuvenated the textile industry and provided lucrative exports to Europe. In 1685, the writer John Aubrey wrote that 'the art of spinning is so much improved within these last 40 years that one pound of wool makes twice as much cloth as it did before the Civil War'.

Declining importance of wool

Sheep and wool were of national importance in the medieval period, and throughout the fifteenth and sixteenth centuries, wool had proved to be England's most profitable commodity and essential to the cloth industry. Despite the introduction of the New Draperies, overproduction and the introduction of Spanish wool to the European market diminished the importance of English wool in the mid-seventeenth century. This led to a considerable fall in price and to make matters worse, Ireland became a major exporter of wool towards the end of the century, with Irish merchants offering cheaper prices than the English. Cloth accounted for 92 per cent of London's exports in 1640, reducing to 74 per cent in 1660 and 72 per cent in 1700. Most of the other 28 per cent of exports in 1700 was made up of re-exports, mainly consisting of products from America and the East (especially sugar and tobacco). During the recurrent depressions of the later seventeenth century, many complaints reached parliament from workers in the cloth industry.

Government strategies to improve the cloth trade

Charles II's government passed laws prohibiting the export of wool to France and several other European countries. The justification for this stemmed from a belief that English wool was of superior quality to wool from elsewhere in Europe, and that freely exporting it would endanger the English cloth trade by providing other countries with good material with which to work. English cloth was sought after mainly because of its variety, from the coarse wool that came from Suffolk sheep to the very fine type found in Herefordshire. Government attempts to keep English wool for English weavers were not entirely successful, as large amounts were smuggled abroad. From this smuggled wool, France was able to work cloth that was re-exported to England and became highly sought after.

The government were well aware that the cloth trade gave employment to many people of both sexes in every corner of England and further action was taken to protect the industry. Native wool faced competition from materials such as calico and muslin (produced from Indian cotton), linen (from flax) and silk (from silkworms). When Louis XIV revoked the Edict of Nantes in 1685 that had formerly provided protection to Protestant **Huguenots**, many of them settled in England. Those new arrivals who were particularly encouraged to migrate had worked in the French cloth industry and in particular with silk. This enabled a silk industry to develop in England. New methods of dyeing were also adopted as a result of Huguenot influence. To further maintain the cloth industry, Acts were passed in the reign of Charles II stating that shrouds were to be made only with wool, and that coach interiors could be lined only with English cloth. In 1676, **medley cloth** was given a much-needed promotion by Charles II, who wore it during a depression to encourage its trade.

Innovations in the cloth industry

The domestic system of cloth production had been in existence for hundreds of years and had essentially changed very little. In an increasing number of areas, village weavers had begun to sell direct to their customers rather than trading with a merchant, and this increased their economic security. Most domestic workers were also supported by their involvement in subsistence farming in the summer months. Labour-saving devices promised to increase the amount of cloth that could be produced. The Dutch frame-knitting machine was introduced after the Restoration and, in 1675, weavers in the east end of London rioted against increased mechanisation in fear of their jobs. The Duke of Monmouth was ordered to suppress the riots and the Attorney General consulted on whether to charge the arrested men with high treason, demonstrating how highly regarded the cloth trade was in the national psyche.

The condition of the cloth trade in 1702

In 1678, the price of wool reached its lowest point in the century at five pence per pound. From here it rose for the next two decades. This rise was due to various causes, including increased exports to Spain and Portugal. Between 1670 and 1700, exports to Portugal trebled in value, in part because of improved relations after Charles II's marriage to Catherine of Braganza. The increase in smuggling, after government attempts to restrict exports to France, actually benefited the price of wool. This was because the smuggled wool became sought after on the Continent and the resultant worked cloth was in high demand in southeast England.

KEY TERMS

Huguenots French Protestants who formed a minority in the sixteenth and seventeenth centuries. They were provided with significant religious and political autonomy before Louis XIV demanded in 1685 that they convert to Catholicism or leave France.

Medley cloth Cloth created by first dyeing wool before spinning to mix the colours.

ONLINE EXTRAS **WWW**
Pearson Edexcel

Test your knowledge of the cloth trade by completing Worksheet 35 at **www.hoddereducation.co.uk/accesstohistory/extras**

SOURCE D

A 'calico printer' at work in London in 1685, from a contemporary woodcut. English woollen cloth was increasingly challenged by the introduction of calico, linen and silk in the late seventeenth century.

SOURCE QUESTION
Study Source D. In what ways do you think the English cloth industry was affected by the diversification of the market?

SUMMARY DIAGRAM

THE CLOTH TRADE

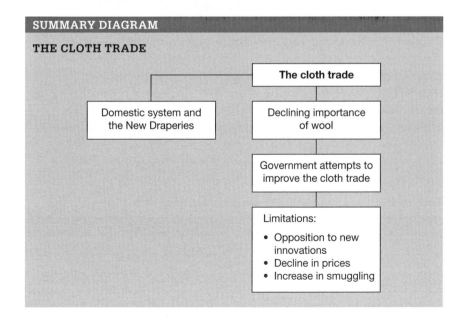

3 Banking and international trade

■ *Why did international trade develop rapidly in the later seventeenth century?*

Since the first European possessions had been claimed in the New World in the late fifteenth century, British merchants had been involved in international trade and this became increasingly lucrative in the Tudor period. However, in the early seventeenth century, the Dutch had begun to dominate many of the markets that had been under British control.

International trade in the late seventeenth century

In 1660, England's trading position looked relatively bleak.

- The Dutch had developed a monopoly on transatlantic trade and had entrenched themselves in the East Indies.
- The Dutch had an abundance of cheap capital and Amsterdam became a major financial centre.
- The yield from the Customs was little different from what it had been in 1640.
- The East India Company, which had been founded in 1600 to promote trade with the East Indies, was increasingly coming into conflict with Dutch traders.
- The African Company, established to promote trade in west Africa, was losing its foothold on the African coast, to the Dutch.

The passing of Navigation Acts (see page 17) in the early 1660s, as well as the growth of banking and an expansion in colonial activity, helped international trade to increase. Both imports and exports increased in the later seventeenth century. The value of imports increased from £2.7 million to £5.8 million between 1640 and 1701 and exports rose from £2.3 million to £4.4 million. These increases were reflective partly of the expansion of British colonies in America and of improved trade in the East. The proportion of imports from America increased from less than one per cent in 1622 to nineteen per cent at the end of the period.

Table 10.2 Estimated value of English overseas trade, 1640–1701

Year	International exports	Imports
1640	£2,300,000	£2,700,000
1663	£3,000,000	£4,000,000
1699–1701	£4,400,000	£5,800,000

Table 10.3 Sources of imports, 1622–1701

Year	Northern Europe	Southern Europe	America	Asia
1622	63%	31%	<1%	6%
1663	45%	31%	24% (combined)	
1699–1701	41%	27%	19%	13%

Table 10.4 Products imported to England, 1622–99

Year	Textiles	Textile raw materials	Other manufactured goods	Other raw materials	Sugar and tobacco	Other food and drink
1622	41%	14%	4%	15%	2%	24%
1663	32%	17%	5%	18%	10%	18%
1699	25%	21%	5%	14%	15%	20%

The North American colonies

Newfoundland (in present-day Canada) was claimed as the first English overseas colony in 1583 and was an important centre for fishing. It was estimated by the government in 1669 that the fisheries there might have produced £50,000 per year in Customs duties and provided employment to 10,000 sailors. These results were never achieved, however, as Newfoundland was not under a settled government in the period. The French held the best harbours in the region and this caused hostility between French settlers and English fishermen.

Other English colonies developed along the east coast of North America, stretching from Newfoundland in the north to Carolina in the south. In 1699, America took thirteen per cent of all English exports. This later rose to 25 per cent in 1752.

Virginia and the tobacco trade

There was a steady increase in the social and economic importance of tobacco in the seventeenth century. Early Stuart monarchs disliked tobacco, but Charles II did much to promote it. Charles I had made repeated efforts to induce the plantation owners of Virginia to turn their attention to other commodities, and high tariffs were placed on imports. After the Restoration, it was at last recognised that the plantations of Virginia were especially suited to growing a crop from which a large revenue could be obtained.

Virginia thus became the most important colony on the mainland of North America. Labour was supplied by **indentured servants** and an increasing number of slaves. Tobacco exports increased from 3 million lbs in 1638 to 25 million lbs in the 1680s and as the trade flourished, taxes in Virginia were frequently paid in tobacco. During the reign of James II tobacco was overproduced, which, coupled with a shortage of shipping, led to economic distress for a number of years before the economy was stabilised after the Glorious Revolution.

KEY TERM

Indentured servants
Workers contracted to provide labour without pay for a fixed period of time. When the fixed period had ended, most were freed.

In 1671, the tobacco trade employed 140 ships of between 150 and 500 tons and the Customs benefited by around £100,000 per year.

Maryland

The colony of Maryland was given its first charter in 1632. It initially became a haven for Catholics fleeing persecution in England, but later, Protestants of all sects were encouraged to settle in order to counteract the Catholic influence. Its prosperity was hampered somewhat by continual hostility between Catholics and Puritans. With few established ports, Maryland suffered even more than Virginia from downturns in the economy. It had a population of 20,000 in 1676 and indentured servants there were offered better conditions than in other colonies. After four years' service they were freed with 50 acres of land, a kit of tools and three suits of clothes.

The Carolinas

The earliest grant of land in the Carolinas – located to the south of Maryland and Virginia – was in 1629, and the first charter was given in 1663. It seems that the original proprietors, who included Anthony Ashley Cooper, intended to attract settlers from Barbados. This was not initially successful as, by 1672, only about 450 had settled in the colony. To encourage growth, the authorities in Carolina secured a stop on Customs duties on wine and silk exported to England for seven years. In addition, promises of religious toleration and equality under the law encouraged 3000 settlers between 1679 and 1688.

New England

The colonies of Massachusetts, Plymouth, Connecticut and New Haven were well-established centres of Puritan settlement by 1660. The Massachusetts Bay Colony was established in 1629 and the New England colonies were all relatively prosperous after the Restoration. Trade was buoyant, particularly with other colonies, and a fleet of 200 merchant ships sailed out of the harbours of Massachusetts and Connecticut by 1670. The colonies were never as lucrative as Virginia and Maryland, although New England merchants became adept at handling the produce of others and transporting it large distances.

The Dutch colony of New Amsterdam, wedged between English possessions in New Jersey and Connecticut, was always a likely target for an attempted capture. Having obtained a royal charter for the operation in March 1664, James, Duke of York, organised an attack and the town fell in August. It was soon renamed New York.

The first governor, Richard Nicholls, allowed the Dutch population to remain and New York was not immediately granted a representative assembly. Instead, all appointments were made by the governor. This caused residents to refuse payment of Customs duties and this caused major disruption to the economy. In 1682, an assembly was finally granted by James.

Pennsylvania

Pennsylvania – named by Charles II in honour of founder William Penn's father – was founded in 1680–2. Penn intended the colony to provide a refuge for his fellow Quakers and its constitution secured religious freedom for all Protestant sects. A shipping industry developed and the fertile land provided a significant amount of grain that became one of its primary exports.

The Caribbean

In the Caribbean, two groups of islands known as the Windward Islands and the Leeward Islands had been colonised by the British:

- The Windward Islands comprised Barbados, St Lucia, St Vincent and Tobago. By far the most important was Barbados, which had a population of 20,000 British planters and 40,000 slaves in 1668. With a militia of 6000 men it was the best fortified of the islands.

- The Leeward Islands comprised Antigua, Montserrat, Nevis and St Christopher.

- A governor-in-chief of all the Caribbean colonies was appointed and the British plantation owners were expected to pay a 4.5 per cent export duty.

Jamaica

The largest and most important of the English colonies was Jamaica, which had an area of over 4000 square miles. It had been captured from Spain in 1655 and its climate suited the production of sugar and coffee. It was given special encouragement from the government and its exports were freed from Customs dues for five years in 1663. Settlers were given 30 acres on the condition that they served in a militia and reserved one-twentieth of mineral rights to the Crown. These incentives produced results. In 1670, 209,000 acres were under cultivation, with 57 sugar refineries in operation.

Sugar

Sugar supplemented the native honey in England and helped to provide a more varied diet, and it became very popular in the middle of the seventeenth century. It was produced in the Caribbean colonies, but overproduction and competition from French and Portuguese sugar colonies led to a steady fall in price after 1660. Between 1660 and 1685, the wholesale price of sugar reduced from 40 shillings per 100 lbs to 20 shillings.

The East India Company

During the early years of Charles II's reign, the East India Company maintained a fleet of 28 ships, of which fourteen were sent to Asia each year. The Company had gained a foothold in China and had trading connections with Persia (present-day Iran) and India.

Bombay (present-day Mumbai) in India was acquired for the Crown in accordance with Charles II's marriage to Catherine of Braganza. Through this gift, the Portuguese intended to encourage English cooperation against the Dutch in the East Indies, while the English intended mainly to develop the commercial possibilities of this new acquisition. In 1662, 500 troops arrived to take possession and Bombay soon became a drain on the exchequer. In December 1667, Charles granted it to the East India Company. Elsewhere in India the foundations of British power were being established. The fort at Madras (present-day Chennai) was strengthened in 1677. The East India Company had a station at Bantam in Java (the largest island of present-day Indonesia), from which it was hoped to develop the **spice trade**. Early in 1683, however, the Dutch expelled the English, which forced the Company to concentrate solely on India.

The Company had about 500 shareholders, including both Charles II and James II. Large dividends were paid out, which averaged 40 per cent in 1663–5. There was a drop during the Anglo-Dutch Wars, but in general the Company became a sound investment. In 1672, the Company was given permission to mint coins in India and in 1675, it became the production source of the Indian rupee. In the 1680s it was usual for annual profits to exceed £600,000.

The changing spice trade

In the early seventeenth century, no kitchen was complete without its supply of saffron, pepper, nutmeg, cloves and cinnamon, all used liberally in the flavouring of dishes at a time when few vegetables were consumed. They were also utilised for their reputed medicinal and preservative qualities. Owing to their small volume and comparatively high price, spices were a key profitable import from the East.

Although the profits of the East India Company increased steadily after the Restoration, fashions were beginning to change. Tea began to be imported in considerable quantities in 1678, while sugar, coffee and tobacco had established themselves and spices were used less frequently to flavour meat. The writer Anthony Wood noted in 1674 that spices were seldom served with meat and that the trade was declining. In some cases, the better quality of meat through improved agricultural practices may account for this change of taste. As a consequence, the East India Company had to diversify and a wider variety of products were carried on their ships.

Africa

Earlier in the seventeenth century, a number of attempts had been made to establish a foothold in west Africa. In 1663, 111 shareholders, led by the Duke of York, founded the Royal African Company as a **joint-stock enterprise**. It was intended to exchange English manufactured goods for gold and ivory. The Company sent an initial 25 ships to the African coast.

The Company soon began trading in slaves, providing a large supply of labour to the islands of the Caribbean. Slaves were sold to planters in Barbados for £16 per head (more than £4000 in today's money), although the very high mortality rates of slaves in transit led to significantly lower profits than projected. The Company faced persistent opposition from the Dutch, who regularly incited their African tribal allies to attack English forts. The Company was restructured in 1672 and was given the right to levy its own army, and set up further military bases and trading posts. This gave them access to ships that were more advanced than their rivals' were.

Banking

Money-lending operations had existed for hundreds of years in England, although under the Tudors they had become more centralised. The first commercial building to cater for the industry was opened in 1571. The Royal Exchange provided a space for **brokers** to carry out business and stimulated the growth in banking.

Before the development of seventeenth-century banking, goods were traded for cash or bartered for bills of exchange:

- Bills of exchange were developed in the Middle Ages and were essentially a form of credit.
- The bills made clear that a purchaser would pay for goods they had received at a future specified time.
- As the supplier of goods was always taking a risk, interest would be added to the loans.

This system of providing credit with interest attached expanded in the seventeenth century and became more formalised. This growth was made possible because of a lowering of interest rates, which continued to fall throughout the century, reaching six per cent in 1651. By 1688, the market rate for a 'good' loan was between four and five per cent, which was below the legal limit. This reduction made credit more attractive and affordable, and brokers established networks of contacts that could provide money, particularly in London.

Money scriveners

The first money scriveners appeared in the 1630s. They specialised in lending and arranging the investment of money on behalf of clients. Robert Abbott established a successful business that flourished in the 1650s, primarily because his services were in demand from royalist landowners who had suffered during the Civil Wars. In the years 1652–5, over £1 million passed through his accounts, with Abbott receiving interest from each transaction he arranged. Abbott's firm was inherited by his nephew, Robert Clayton, and in the 1670s Clayton was one of the foremost money-lenders in London. The first cheque was written by Clayton and his business partner, John Morris, in 1659.

KEY TERM

Broker A person who arranges the buying and selling of goods or assets on behalf of others.

Table 10.5 Legal limits of interest rates, 1571–1714

Years	Maximum interest rate
1571–1624	10%
1624–51	8%
1651–1714	6%

KEY TERM

Goldsmith Someone who makes items out of gold and silver for sale.

Goldsmith bankers

Merchants turned to the **goldsmiths** of London to deposit their money after Charles I seized the Royal Mint in 1640. Previously, the Mint was viewed as the safest place to store money, but after Charles lost the trust of the merchants, the secure vaults of the goldsmiths provided a reliable alternative. The goldsmiths made loans with the money they held in storage, and in 1670, 32 goldsmiths were active in London. This rose to 44 in 1677. They tended to borrow at around four per cent and offer short-term loans at rates above six per cent.

The impact of the Stop of the Exchequer

When, in 1672, Charles II suspended payments to his creditors, in what became known as the Stop of the Exchequer (see page 35), the finances of the nation were not put under threat, but rather Charles's debts to the London bankers. In particular, Charles was heavily indebted to a group of goldsmiths, who had lent him money at a rate of ten per cent. The bankers lost around £1 million as a result, and in 1674 they were given a payment of two years' additional interest as compensation.

There were three main consequences of the Stop of the Exchequer:

- Charles reformed banking in 1672 so that loans to the Crown were levied from the general public. This resulted in his paying a lower rate of interest.
- The goldsmiths received notification that the funds deposited by them at the royal treasury had been confiscated, and they were not refunded.
- The breakdown in trust meant that further financial experiment was postponed until after the Glorious Revolution.

The importance of London to banking and trade

At the end of the seventeenth century, London continued to dominate both the transatlantic and African trades and the merchant vessels leaving its port sailed along increasingly complex trading routes. London was still overwhelmingly the centre for trade and finance. The wealth of London businessmen still far exceeded that of their counterparts in other towns, but its relative importance was gradually declining as the western ports expanded. These western ports – including Liverpool, Bristol, Glasgow and Whitehaven – increased their transatlantic activities as an extension of their existing arrangements with Ireland.

Insurance

Successful trade after the Restoration was made possible in part because of the growth of insurance. Financial coverage was required, in particular against risks to shipping, and this was provided by marine insurance. Although a developed industry did not appear until after 1688, Italian merchants had introduced the practice to Britain in the fifteenth century and the insurers Filippo Borromei & Co. had a branch in London. The high premiums demanded by insurers suppressed the confidence of merchants before 1650 and it was common for them not to insure their ships at times when the threat from foreign powers was low.

From 1657, English brokers were regularly involved in insuring Dutch ships and the London merchants began to replicate the Dutch in viewing the calculation of risk as a wise practice. Marine insurance prices soon dropped as the industry became more established and London became the leading insurance market in the world. In 1688, Edward Lloyd opened a coffee house in London, which served as a venue for brokers, merchants and bankers to conduct business. As more insurance brokers began to descend on his coffee house, he moved to larger premises in 1691 and his business eventually developed to become the world's first insurance market, Lloyd's of London.

The growth of literacy and the press also increased the amount of insurance activity. The *City Mercury* newspaper was the principal London publication that provided shipping announcements and shared the latest information on the prices of tradable commodities. From 1680, advertisements for insurance services began to appear.

ONLINE EXTRAS WWW
Pearson Edexcel

Test your understanding of international trade by completing Worksheet 36 at **www.hoddereducation. co.uk/accesstohistory/extras**

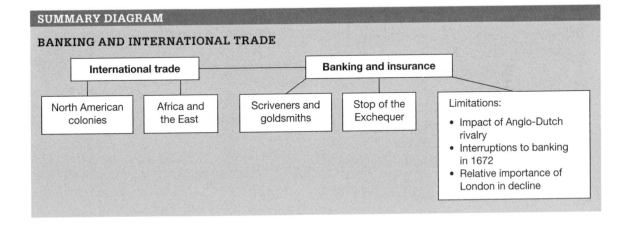

SUMMARY DIAGRAM

BANKING AND INTERNATIONAL TRADE

- International trade
  - North American colonies
  - Africa and the East
- Banking and insurance
  - Scriveners and goldsmiths
  - Stop of the Exchequer
  - Limitations:
    - Impact of Anglo-Dutch rivalry
    - Interruptions to banking in 1672
    - Relative importance of London in decline

CHAPTER SUMMARY

The seventeenth century marked a period of agricultural progress that helped to meet the demands of a growing population. Innovations such as land reclamation and the introduction of new crops helped to increase the yield from farms, although many agricultural improvements were only made possible because of the expansion of large farms at the expense of smallholders. The cloth industry that had provided much of England's wealth in the Middle Ages continued to play a central role in the development of the economy. The domestic system of cloth production continued as it had done for hundreds of years, although new products, techniques and machinery were introduced by the Dutch into England.

From a relatively bleak position in 1660, England's trading position improved drastically. The North American colonies provided a variety of products that were exported to England and elsewhere, with tobacco and sugar proving to be particularly lucrative. The East India Company was challenged by a changing spice trade. Fashions began to change and the Company was compelled to diversify. The improved trading environment was made possible by the ease with which merchants could acquire loans.

Refresher questions

Use these questions to remind yourself of the key material covered in this chapter.

1 What was enclosure?

2 What was the impact of enclosure?

3 What were the successes of land reclamation?

4 In what ways were agricultural techniques improved?

5 How far did agriculture undergo change?

6 In what ways were road and water transport improved?

7 What were the New Draperies?

8 Why was wool declining in importance?

9 In what ways did Charles II attempt to improve the cloth trade?

10 Why was England's trading position in 1660 relatively weak?

11 Why was Virginia successful?

12 What were the key features of the following colonies: Maryland, the Carolinas, New England, Pennsylvania?

13 What economic contribution did the Caribbean colonies make?

14 Why did the East India Company have to diversify in the later seventeenth century?

15 What were money scriveners?

16 Why did goldsmiths become money-lenders and bankers?

17 What impact did the Stop of the Exchequer have on banking?

18 How successful was the insurance industry?

Question practice: Pearson Edexcel

Essay questions

1 How far was the economy transformed in the years 1625–88? [AS level]

EXAM HINT Examine economic conditions in 1625, and explain the extent of change by 1688. Relevant factors might include changes in commercial development, agriculture, and the considerable growth of imperial trade. Reach a conclusion on 'how far'.

2 To what extent was the cloth trade improved in the years 1625–88? [AS level]

EXAM HINT Note the importance of Protestant refugees, the development of New Draperies, and the spread of the textile industry from East Anglia to Manchester and the northwest. Reach a judgement on the extent of improvement.

3 How far do you agree that the growth of London was the most important cause of increased international trade in the years 1625–88? [A level]

EXAM HINT Examine the growing role of London as a banking and commercial centre. Other causes of increased international trade might include the Navigation Acts and trade with imperial possessions. Reach a judgement on the most important cause.

4 To what extent were agricultural innovations responsible for the growth of the Stuart economy in the years 1625–88? [A level]

EXAM HINT Assess a number of innovations, such as growing specialisation in farming and the introduction of new crops. Evaluate other factors, including banking, imperial trade, and the growth of the cloth trade.

Exam focus: AQA

Essay guidance

At A level for AQA Component 1: Breadth Study: Stuart Britain and the Crisis of Monarchy, 1603–1702, you will need to answer an essay question in the exam. In Section B, you will need to answer two essay questions from a choice of three, and each essay question is marked out of 25.

There are several question stems which all have the same basic requirement: to analyse and reach a conclusion, based on the evidence you provide.

The A level questions give a quotation and then ask whether you agree or disagree with this view. Almost inevitably, your answer will be a mixture of both. Detailed essays with accurate deployment of dates and own knowledge are more likely to do well than vague or generalised essays.

The mark scheme for A level emphasises the need to analyse and evaluate the key features related to the periods studied. The key feature of the highest level is sustained analysis: analysis that unites the whole of the essay. Opposite is a summary of the mark scheme but it is always worth checking the full version on the AQA website.

Essay questions for Paper 1 (Breadth Studies) will relate directly or indirectly to one of the six key issues listed at the beginning of the syllabus:

- How far did the monarchy change?
- To what extent and why was power more widely shared during this period?
- Why and with what results were there disputes over religion?
- How effective was opposition?
- How important were ideas and ideology?
- How important was the role of key individuals and groups and how were they affected by developments?

Level 5	Well-selected, specific and precise use of knowledge
	Fully analytical with a balanced argument
	A well-substantiated judgement
Level 4	Well organised
	A good range of supporting information
	Mainly analytical
	There is some judgement and balance
Level 3	There is some use of accurate information but parts lack precise detail
	Some comments are general and not fully focused on the question
	There is some analysis and balance
Level 2	Descriptive
	There is some appropriate information and some understanding but there is inaccuracy and irrelevance
	Comments may be unsupported and generalised
Level 1	Limited organisational and communicational skills
	Limited knowledge and irrelevance
	Unsupported and vague comments

Writing an essay: tips from examiners' reports

Focus and structure

- Be sure what the question is asking and plan what the paragraphs should be about.
- Especially on Paper 1 breadth essay questions, it is important that the whole of the time period in the question is considered. Essay titles in breadth essay questions will cover at least twenty years. Do not just focus on the beginning or the end of the period. A response that fails to cover the full date range set in the question will struggle to reach the higher levels.
- Your introduction to the essay should be focused and outline the overall argument of the essay. It is not the place to talk about different definitions of

what it meant by absolutism, for example. Make sure that you clearly state what your opinion is and why you think that.

- Be sure that each paragraph highlights the structure of the answer, for example the opening sentence should be analytical and not descriptive.

- Make sure that the introductory sentence of each paragraph relates directly to the focus of the question.

- Avoiding writing a narrative (an account of what happened). Simply listing events and telling the story will result in a low-level mark.

Use detail

- Make sure that you show detailed knowledge – but only as part of an explanation being made in relation to the question. No knowledge should be standalone; it should be used in context.

- For every piece of detailed knowledge think 'so what?' Why have you added this piece of information? What role is it playing in advancing your argument?

Explanatory analysis and evaluation

Consider what words and phrases to use in an answer to strengthen the explanation. A good place to start is to use adjective qualifiers (words that precede an adjective that increase or decrease the quality signified by the word they modify).

Use of primary sources and references to historians

- Primary sources can be referred to in your answer in order to add substance to an explanation.

- The views of historians can also be used *but* do not parade knowledge about several historians who do not always agree with each other unless you are actively using their views to augment your own argument. Extensive historiography is not wanted. Indeed, an answer can be in the top level and make no mention of historians whatsoever.

Balance

- Your answer must be a balanced response. This does not mean giving two alternative viewpoints and sitting on the fence or in the middle – you will need to consider a variety of factors and make a judgement. You will need to explain why the alternative view or factors are not as important or valid as the one you are advancing.

Argument and counter-argument

- Think of how arguments can be juxtaposed as part of a balancing act to give contrasting views.

- Think how best to 'resolve' contradictory arguments.

Relative significance and evaluation

- Think how best to reach a judgement when trying to assess the relative importance of various factors, and their possible interrelationship.

Planning an essay

Practice question 1

To what extent were the political problems faced by the monarchy in the years 1660–85 caused by religious issues?

This question requires you to analyse why the monarchy faced political problems. You must discuss:

- how religious issues caused political problems (your primary focus)

- the other factors that caused this (your secondary focus).

A clear structure makes for a much more effective essay and is crucial for achieving the highest marks. In addition to an introduction and a conclusion, you need three or four paragraphs to structure this question effectively. In each paragraph you will deal with one factor. One of these *must* be the factor in the question. If you don't address the factor (in this case religious issues) you aren't answering the question and will only score a low level.

A very basic plan for this question might look like this:

- Paragraph 1: the effects of religious issues.
- Paragraph 2: the effects of the Restoration Settlement, in particular the inadequacy of the financial settlement and issues created by the political settlement, such as the revised Triennial Act of 1664.
- Paragraph 3: Charles II's desire for absolutism and his pro-French foreign policy.

It is a good idea to cover the factor named in the question first, so that you don't run out of time and forget to do it. Then cover the others in what you think is their order of importance, or in the order that appears logical in terms of the sequence of paragraphs.

The introduction

Maintaining focus is vital. One way to do this from the beginning of your essay is to use the words in the question to help write your argument. The first sentences of your answer to question 1, for example, could look like this:

> Religious issues – particularly those that divided the pro-Anglican parliament from a monarch who desired religious toleration – were vital in causing political problems during the reign of Charles II. There were, however, other factors that explain these problems.

This opening sentence provides a clear focus on the demands of the question, although it could, of course, be written in a more exciting style. Then go on to outline the argument of the essay – anticipating the conclusion. The rest of the essay should flow from these opening statements because you have indicated a clear sense of direction.

Focus throughout the essay

Structuring your essay well will help with keeping the focus of your essay on the question. To maintain a focus on the wording in question 1, you could begin your first main paragraph with a reference to 'religious issues'.

> Religious issues were one very important factor in causing political problems.

- This sentence begins with a clear point that refers to the primary focus of the question (political problems) while linking it to a factor (religious issues).
- You could then have a paragraph for each of your other factors.
- It will be important to make sure that each paragraph focuses on analysis and includes relevant details that are used as part of the argument.
- You may wish to number your factors. This helps to make your structure clear and helps you to maintain focus. However, this can make the essay appear to be concerned with a list, and not encourage links between paragraphs.

Deploying detail

As well as focus and structure, your essay will be judged on the extent to which it includes accurate detail. There are several different kinds of evidence you could use that might be described as detailed. These include correct dates, names of relevant people, statistics and events. You can also make your essays more detailed by using the correct technical vocabulary. For example, for sample question 1 you could use terms such as royal absolutism, exchequer, Whigs and Tories. You might also be able to use specific primary sources, including brief quotations, and references to the views of particular historians who support your arguments. However, the quotations and arguments of historians must be relevant. There is no point in learning historians' quotes and squeezing them in somewhere just because you have learnt them. This will not gain you marks – they need to relate to your argument.

Analysis and explanation

'Analysis' covers a variety of high-level skills including explanation and evaluation; in essence, it means breaking down something complex into smaller parts. A clear structure which breaks down a complex question into a series of paragraphs is the first step towards writing an analytical essay.

The purpose of explanation is to account for why something happened, or why something is true or false. An explanatory statement requires two parts: a *claim* and a *justification*.

For example, for question 1, you might want to argue that one important reason was Charles II's sympathy with Catholics. Once you have made your point, and supported it with relevant detail, you can then explain how this answers the question. For example, you could conclude your paragraph like this:

> Charles II's sympathy with Catholics is important in understanding the political problems of the period[1] because this led the King to follow pro-Catholic policies[2], such as the second Declaration of Indulgence in 1672, which in turn alienated many members of the Cavalier Parliament, which was overwhelmingly Anglican[3].

1 Claim. **2** Relationship. **3** Justification.

- The first part of this sentence is the claim while the second part justifies the claim.

- 'Because' is a very important word to use when writing an explanation, as it shows the relationship between the claim and the justification.

Evaluation

Evaluation means considering the importance of two or more different factors, weighing them against each other and reaching a judgement. This is a good skill to use at the end of an essay because the conclusion should reach a judgement which answers the question. Ideally this will have been anticipated in the introductory paragraph, thus ensuring that the essay has a clear sense of direction from beginning to end. For example, your conclusion to question 1 might read:

> Clearly[1], religious issues meant that political conflict was inevitable between 1660 and 1685. However[2], many of these conflicts could have been avoided if Charles had not emulated the absolutist policies of Louis XIV. Many MPs favoured a pro-Dutch policy, whereas Charles became closer to France throughout the 1660s

> and ultimately signed the Treaty of Dover in 1670, committing England to a pro-French military alliance. Therefore[3], the issues of religion and foreign policy are closely linked in this period and were both responsible for political problems.

1 Clearly. **2** However. **3** Therefore.

Words like 'however' and 'therefore' are helpful to contrast the importance of the different factors.

Complex essay writing: argument and counter-argument

Essays that develop a good argument are more likely to reach the highest levels. This is because argumentative essays are much more likely to develop sustained analysis. As you know, your essays are judged on the extent to which they analyse.

After setting up an argument in your introduction, you should develop it throughout the essay. One way of doing this is to adopt an argument–counter-argument structure. A counter-argument is one that disagrees with the main argument of the essay. This is a good way of evaluating the importance of the different factors that you discuss. Essays of this type will develop an argument in one paragraph and then set out an opposing argument in another paragraph. Sometimes this will include juxtaposing the differing views of historians on a topic.

Good essays will analyse the key issues. They will probably have a clear piece of analysis at the end of each paragraph. While this analysis might be good, it will generally relate only to the issue discussed in that paragraph.

Excellent essays will be analytical throughout. As well as the analysis of each factor discussed above, there will be an overall analysis. This will run throughout the essay and can be achieved through developing a clear, relevant and coherent argument.

A good way of achieving sustained analysis is to consider which factor is most important. Here is an example of an introduction that sets out an argument for question 1:

> Political problems were rife in the years 1660-85, particularly the conflict between Charles II and parliament[1]. This conflict came to a head

in the years 1679-81 with the Exclusion Crisis and the political nation was still not settled when Charles died in 1685. Religious issues were prevalent throughout the period and were vital in understanding this conflict because of the fundamental disagreement between Charles, who followed a policy of religious toleration, and parliament, which was generally made up of Anglicans. However, this was not the only reason for political problems. Charles pursued a pro-French foreign policy which meant he was accused of attempting to impose absolutism in England[2]. The most important reason, however, was undoubtedly the inadequate Restoration Settlement, because this left many religious, financial and political problems unresolved. If these problems had been solved in the early 1660s, many of the later conflicts could have been avoided[3].

1 The introduction begins with some context on the period and a claim.

2 The introduction continues with another reason.

3 Concludes with an outline of an argument of the most important reason.

- This introduction focuses on the question and sets out the key factors that the essay will develop.

- It introduces an argument about which factor was most significant.

- However, it also sets out an argument that can then be developed throughout each paragraph, and is rounded off with an overall judgement in the conclusion.

Complex essay writing: resolution and relative significance

Having written an essay that explains argument and counter-arguments, you should then resolve the tension between the argument and the counter-argument in your conclusion. It is important that the writing is precise and summarises the arguments made in the main body of the essay. You need to reach a supported overall judgement. One very appropriate way to do this is by evaluating the relative significance of different factors, in the light of valid criteria. Relative significance means how important one factor is compared to another.

The best essays will always make a judgement about which was most important based on valid criteria. These can be very simple – and will depend on the topic and the exact question.

The following criteria are often useful:

- Duration: which factor was important for the longest amount of time?

- Scope: which factor affected the most people?

- Effectiveness: which factor achieved most?

- Impact: which factor led to the most fundamental change?

As an example, you could compare the factors in terms of their duration and their impact.

A conclusion that follows this advice should be capable of reaching a high level (if written in full, with appropriate details) because it reaches an overall judgement that is supported through evaluating the relative significance of different factors in the light of valid criteria.

Having written an introduction and the main body of an essay for question 1, a concluding paragraph that aims to meet the exacting criteria for reaching a complex judgement could look like this:

Thus, the causes of political problems in the years 1660-85 are complex with several interrelated factors responsible. There is no doubt that Charles II's behaviour caused an increase in opposition, as evidenced in his actions during the Exclusion Crisis, where he staunchly defended his Catholic brother James. The serious religious divisions seen in the period were not inevitable. They were exacerbated by the inadequacy of the Restoration Settlement. The fact that the Clarendon Code defined uniformity on a very narrow basis meant that anyone outside this was viewed with suspicion, and these were the exact groups that Charles hoped to give toleration to.

Interpretations guidance

Section A of the examination for AQA Component 1: Breadth Study: Stuart Britain and the Crisis of Monarchy, 1603–1702 contains extracts (approximately 120–150 words) from the work of historians. This section tests your ability to analyse and evaluate different historical interpretations. Therefore, you must focus on the interpretations outlined in the extracts. The advice given here is for the A level exam:

■ you will be given three extracts and will be asked how convincing each of the arguments in the extracts are in relation to a specified topic (30 marks).

An interpretation is a particular view on a topic of history held by a particular author or authors. Interpretations of an event can vary, for example, depending on how much weight a historian gives to a particular factor and largely ignores another one. For example, the Whig view that the Glorious Revolution simply marked the restoration of an 'ancient constitution' is no longer accepted by most historians.

Interpretations can also be heavily conditioned by events and situations that influence the writer. For example, judging the impact of the Glorious Revolution will tend to produce different responses. Someone writing shortly after the Revolution may have seen the events as positive. A Marxist historian writing the mid-twentieth century will see the Revolution in a negative light.

The interpretations that you will be given will be largely from recent or fairly recent historians, and they may, of course, have been influenced by events in the period in which they were writing.

When looking at a historian's argument you will need to consider the following questions:

■ What is the main argument/interpretation that the historian is putting across?

■ How good is the argument?
■ What factors does the historian consider?
■ What evidence does the historian use?
■ What subsidiary arguments does the historian make?

Interpretations and evidence

The extracts will contain a mixture of interpretations and evidence. The mark scheme rewards answers that focus on the *interpretations* offered by the extracts much more highly than answers that focus on the *information or evidence* mentioned in the extracts. Therefore, it is important to identify the interpretations. The main interpretation could be anywhere – it might not be the first line that you read. It could be towards the end of the extract or just an overall feeling throughout the extract.

■ *Interpretations* are a specific kind of argument. They tend to make claims such as 'Charles II was an absolutist monarch who saw no need for a parliament at all'.

■ *Information or evidence* tends to consist of specific details. For example: 'Danby's methods of raising revenue meant that Charles did not have to worry about calling parliament'.

■ *Arguments and counter-arguments*: sometimes in an extract you will find an interpretation which is then balanced in the same paragraph with a counter-argument. You will need to decide with which your knowledge is most in sympathy.

Fact and opinion

It is important to be able to identify the difference between a fact and an opinion. For example, a weak candidate will write 'the historian says that Charles was in a weak financial position. I know this to be true.' However, the task is not to assess how accurate the historian is, but how convincing the argument is.

The importance of planning

At A level you are allowed one hour for this question. It is the planning stage that is vital in order to write a good answer. You should allow at least one-quarter of that time to read the extracts and plan an answer. If you start writing too soon, it is likely that you will waste time trying to summarise the *content* of each extract. Do this in your planning stage – and then think how you will *use* the content to answer the question.

EXTRACT A

From J.R. Jones, *The First Whigs: The Politics of the Exclusion Crisis, 1678–1683*, Oxford University Press, 1961, p. 64. Charles gained French support in order to bypass parliament.

In order to stifle the progress of the First Exclusion Bill, Charles prorogued parliament and dissolved it shortly afterwards. His action encouraged supporters to rally round the Crown, but the elections of August and September saw the Whigs strengthened, not weakened. When parliament did meet in October 1680 the Whig hold was stronger than ever. Unknown to the Whigs the turning-point in the crisis had already been passed. Having failed to significantly reduce their strength, the King preferred to become the client of France rather than the dependant of his own subjects. A secret agreement assured him of French support, and with this behind him he had no immediate need to call parliament at all.

EXTRACT B

From John Miller, *Popery and Politics in England: 1660–1688*, Cambridge University Press, 1973, p. 188.

There was not the same alienation of king and nation in 1678–81 as there had been in 1640–2 or as there was to be in 1688. Charles kept the support of a substantial section of the political nation and was able to exploit the Tory backlash for all it was worth. The Plot and the eventual confrontation over exclusion, though causally linked, were separated in time; the emotional excitement generated by the first had waned by the time of the second. The threat from Popery and arbitrary government seemed immediate in 1640–2 and in 1688; in 1679–81 it was only a possible threat, somewhere in the future. This lower level of intensity and of immediacy made the battles of the Exclusion Crisis more superficial than they might appear at first sight.

EXTRACT C

From Nicholas Fellows, *Charles II and James II*, Hodder & Stoughton, 1995, p. 80. Weaknesses of the Whigs.

Throughout the period the Whigs faced a very difficult task. They had expected popular pressure to be sufficient to persuade Charles to give way. Once it became apparent that it was not, their position became much weaker. It was very difficult to maintain the momentum of the campaign when they appeared to be getting nowhere. When parliament was either dissolved or prorogued the Whigs found it hard to maintain the nation's interest, despite pamphlets, tours and pope-burning ceremonies. The Whig cause was further weakened by divisions within their own ranks. If James was to be excluded who should succeed? In the end Shaftesbury came down on the side of Charles's illegitimate son, Monmouth, but not all agreed with this choice. Charles had been able to exploit this and play upon the potential divisions within the opposition.

Analysing interpretations: A level (three extracts)

For the AQA A level exam, Section A gives you three extracts, followed by a single question.

Using your understanding of the historical context, assess how convincing the arguments in each of these three extracts are in relation to the reasons for the failure of Exclusion in the years 1678–81. (30 marks)

Analysing Extract A

From the extract:

- Charles prorogued parliament in order to prevent the first Exclusion bill passing.

- Whig power in parliament increased in the election of October 1680.

- Charles made a secret agreement with France so he could avoid calling parliament in the future.

Assessing the extent to which the arguments are convincing:

- Deploying knowledge to corroborate that Charles's personal actions were responsible for his survival.

- Deploying knowledge to highlight the limitations of the evidence in favour of Charles being responsible.

- The extract is highly selective because it is designed to portray Charles as the main actor in the Exclusion Crisis.

- The extract omits any reference to the weaknesses of the Whigs.

Analysing Extract B

From the extract:

- Charles was not alienated from the nation in the way his father had been in 1640–2.

- The Popish Plot and Exclusion Crisis were separated in time.

- Enthusiasm for Exclusion was not great because excitement about the Popish Plot had died down.

Assessing the extent to which the arguments are convincing:

- Deploying knowledge to agree with the assessment that Charles was in a stronger position than his father had been in 1640–2.

- Deploying knowledge to highlight the waning of enthusiasm for the Popish Plot.

- Juxtaposing the actions of Charles to prevent Exclusion (Extract A) against the lack of enthusiasm for Exclusion (Extract B).

Comparing the analysis of each extract should give the direction of an overall conclusion and judgement about which of the extracts is more convincing. In this case it may be that Extract B is more convincing because it does try to present a balanced view.

Analysing Extract C

From the extract:

- The Whigs expected Charles to give way under popular pressure, but this did not happen.

- Despite active campaigning against Exclusion, the Whigs found it difficult to maintain momentum when parliament was prorogued (linking to Charles's actions as presented in Extract A).

- There were divisions within the ranks of the Whigs.

- The Whigs could not agree on who would take James's place as king.

Assessing the extent to which the arguments are convincing:

- Deploying knowledge to corroborate the argument that the Whigs were in a weak position.

- Deploying knowledge to explain the divisions among the Whigs.

- The extract minimises the role of Charles II.

Writing the answer for A level

First, make sure that you have the focus of the question clear – in this case, the focus is on the reasons for the failure of Exclusion and how convincing the extracts are on that subject. Then you can investigate the three extracts to see how convincing they are.

You need to analyse each of the three extracts in turn. A suggestion is to have a large page divided into nine blocks.

Extract's main arguments	Knowledge to corroborate	Knowledge to contradict or modify
A		
B		
C		

- In the first column, list the main argument and any subsidiary arguments each uses.

- In the second column, list what you know that can corroborate the arguments.

- In the third column, list what might contradict or modify (you might find that you partly agree, but with reservations) the arguments.

- You may find, of course, that some of your knowledge is relevant more than once.

Hints from examiners' reports: how to write a 'good answer'

There is no one correct way to organise an answer. It is the overall argument(s) that you are being judged on.

- Briefly refer to the focus of the question.

- For each extract in turn, set out the main argument and any subsidiary ones, corroborating and contradictory evidence.

- Do this by treating each argument (or group of arguments) in turn.

- Refer to the content of an extract directly – perhaps by a brief quotation – but do not copy out whole sections.

- The argument that has been summarised should be related to the focus of the question, not simply a summary of the extract.

- Your own knowledge must only be used to support or refute an argument in the extract, not presented as a separate entity.

- Do *not* wander into provenance or value. You are only concerned with the content of each extract. You do not need to know anything about the historian or schools of history (for example Marxist, post-revisionist and so on). Evaluate the extract, not the historian!

- Do *not* attempt to analyse the extract by focusing on what is not there. Focus on what you are given to analyse.

- Make comparisons between the extracts if this is helpful. The mark scheme does not explicitly give credit for doing this, but a successful cross-reference may well show the extent of your understanding of each extract and add to the weight of your argument. Bear in mind, this is a high-level skill so only do this if you feel particularly confident with this approach.

- Write a brief judgement at the end of the analysis on each extract. Do not write an introduction or an overall conclusion saying which was most convincing.

- This is not an exercise in English literature so do not stray into focusing on tone or particular use of emotive language. If the historian comes across as angry, for example, this does not make the argument any less or more convincing.

The mark scheme for A level

For each of the three extracts, the mark scheme makes it clear that a good answer will:

- Identify the arguments presented in each extract.

- Assess the extent to which the arguments are convincing, using your own knowledge.

- Take every opportunity to make a balanced answer wherever this is appropriate, by corroborating and contradicting the arguments in each extract. An unbalanced answer will be that the interpretation is completely convincing or, conversely, completely unconvincing.

The mark scheme progresses upwards like this:

- Level 1: general comments about the three extracts or accurate understanding of one extract.

- Level 2: some accurate comments on the interpretations in at least two of the three extracts, but with limited comments or with description.

- Level 3: some supported comments on the interpretations, putting them in their historical context. Some analysis of the content of the extracts, but little attempt to evaluate them.

- Level 4: good understanding of the interpretations provided in the extracts, with knowledge to give a good analysis and some evaluation.

- Level 5: very good understanding and strong historical awareness to analyse and evaluate.

Notice that there is no reference in the A level mark scheme to *comparing* the extracts or reaching a judgement about the most convincing.

Exam focus: Pearson Edexcel

Overview

Pearson Edexcel's Paper 1, Option 1C: Britain, 1625–1701: conflict, revolution and settlement, is assessed by an exam comprising three sections:

- Sections A and B test your knowledge of the period 1625–88. The questions test your breadth of knowledge of four key themes:
  - ☐ The quest for political stability, 1625–88
  - ☐ Religion, conflict and dissent, 1625–88
  - ☐ Social and intellectual challenge, 1625–88
  - ☐ Economy, trade and empire, 1625–88.
- Section C tests your depth of knowledge regarding a key historical debate: How revolutionary, in the years to 1701, was the Glorious Revolution of 1688–89?

Sections A and B

The questions in Sections A and B are essay questions, but their demands are different:

- Section A of the exam paper contains two questions, and you have to complete one. The questions in Section A target a short period of time: they test the breadth of your knowledge by focusing on at least ten years.
- Section B of the exam paper also contains two questions, and you have to complete one. Questions in Section B cover a much broader timespan (at least one-third of the period that you have studied). This means you should plan your answer carefully and select material to deploy.

Neither Section A nor B requires you to read or analyse either sources or extracts from the work of historians.

Skills

Questions in Sections A and B require you to deploy a variety of skills. The most important of these focus on the question, selection and deployment of relevant detail, analysis and, at the highest level, prioritisation.

Questions in Sections A and B include a second-order concept. These are:

- cause
- consequence
- change/continuity
- similarity/difference
- significance.

Therefore, the questions will typically begin with one of the following stems:

- How far …
- How accurate is it to say …
- To what extent …
- How significant …
- How successful … .

You should identify the second-order concept in the question and link your answer to that concept.

Dual focus questions

Some questions will have a dual focus, for example:

How far do you agree that the cloth trade was more successful than agriculture in Britain in the years 1625–88?

Your answer should focus only on the two statements in the question: do not attempt to introduce a third. You should ensure a balance of coverage of the two issues.

Section C

Section C of the exam paper is different from Sections A and B. While Sections A and B test your own knowledge, Section C tests both your own knowledge and your ability to analyse and evaluate interpretations of the past in the work of historians. Section C contains two extracts from the work of historians, and there is one compulsory question.

Section C focuses on an interpretation related to the following controversy:

How revolutionary, in the years to 1701, was the Glorious Revolution of 1688–89?

It looks at the following aspects of the interpretation:

- The significance of revolutionary ideas in the establishment of a constitutional monarchy.
- The impact of the Toleration Act of 1689 and the end of Anglican supremacy.
- The significance of the Triennial Act of 1694 and the growth of parliamentary power.
- The importance of William III's wars in the development of a financial revolution.

Skills

Section C tests your ability to analyse and evaluate different historical interpretations in the light of your own knowledge. Therefore, it tests a variety of skills including:

- identifying the interpretation
- writing a well-structured essay
- integrating own extracts with own knowledge
- reaching an overall judgement.

The AS level exam

Paper 1

The AS exam tests the same content as the A level exam and is structured in exactly the same way. However, there are differences between the two exams.

Sections A and B

There are three key differences between A level and the AS in Sections A and B.

Wording

The wording of AS level questions will be less complex than the wording of A level questions. For example:

A level question	AS level question
To what extent was the discontent faced by the Stuart monarchy in the years 1660–88 caused by a desire from Charles II and James II to become absolute monarchs?	Was the fear of Catholicism the main reason for the lack of political stability in the years 1660–85?
'Improved international trade was the most important influence on the economy in the years 1625–88.' How far do you agree with this statement?	How far do you agree that the growth of London was the main reason for improvements in the Stuart economy in the years 1625–88?

Focus

Section A questions can focus on a more limited range of concepts at AS than at A level. Specifically, at AS level, Section A questions can only focus on *cause* and *consequences* (including success and failure), whereas A level questions can focus on a wider variety of concepts.

Mark scheme

The A level mark scheme has five levels, whereas the AS level mark scheme only has four. This means that full marks are available at AS for an analytical essay, whereas sustained analysis is necessary for full marks at A level.

Section C

Section C of the AS exam focuses on the same aspects of the same debate: 'How revolutionary, in the years to 1701, was the Glorious Revolution of 1688–89?' As in the A level exam, you have to answer one compulsory question based on two extracts. The AS level exam is different from the A level exam in the following ways.

The question

The AS level question is worded in a less complex way than the A level question. For example:

A level	AS level
In the light of differing interpretations, how convincing do you find the view that the power of the monarchy increased as a result of the Glorious Revolution?	Historians have different views about how revolutionary, in the years 1701, the Glorious Revolution was. Analyse and evaluate the extracts and use your knowledge of the issues to explain your answer to the following question.
To explain your answer, analyse and evaluate the material in both extracts, using your own knowledge of the issues.	How far do you agree with the view that the Glorious Revolution transformed the role of parliament?

The extracts

At AS, the extracts will be slightly shorter and you may get extracts taken from textbooks as well as the work of historians. In this sense, the extracts at AS level should be slightly easier to read and understand.

The mark scheme

The A level mark scheme has five levels, whereas the AS level mark scheme only has four. This means that full marks are available at AS for an analytical essay, whereas sustained analysis is necessary for full marks at A level.

Essay guidance for Sections A and B

Understanding the question

In order to answer the question successfully you must understand how the question works. Each essay question has three components:

- an invitation to reach a judgement …
- … on a subject from your course of study …
- … and a clearly defined time period.

For example:

To what extent … was the Restoration Settlement responsible for the political instability experienced in England … in the years 1660–85?

Overall, *all* Section A and B questions ask you to make a judgement about the extent of something, in a specific period. In order to focus on the question you must address all three elements. The most common mistakes come from misunderstanding or ignoring one of these three key elements.

Planning your answer

Do not plan a narrative answer; instead you should:

- focus on the exact demands of the question
- note any key terms in the question
- note the timescale in the question.

Do not simply consider one part of the chronology and do not go beyond the dates provided.

All of your examined essays will be judged on how far they focus on the question and the quality of their structure. The better your focus and the clearer your structure the better your chance of exam success.

Your essay should be made up of three or four paragraphs, each addressing the reasons for political instability. Your essay plan might look something like this:

- paragraph 1: the Restoration Settlement, 1660–4 (stated factor)
- paragraph 2: religious issues
- paragraph 3: financial problems
- paragraph 4: foreign policy.

In addition to your three or four main points, you should begin your essay with a clear introduction and end with a conclusion that contains a focused summary of your essay.

Creating a strong introduction

Here is an example introduction in answer to the question. The commentary reveals how to ensure your essay gets off to a good start.

To what extent was the Restoration Settlement responsible for the political instability experienced in England in the years 1660–85?

Between 1660 and 1685, England experienced much political instability. There were disagreements in parliament over religious issues, finance and foreign policy and many of these issues arguably stem from the inadequate political settlement of 1660-4[1]. In addition, religion and, in particular, the fear of Catholicism, did much to increase political tensions, especially after Charles II made an alliance with Louis XIV in 1670 and it became clear that the Crown's foreign policy was steadfastly pro-Catholic and pro-French. Financial problems also dogged the Crown in these years, and Charles's solutions to these problems made him more enemies, particularly when this meant that he was compelled to seek a closer alliance with France[2]. All of these factors were important in causing political instability, but the most dramatic impact came from the religious divisions that existed between Crown and parliament. The divisions between the pro-Anglican parliament and pro-Catholic Royal Court meant that other issues including finance and foreign policy were extremely difficult to resolve[3].

1 The essay starts with a clear focus on the question.

2 These two sentences introduce alternative factors to the Restoration Settlement and give a sense of the links between them.

3 This sentence indicates that the essay will argue that religious issues were the most important factor and gives some justification.

Reaching an overall judgement

In addition to focus, structure, the level of relevant detail and analysis, your exam essays will be assessed on how far you reach a supported overall judgement. The clearer and better supported your judgement, the better your mark is likely to be.

The mark scheme distinguishes between five levels of judgement:

Level 1 (low)	No overall judgement
Level 2	Stated overall judgement, but no support
Level 3	Overall judgement is reached, with weak support
Level 4	Overall judgement is reached and supported
Level 5 (high)	Overall judgement is reached and supported by consideration of the relative significance of key factors

As you know, your essays are judged on the extent to which they analyse. The mark scheme distinguishes between five different levels of analysis:

Level 1 (low)	Simplistic or no analysis
Level 2	Limited analysis of key issues
Level 3	Some analysis of key issues
Level 4	Analysis of key issues
Level 5 (high)	Sustained analysis of key issues

The key feature of the highest level is sustained analysis: analysis that unites the whole of the essay.

Below is a sample paragraph for the essay title above. This paragraph highlights the use of relevant detail, analysis and a well-supported judgement.

The Restoration Settlement caused a number of political problems that would continue until the death of Charles II in 1685 and beyond[1]. The power of the monarch was not fully clarified and it could be argued that the balance of power between monarch and parliament had not changed since the days of Charles I. A revised Triennial Act was issued in 1664 and although it recommended that parliament should meet at least once every three years, there was no legal mechanism to enforce this. This meant that Charles had the freedom to bypass the expectation that he held triennial parliaments after 1681, during the period known as the 'Tory reaction'. In addition, the financial settlement was inadequate because the Crown was unable to collect enough money to adequately fund the government. The £1.2 million offered by the Cavalier Parliament in 1661 turned out to be much less than anticipated in the 1660s, leading to the sale of Dunkirk to the French for £320,000. Later in the period, this inadequate financial settlement led to Charles adopting a militantly pro-French foreign policy, culminating in the Treaty of Dover in 1670. Charles's apparent desire to copy the absolutism of Louis XIV was resented in England, which was reflected in the attitude of parliament towards his Declaration of Indulgence in 1672 [2]. The most significant aspect of the Restoration Settlement, however, was the religious settlement. The Clarendon Code of 1661-5 enforced a narrow Anglican settlement on the Church of England, reflecting the religious convictions of the members of the Cavalier Parliament. This attitude conflicted with that of the King, who favoured religious toleration and had a lenient attitude towards Catholics. When he attempted to provide toleration for Catholics in 1662, this was immediately opposed by parliament, meaning that Charles had to explore non-parliamentary methods in order to achieve his religious objectives [3].

1 The paragraph starts with a clear focus on the question and indicates that this paragraph will cover the Restoration Settlement.

2 The paragraph has analysed the political and financial aspects of the Revolution and the links between these and other events in the period.

3 The last sentences serve as a good example of detailed substantiation, signalled by relevant dates and events.

Interpretation guidance for Section C

Identify the interpretations

Section C is different from Sections A and B. It presents two extracts from the works of historians. You are expected to use the extracts and your own knowledge to examine the views presented in the extracts and reach conclusions in answer to the question.

Questions in Section C are *not* source analysis questions. You must *not* carry out source analysis on the extracts. There is no credit for issues such as provenance or reliability.

Most questions will offer two extracts with sharp disagreements between them. You must consider the extent to which they disagree and attempt to reconcile these disagreements.

Planning your answer

Below are some issues for you to bear in mind when planning your answer:

- Consider the precise demands made by the question and make detailed use of the two extracts.
- Use the two extracts together at some stage:
  - consider their differences
  - compare and contrast their arguments
  - evaluate their merits
  - remember to devote equal attention to both extracts.

Make careful use of your own knowledge. This should not form a narrative, nor should it simply be tacked on to the points raised by the extracts. Your own knowledge should be used to relate to the issues raised in the extracts.

The following guide may be helpful in framing your answer:

- Analyse and evaluate the points made by the author of the first extract.
- Analyse and evaluate the points made by the author of the second extract.
- Use your own knowledge and the material in the extracts to support the proposition made in the question.
- Use your own knowledge and the material in the extracts to modify or challenge the proposition made in the question.

For the highest levels of attainment, use the two extracts as a set and draw reasoned conclusions on the question.

Strong conclusions

Good answers will end with a strong conclusion. This does not necessarily have to be exhaustive in length, but should offer a clear and reasoned judgement linked back to the analysis of the viewpoint, including the extracts.

Sample answer

Here is a sample Section C question with a worked answer to guide you. Study Extracts 1 and 2 before you answer this question.

In light of the differing interpretations, how convincing do you find the view that the Glorious Revolution increased the power and importance of parliament? To explain your answer, analyse and evaluate the material in both extracts, using your own knowledge of the issues.

EXTRACT 1

From Christopher Hill, *The Century of Revolution 1603–1714*, Routledge, 1969, pp. 237–9.

The revolution of 1688 saw a restoration of power to the traditional ruling class, the Shire gentry, and town merchants, as well as a change of sovereigns. Borough charters were restored. The militia was returned to safe hands, and was used henceforth chiefly against any threat from the lower classes.

The revolution demonstrated the ultimate solidarity of the propertied class. Whigs and Tories disagreed sharply about whether James had abdicated or not, whether the throne should be declared vacant, whether Mary alone or William and Mary jointly should be asked to fill it, or declared to have filled it. But these differences were patched up, and the Declaration of Rights simply stated both positions and left it to individuals to resolve the contradictions as they pleased. One reason for this solid front was the behaviour of James and William. The latter, so far from remaining inscrutably in the background, made it perfectly clear that he was determined to have the title of King. But a second reason for agreement was men's recollections of what had happened forty-five years earlier, when unity of the propertied classes had been broken.

EXTRACT 2

From John Miller, *The Stuarts*, Hambledon Continuum, 2006, p. 242.

The Revolution had effectively removed the threat from the royal prerogative. Kings had to rule as Parliament expected. The Triennial Act of 1694 laid down that there had to be a general election at least every three years. This was intended to deny ministers the time to build up a substantial 'court party' in the Commons. In fact the danger was never quite as great as it appeared. William, Anne and their managers did not want either party to win sweeping electoral victories. An evenly balanced House of Commons was easier to manage than a heavily partisan one and allowed the monarch more scope to appoint moderates and neutrals to office. Within the 'crown', the monarch exercised less and less personal power as ministers ruled in his or her name. These ministers derived their power over the monarch from their ability to push government bills (especially money bills) through Parliament, but also from the support that they enjoyed in the wider society.

Here is an example of a worked answer:

> In some ways, both extracts could be considered to agree that the power and importance of parliament was enhanced as a result of the Glorious Revolution. In Extract 1, 'the propertied classes' were restored to their former status and they are presented as holding the balance of power, while Extract 2 claims that 'kings had to rule as parliament expected'. However, Extract 2 suggests that increased parliamentary activity was beneficial to the Crown, with the argument that 'an evenly balanced House of Commons' was easier for the monarch to manage being quite convincing[1].
>
> There is evidence to suggest that the position of parliament improved after 1688. Extract 1 reminds us that Whigs and Tories 'patched up' their differences in order to offer William and Mary the Declaration of Rights. However, there is much evidence to show that parliament was not united in the period and that the conflicts between Whigs and Tories were counter-productive to the parliamentary cause. There was an increase in election contests, with 45 per cent of constituencies being contested in the 1698 election, and contemporaries felt that the increased frequency of elections endangered traditional gentry influence in the localities as outsiders became more likely to intervene. This contradicts Hill's view that the propertied classes maintained their pre-eminent position in society[2].
>
> Extract 1 indicates that the ruling classes in parliament worked together in order to combat any sort of disorder because of 'what had happened forty-five years earlier' during the Civil War. It is true that the Convention Parliament united in order to state that a Catholic king was inconsistent with a Protestant state and it could be argued that the Declaration of Rights is evidence of parliament attempting to claw back some control and avoid chaos. However, many of the powers that James II enjoyed were left untouched, including the right of the monarch to choose their ministers, appoint bishops and peers, and veto legislation. William used the royal veto five times, including his blocking of an early version of the Triennial Act that he was also
>
> not satisfied with, and a bill for regulating elections[3]. In addition, William focused on including a balance of Whigs and Tories in his administration in order to maintain stability. The rise to prominence of the 'Whig Junto' from 1692 demonstrates the vital power that the monarch continued to have in the constitution. As well as this, the Association was presented to MPs in 1696. This oath of allegiance to William was passed in the Commons by 364 votes to 89, demonstrating William's strong position[4].
>
> Despite the fact that the monarch continued to wield much power within the political system, Extract 2 suggests that a genuine constitutional monarchy was established with a more prominent role for parliament. Miller states that 'the Revolution had effectively removed the threat from the royal prerogative', which suggests that monarchs were no longer able to rule in an arbitrary way in the manner of James II and to an extent, Charles I and Charles II. The Declaration of Rights contained several clauses aimed at achieving this, including those designed to limit the Crown's right to levy taxes without parliament's consent, limit their right to interfere with elections and prevent any return to arbitrary government. It could be argued, however, that the Bill of Rights did not go far enough in the eyes of many parliamentarians. Some clauses from the Declaration never received the royal assent, such as the suggestion that the national Church become more unified and measures to more closely monitor judges. In addition to the Declaration of Rights, the Act of Settlement of 1701 further clarified the powers of monarch and parliament. Excessive royal influence over the House of Commons was curbed by the exclusion of MPs from government posts, and judges could only be dismissed with the consent of parliament. The Mutiny Acts, first passed by parliament in 1689, ensured that the monarch could not court-martial soldiers without the consent of parliament[5].
>
> The two extracts do agree on some aspects of the constitutional settlement. They both give a sense that despite the fact that parliament's power and influence were increased, William III was able to use this to his advantage. Extract 1 states that William 'was determined to have the

title of King' and that the propertied classes rallied round him for safety, while Extract 2 gives the impression that as ministers began to rule in William's name, the power of the government was increased. Extract 2 states that the Crown enjoyed 'less and less personal power', but fails to acknowledge many of the personal accomplishments of William, especially his role in leading the Nine Years' War, particularly in Ireland where he defeated a Jacobite army to secure his power. Extract 1, on the other hand, focuses almost exclusively on the class aspect of the Glorious Revolution, suggesting that the lower classes were feared by both parliament and king and that the militia was used against only this group. This fails to recognise the restrictions placed on the militia by parliament, where it was ultimately agreed to fund an army of just 7000 men[6].

There is no doubt that the Glorious Revolution increased the power of parliament, as Extract 2 reminds us, but Extract 1 is convincing in suggesting that the Revolution marked simply 'a change of sovereigns' without doing much to change existing power structures. The Revolution marked the beginnings of a modern constitutional monarchy, but there were still many ways in which the monarch could bypass parliament if they wished to[7].

1 The introduction demonstrates immediate focus on the question, sets out where the extracts stand, and suggests what the essay will ultimately argue.

2 Extract 1's claim that political differences were cast aside is evaluated through a proven reminder that Whigs and Tories were deeply partisan.

3 While it is acceptable to deal with the extracts one at a time, reaching the highest levels of attainment requires exploring the two extracts together.

4 Own knowledge is used to challenge the proposition made in the question.

5 Own knowledge is used to support and challenge the claim made in Extract 2 that the royal prerogative was reduced.

6 The two extracts are used together to explain where they overlap and their views are criticised with own knowledge.

7 The conclusion sums up the opinions of both extracts and follows the argument first set out in the introduction.

Timeline

Year	Ruler	Domestic events	Foreign events
1660	Charles II	Restoration of the monarchy	
1660		Declaration of Breda	
1662		Act of Uniformity	
1664		Triennial Act Conventicle Act	
1665		Five Mile Act	
1665–6		Great Plague	
1666		Great Fire of London	
1667		Fall of Clarendon End of Second Anglo-Dutch War	
1669		James converted to Catholicism	
1670		Treaty of Dover Conventicle Act	
1672		Declaration of Indulgence	William of Orange became *Stadtholder* of Holland
1673		Test Act Rise of Danby	
1676		Compton Census	
1677			Marriage of William and Mary
1678		Test Act	
1678–81		Popish Plot Exclusion Crisis	
1681		Oxford Parliament	
1683		Rye House Plot	
1685	James II	Monmouth Rebellion	Revocation of the Edict of Nantes
1686		*Godden* v. *Hales*	
1687		Declaration of Indulgence	
1688	William III and Mary II		
1688		Start of the Nine Years' War	
1688–1701		Glorious Revolution	
1689		Bill of Rights Toleration Act	
1690		Battle of the Boyne	
1691		Public Accounts Commission was established	
1693		Glencoe Massacre	
1694	Death of Mary II; William III ruled alone for the rest of his reign	Bank of England was founded Triennial Act	
1697		End of the Nine Years' War	
1698		Establishment of the Civil List	
1701		Act of Settlement	
1702	Death of William III Accession of Anne		

Glossary of terms

Aldermen High-ranking members of a borough council.

Almshouse A house supported by charity to provide for the poorest and most vulnerable.

Anglican The Church of England.

Arable land Land suited to growing crops.

Arminian A follower of the Dutch theologian Jacobus Arminius. Arminians were associated with 'high-church' practices (similar to those of the Catholic Church), such as the use of organs, hymns and bowing to the cross.

Baptists A Protestant sect that practised adult baptism.

Bill of attainder An Act of parliament confirming a decision to find someone guilty of a crime without the need for a trial.

Book of Common Prayer The English prayer book, first introduced in 1549.

Book of Rates A document that listed how much tax was due to be paid on all items that could be imported into, and exported from, England.

Borough charter A document granting a town certain privileges and allowing it to control some of its own affairs.

Broker A person who arranges the buying and selling of goods or assets on behalf of others.

Bubonic plague The most common form of plague, typified by fever and swollen lymph nodes (called buboes). The disease killed around half of those who contracted it in the seventeenth century.

Catholicism The dominant form of Christianity under papal (the pope's) authority in Europe before the Protestant Reformation. The Catholic Church was founded on the belief that bishops were the successors of Christ's apostles and that the pope was the successor to Saint Peter.

Clan A large group of families who claim descent from a common ancestor and share a common identity.

Cleaning crop Any crop suited to growing in place of weeds in order to 'clean' the soil.

Common land Land that can be used by all residents of a parish to graze animals and collect firewood.

Comprehension The process of accepting different religious denominations into the national Church.

Constituency An area whose voters elect a representative to parliament.

Constitutional monarchy A system of government where the power of a monarch is limited by a constitution.

Constitutional Royalists A group which believed that the concessions won by parliament in the years 1640–2 were adequate and that the King's powers should not be limited any further. Many had fought for Charles I in the Civil War.

Conventicles Religious meetings outside the Church of England.

Convention Parliament An irregular parliament that assembles without being summoned by a monarch.

Convocation A formal assembly of bishops and clergy that meets to consider matters of Church policy.

Cottage industry A manufacturing activity carried out in people's homes.

Council of Officers An organisation first established to coordinate the activities of the New Model Army in the Civil War. By the late 1650s, it had become an influential and politicised body of senior commanders.

Council of State An administrative body responsible for deliberating on matters of government policy.

Council of the North An institution established to enhance government control over the north of England.

Court of High Commission A religious court established in the sixteenth century. It could be convened by the sovereign at any time and one of its main responsibilities was implementing the laws against both Puritans and Catholics.

Court of quarter sessions A criminal court held four times a year empowered to try all but the most serious offences and hear appeals.

Demographics Statistical data relating to a population and particular groups within it.

Dispensing power A long-standing prerogative power allowing monarchs to discard laws in certain cases. It was exercised widely in the medieval and Tudor periods, but came under attack during the reigns of James I and Charles I.

Dissenting academies Educational institutions established to teach Dissenters. As Oxford and Cambridge barred Dissenters from taking degrees, the academies were the only places where they could receive a formal education.

Divine right of kings The belief that the power of kings is ordained by God.

Episcopacy Government of a Church by bishops.

Executive The branch of government holding authority and responsible for the day-to-day running of the state.

Fertility rate The number of live births occurring in a population.

Feudal dues Taxes traditionally paid by a lower class to a higher class under the feudal system.

Fifth Monarchist A radical Puritan sect whose members believed that Christ's return to

Earth was imminent. They had supported the Republic at first, but turned against one-man rule under Cromwell. They wanted a new parliament to be elected based on godly principles.

Fuller A worker who cleans wool by eliminating oil or dirt and thickens it by matting the fibres together.

Goldsmith Someone who makes items out of gold and silver for sale.

Goldsmith bankers The London goldsmiths were able to provide safe storage for valuable items and in the early seventeenth century began to accept deposits and made loans with the funds they kept. After the Stop of the Exchequer a number of goldsmith bankers went out of business completely.

Good Old Cause A phrase used by former parliamentarians and republicans in reference to the reasons that motivated them to fight during the English Civil Wars.

Grand jury A jury selected to investigate whether criminal charges should be brought prior to a trial.

Great Tew Circle A group that assembled at the house of Lucius Cary, Viscount Falkland, in the 1630s. Many of its members had unorthodox and tolerant religious beliefs, although they tended to support a strong monarchy.

Green Ribbon Club A loosely organised political group consisting of MPs, peers, radicals and former Cromwellian supporters. They were alarmed by the apparent drift towards Catholicism and arbitrary government. Many of its members became active Whig supporters.

Hackney coaches Horse-drawn carriages hired to carry passengers in London.

Huguenots French Protestants who formed a minority in the sixteenth and seventeenth centuries. They were provided with significant religious and political autonomy before Louis XIV demanded in 1685 that they convert to Catholicism or leave France.

Indentured servants Workers contracted to provide labour without pay for a fixed period of time. When the fixed period had ended, most were freed.

Independents People who believed in the local control of churches without a national hierarchy.

Inductive reasoning A type of reasoning where theories are based on evidence and observed fact.

Inns of Court The four legal societies given the right to confer the title of barrister on law students.

Jesuit A member of the Roman Catholic religious order of the Society of Jesus, founded in 1534. Jesuits were renowned for the intensity of their religious commitment.

Joint-stock enterprise A business owned collectively by its shareholders.

Justices of the peace Magistrates who were responsible for ensuring that law and order was upheld at a local level. They were typically members of the lower gentry.

Laity People who belong to a religion, but are not members of the clergy.

Levellers A radical movement that was particularly popular in the New Model Army.

Libel A written statement that is damaging to a person's reputation.

Lord Keeper A high-ranking Privy Councillor with particular responsibility for the care of the king's great seal, with the authority to affix it to public documents.

Low Countries The coastal lowland region of northwest Europe, consisting of modern-day Belgium, the Netherlands, Luxembourg and parts of northern France.

Lucerne A grazing crop, which converts large amounts of nitrogen from the air to enrich soil.

Man-of-war A heavily armed warship.

Mayor The head of a town or borough council.

Medley cloth Cloth created by first dyeing wool before spinning to mix the colours.

Mercantilism A economic policy that attempts to achieve self-sufficiency and surplus wealth for a state by regulating trade and acquiring overseas possessions and colonies.

Monopoly The exclusive control of trade in a commodity.

Muster A formal gathering of troops.

Non-Trinitarians Christians who do not believe in the doctrine of the Trinity; the notion that divinity exists within God, Jesus and the Holy Spirit equally.

Numerology The belief in the mystical power of numbers and patterns of numbers in dictating events on Earth.

Open-field system The traditional medieval system of farming. Land was divided into strips and managed by tenants or peasants, with areas set aside for common grazing.

Ordain To make someone a priest or minister.

Petition A formal written request appealing to authority in respect of a particular cause.

Political nation People able to take part in politics and vote in elections.

Polymath Someone who possesses significant knowledge about a wide variety of subjects.

Poorhouse Also known as a workhouse, an institution funded by parish taxes to provide accommodation for the poor.

Pope-burning The practice of burning an effigy of the pope.

Prerogative of mercy The power of the monarch to grant royal pardons to convicted criminals.

Prerogative powers Powers that are unique to the monarch.

Presbyterian A Church governed by a council of elders rather than a hierarchy of bishops.

Privateers Privately owned armed ships with government authority to capture foreign merchant vessels.

Privy Council A body of advisers appointed by the monarch.

Protestants Followers of the Christian Churches that had separated from the Catholic Church. They focused on the belief that faith alone was required to enter heaven.

Protestant Dissenters Members of Nonconformist churches who did not follow the Church of England.

Puritans Protestants who believed that the Reformation of the Church under Elizabeth I had not gone far enough, and sought to simplify worship and 'purify' it.

Quakers Members of the Religious Society of Friends, a movement founded by George Fox in the early 1650s. Central to their beliefs is the doctrine of the 'Inner Light' of the Holy Spirit that can be accessed by anyone. As a result, their meetings did not follow the same pattern as church services and their organisation did not have a hierarchical leadership structure.

Recusant A person who refused to attend Anglican Church services.

Regent A person appointed to administer a government in place of the legitimate ruler, normally when the monarch is incapacitated or too young to rule alone.

Regicide The action of killing a king.

Republic A state in which power is vested in elected representatives rather than a monarch.

Sainfoin A drought–resistant grazing crop.

Sectaries Members of Nonconformist Protestant groups.

Sovereignty Supreme power or authority in a political system.

Spice trade The trade in spices between East Asia, the Middle East and Europe that had been established in ancient times and was increasingly dominated by Europeans in the seventeenth century.

Stop of the Exchequer The suspension of loan repayments to creditors. Charles used a loophole in the law to declare his debts illegal and void because they were charged at a rate of more than six per cent.

Stratified Arranged into groups or classes.

Subsistence work Work that provides the minimal amount of income necessary for survival.

Thirty-nine Articles A document from 1571 that set out the doctrines of the Church of England.

Tithe A tax paid to support the Church and the clergy.

Tontine loan A loan provided by a group of investors who each receive an annual dividend on their investment. As each investor dies, their share is divided between the survivors.

Transubstantiation The belief that the bread and wine consumed during Holy Communion change their essence to become the body and blood of Christ.

Turnpike A gate or barrier that prevented passage on a road until a toll had been paid.

Tyburn The site of London's gallows, where public hangings took place.

Universal male suffrage The vote for all men aged over eighteen.

Whig historians Historians who presented the seventeenth century as the inevitable rise of a constitutional monarchy and increased religious liberty. They believed that the Stuart kings who attempted to block reform were tyrants, and tended to revere institutions such as parliament and the legal system as the key components of a balanced constitution.

Further reading

Chapter 1: general texts on the period

B. Coward, *A Companion to Stuart Britain* (Blackwell, 2008)
A collection of articles from leading scholars providing an up-to-date view of the Stuarts

B. Coward and P. Gaunt, *The Stuart Age* (Routledge, 2017)
An accessible and detailed account of the years 1603–1714

C. Hill, *God's Englishman: Oliver Cromwell and the English Revolution* (Penguin, 1990)
A classic biography of Cromwell that traces his life from his beginnings to his political rise and fall

D. Hirst, *England in Conflict, 1603–1660* (Hodder Arnold, 1999)
An excellent study of the causes and consequences of conflict before the Restoration

M. Kishlansky, *A Monarchy Transformed, Britain 1603–1714* (Penguin, 1997)
A very accessible and clear overview of the key political events of the period

J. Morrill, *Stuart Britain: A Very Short Introduction* (Oxford University Press, 2000)
Sets the revolutionary events of the century into their political and social context

Chapter 2

R.M. Bliss, *Restoration England: Politics and Government 1660–1688* (Routledge, 1985)
A brief, but very informative, analysis of the years immediately after the Restoration

A. Fraser, *King Charles II* (Weidenfield & Nicolson, 2002)
A detailed and comprehensive biography of Charles II with some useful commentary on the build-up to the Restoration

R. Hutton, *The Restoration: A Political and Religious History of England and Wales, 1658–1667* (Clarendon Press, 2004)
A detailed study of manuscript sources to provide a fresh account of the period

N.H. Keeble, *The Restoration: England in the 1660s* (John Wiley, 2002)
Challenges the view that the Restoration settlement was marked by stability and order

J. Miller, *The Restoration and the England of Charles* (Routledge, 1997)
Includes an excellent section on the key features of the Restoration settlement

J. Uglow, *A Gambling Man: Charles II and the Restoration* (Faber & Faber, 2009)
Traces Charles II's life in the years 1660–1670

Chapter 3

T. Harris, *London Crowds in the Reign of Charles II: Propaganda and Politics from the Restoration until the Exclusion Crisis* (Cambridge University Press, 1990)
Traces the political attitudes of ordinary Londoners and their reaction to political propaganda before the Exclusion Crisis

T. Harris, *Restoration: Charles II and his Kingdoms, 1660–1685* (Penguin, 2006)
Traces the political history of the monarchy after the Restoration

J.R. Jones, *The Anglo-Dutch Wars of the Seventeenth Century* (Routledge, 1996)
Full coverage of the three Anglo-Dutch Wars, including their political and economic impacts

A. Patterson, *The Long Parliament of Charles II* (Yale University Press, 2008)
A study of the Cavalier Parliament of 1661–79 that traces its origins from a compliant assembly to its later years as a source of Whig opposition

Chapter 4

J. Rose, *Godly Kingship in Restoration England* (Cambridge University Press, 2014)
Deals with tensions in the Church and issues of toleration and Dissenters

J. Spurr, *England in the 1670s* (John Wiley, 2000)
A detailed examination of the 1670s that introduces many of the key religious issues

Chapter 5

J.R. Jones, *The First Whigs: The Politics of the Exclusion Crisis* (Greenwood Press, 1985)
A classic account of the Exclusion Crisis and the emergence of the Whigs

J.P. Kenyon, *The Popish Plot* (Phoenix, 2000)
The most thorough and authoritative work on the Popish Plot

Chapter 6

J. Miller, *James II* (Yale University Press, 2000)
A reassessment of James's reign that presents the King's positive attributes and explains his reign as one of bad luck and misunderstanding

D. Ogg, *England in the Reigns of James II and William III* (Oxford University Press, 1969)
Places the reign of James II in its social, political and economic context

G. Tapsell, *The Personal Rule of Charles II: Politics and Religion in an Age of Absolutism* (Boydell Press, 2007)
A detailed study of the final four years of the reign of Charles II

D. Womersley, *James II: The Last Catholic King* (Penguin, 2015)
A short and accessible overview of the reign of James II

Chapters 7 and 8

T. Claydon, *William III* (Routledge, 2002)
An in-depth biography of William that presents his achievements in their wider context

T. Harris, *Revolution: The Great Crisis of the British Monarchy, 1685–1720* (Penguin, 2007)
Presents the Glorious Revolution as an event that completely changed Britain and one that was marked by violence in Ireland and Scotland

S. Pincus, *1688: The First Modern Revolution* (Yale University Press, 2011)
Argues that the Glorious Revolution had much wider repercussions than historians once thought, including in areas of religion and the economy

G.M. Trevelyan, *The English Revolution, 1688–1689* (Oxford University Press, 1968)
Presents the traditional Whig view of the Glorious Revolution

E. Vallance, *The Glorious Revolution: 1688 – Britain's Fight for Liberty* (Abacus, 2007)
Full coverage of all the key events of 1688 and the political impact of the Revolution

Chapter 9

N. Heard, *Stuart Economy and Society* (Hodder Education, 1995)
A straightforward and informative analysis of the key features of Stuart economy and society

S. Hindle, *On the Parish? The Micro-Politics of Poor Relief in Rural England, c.1550–1750* (Oxford University Press, 2009)
An in-depth study of the allocation of poor relief

E. Howe, *The First English Actresses: Women and Drama, 1660–1700* (Cambridge University Press, 1992)
Explores the role of women in the theatre after 1660

Chapter 10

D.C. Coleman, *The Economy of England, 1450–1750* (Oxford Paperbacks, 1977)
A survey of economic developments over a long period that sets the later Stuart era in context

M. Overton, *Agricultural Revolution in England: The Transformation of the Agrarian Economy, 1500–1850* (Cambridge University Press, 1996)
A survey of English agriculture that sets the changes of the late seventeenth century in context

Index